Commerce

Fifth Edition

D. Treharne Williams, B.A., B.COM.

Formerly Head of the Commerce Department
at Sparkhill Commercial School and
Hall Green Bilateral School, Birmingham

Edited by Millie Pincott, B.A., L.R.A.M., F.S.C.T.

Lecturer at Auckland Technical Institute,
New Zealand

Longman
London and New York

Longman Group Limited London

Associated companies, branches and representatives throughout the world

Published in the United States of America by Longman Inc., New York

First published 1956

Library of Congress Cataloging in Publication Data
Williams, David Treharne.
  Commerce.

  1. Business. 2. Finance. I. Pincott, Millie.
II. Title.
HF5500.W585   1978   658.4   77-21279
ISBN 0-582-41012-6

Filmset in 'Monophoto' Times 9 on 11 pt. and printed in Great Britain by
Richard Clay (The Chaucer Press), Ltd., Bungay, Suffolk

Second Edition 1962
Third Edition 1967
Fourth Edition 1971
Fifth Edition 1978

ISBN 0 582 41012.6

Contents

Preface to the fifth edition

It has been my privilege to prepare this latest edition of the late D. Treharne Williams' popular textbook. Like a great many teachers of commerce, I found his book, over the years, invaluable in the teaching of the subject.

Most of the original material in this highly esteemed text has been retained, but some amendments and additions have been necessary in the process of updating it. Several new chapters have been added to cover the wide field of knowledge now expected from candidates by the examining bodies.

My thanks are due to the following boards for permission to use questions set in their examinations:

Associated Examining Board;
Associated Lancashire Schools Examining Board;
Joint Matriculation Board;
London Chamber of Commerce & Industry;
Metropolitan Regional Examinations Board;
Royal Society of Arts Examinations Board;
Southern Regional Examinations Board;
University of Cambridge Local Examinations Syndicate;
Welsh Joint Education Committee;
West Midlands Examinations Board.

M.P.

Chapter 1

Producers and consumers

All people, however simply they live, require at least food, clothing and shelter. To some extent we can satisfy our wants by growing, for example, our own food, but for the most part we rely on others to provide our wants in return for money. Those who satisfy wants by providing goods and services are **producers**, and those who use these goods and services are **consumers**.

Producers include not only workers who make goods or grow crops, but also those who give services in offices, banks, hospitals, etc. A factory worker may think clerks and engine drivers are not producers because they do not make goods which can be sold for the money required to pay their wages. But without the railway men, the lorry drivers, the typists and many others, the factory would soon come to a standstill, unable to obtain supplies and to sell what it had already made.

We are all, without exception, **consumers**, for we all want goods and services from others. Save for a few criminals, invalids and beggars, who do not provide anything the rest of us are prepared to pay for, we are also producers, earning our living by selling what we can provide.

Producers can be divided into three groups as follows:

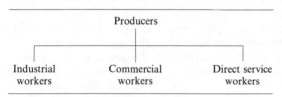

The **industrial workers** obtain raw materials from Nature and convert them into other kinds of products. Those who obtain the raw materials in the first place are extractive industrial workers such as miners, farmers, lumbermen. Those who use these materials for making gas, cotton cloth and furniture are the manufacturing industrial workers, while those who employ the materials for building such things as roads, docks and piers are constructive industrial workers.

Those who perform **direct services** deal directly with the consumers. Coal can be bought and sold several times before it is finally burned by the consumer, but a doctor must be called in to give his services directly to the patient and no one can come between them. Similarly, a hairdresser must cut his customer's hair without any third person coming between them, but a customer could obtain hair cream without even seeing the hairdresser.

The third group of workers or producers, comprising those engaged in commerce, is the group with which we are concerned in this book. What work do they do?

Let us suppose that I, a consumer, want a packet of tea. The grower is a very long way away – in India, perhaps. Obviously I cannot travel there in order to obtain a packet of tea. The grower, too, would not find it worth while to grow tea for sale in such small quantities. How can the tea be brought from the grower to the consumer? It is done by means of the **commercial workers**, those people engaged in shipping, railways and all forms of transport, warehousing, shops, etc.

As I cannot very well buy tea from the grower himself, I must pay others to do it for me. These are the **traders** who buy and sell at a profit, the profit being what they earn for their work. The tea may pass through the hands of many traders before it reaches me, the final buyer. I obtain it from the local grocer. He is the retail trader who sells me the small quantities I want. As he serves many customers he has to buy large quantities from the wholesaler who, in turn, supplies many retailers, and buys still larger quantities from the importer, who, again, has to supply many wholesalers and must therefore have shipped to him many thousands of chests of tea.

Trade alone, however, cannot satisfy my desire for tea. **Trade** is merely buying and selling. It only changes the owners of the goods. No one in this country would become the owner of tea in India unless it could be brought over the long distance that separates producer and consumer. The various forms of **transport** enable this to be done. In the days when there were no railways, no canals and no steamships there was much less trade than there is today.

Another difficulty the trader has to face is the risk he runs. The ship carrying the tea may be sunk and the trader ruined. Many would be unwilling to trade if there were no means of protecting themselves against this risk of loss. Nowadays **insurance** gives protection against all kinds of risk.

When the tea arrives in this country, all of it is not required at once and the importer is faced with the difficulty of keeping it for a time, until other traders are ready to buy it. It cannot be left just anywhere, and suitable **warehouses** have to be provided at convenient points.

Another hindrance to trade is caused by the different kinds of money used by different countries. The grower of tea in India wants to be paid in

		Maker	
Difficulties			*Aids*
Distance			Transport
Risk			Insurance
Time	Goods		Warehousing
Finance			Banking
Information			Advertising
		↓	
		Consumer	

that country's money and not in English £1 notes. At times the trader may be short of money and may wish to borrow in order to be able to carry on his business. In such cases the trader can obtain help from **banks** and other financial institutions.

Persons wishing to buy tea must know where it can be obtained while those with tea to sell must let them know that they can satisfy their wants. **Advertising** overcomes this difficulty by giving information about goods and services to buyers and sellers who can then get in touch with one another.

We can now say that **commerce** means trade and anything that helps to distribute or to bring the goods from the maker to the consumer. It tries 'to deliver the right goods, to the right person, at the right place, at the right time, and at the right price'. To succeed in this it must employ a large number of workers, all of whom must be paid. In this country when a consumer spends a pound he is paying as much as 50p for the work of bringing the goods from the maker.

Commerce can be divided into the following branches:

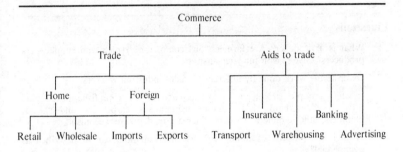

Many people do more than one kind of work. A farmer, for instance, would be placed in the extractive industries group although he also manufactures butter and cheese, builds barns, trades in the products of his farm and may give direct services by writing articles on farming.

Analysis of civil employment in Britain, mid-1974

Occupation	Employed (million)
Manufacturing	7.9
Professional, financial, miscellaneous	6.0
Distributive trades	2.8
Transport and communications	1.5
Building and contracting	1.3
Public administration	1.6
Agriculture, forestry and fishing	0.4
Mining and quarrying	0.3
Gas, electric and water	0.4
Hotels and catering	0.5

Occupations are classified for convenience only. They can be grouped in different ways. The classification in the chart is the one that suits our purpose best. It shows the place occupied by commerce in the general scheme of production and gives us the main types of commercial workers.

The lower table on page 3 adopts a different classification. It shows how nearly 23 million people in civil employment are distributed over ten groups. About one-third of the total employed are women. Out of every five workers one is employed in the distributive trades of retailing and wholesaling, or in transport and communications. Many in the professional and other groups, such as bankers and accountants, are also engaged in commercial work.

Businesses like hotels, garages and laundries are known as **service trades**.

As we all know something about the retail trade, we shall begin studying that branch in the next chapter.

Questions

1. What is a producer? Are farmers, bus conductors, typists and shopkeepers producers? Give reason for your answers.

2. Describe the work done by different kinds of industrial workers.

3. In which group of producers would you place the following: fishermen, engine drivers, sailors, bank clerks, actors, fishmongers, carpenters, undertakers, plumbers, tailors, miners, warders, cinema attendants, tobacconists?

4. What is the purpose of commerce? Which occupations can be described as commercial?

5. Draw a diagram illustrating the main divisions of commerce. Using one commercial transaction as an example, describe how these divisions of commerce each play a part in completing the transaction.   (R.S.A.)

6. Trade forms a large part of commerce. Expand this statement.   (U.C.L.E.S.)

7. What are the subdivisions of trade? Show how the different kinds of trade you mention differ from one another.

8. What are the distributive trades? Why are so many employed in these trades and in transport?

9. Name five aids to trade and show in what ways they help trade.

10. What risks do (*a*) greengrocers, (*b*) drapers, (*c*) booksellers, have to bear?

11. Name some products that must be kept for a considerable time, and find out what kind of warehouses they require.

12. What is a service trade? Name six examples. Are they productive? Why has the demand for such services increased in recent years?

13. Describe the contribution made by commercial activities in the passage of any article, e.g. a washing machine, from the factory to the user.   (W.M.E.B.)

14. To what extent does the owner of a fishing vessel engage in commerce and make use of the services of others so engaged?   (W.J.E.C.)

15. Explain the contribution to the production of goods and services of (*a*) land, (*b*) labour, (*c*) capital and (*d*) enterprise. (L.C.C. & I)

16. (*a*) Explain the meaning of (i) trade and (ii) commerce, (*b*) Show how commerce aids trade. (L.C.C. & I.)

17. 'Human wants are satisfied by the production of goods and services.' Briefly explain this statement and indicate how commerce assists in the satisfaction of human wants. (U.C.L.E.S.)

Chapter 2

The retailer

The word **'retail'** means to cut up or off, and cutting up big lots into small lots is the main service given by the retailer in return for his profit. The makers and wholesalers like to sell in big quantities and do not want to sell in ones and twos. No one would think of going into a big factory to buy one packet of chocolate, for instance, but the retailer will gladly supply one packet. He buys 'wholes' from the wholesaler and then splits them up into the sizes that will suit his customers.

He also **weighs, measures and packages** the goods. In recent years the makers have been doing more and more of this weighing and packaging instead of leaving it to the retailer. They can do it cheaply by means of machinery, and as they package all that they make they have enough work to keep the machines busy all the time. One retailer has not enough work for these machines, because he handles only a small part of the factory's output. By carrying out the packaging themselves the makers are sure that their names are advertised on the packets and they can claim that their goods are 'untouched by hand' and clean. The customers, too, can see that they are obtaining the make they ask for, and different makes cannot be mixed together. The development of self-service since 1945 (see p. 74) has made pre-packaging of many goods by the makers essential.

The retailer opens his shop in a **convenient spot** near to his customers so that there is no need for anybody to travel a long way in order to obtain what he requires. His shop is open for most of the day, and although he may have hardly any customers at certain times, he is spending his time waiting for them to come when it suits them.

The customer sometimes does not know exactly what he wants and relies on the retailer to give him **advice**. He expects the retailer to show him articles of different makes and prices so that he can choose the one he likes best. He also expects the retailer to show him the newest and most up-to-date goods. If he desires something unusual, not generally kept in stock, he asks the retailer to obtain it for him.

Besides providing goods, most retailers give some **services** to their customers. They deliver goods and the roundsman may take orders, provide an after-sales service, and alter something to suit a customer's special requirements, such as shortening or lengthening a coat.

Many retailers allow their customers to have the goods now and to pay for them when they can, i.e. they give **credit**.

Makers and wholesalers expect the retailer to bring their goods to the notice of their customers, and may pay the expenses of a special **display** or 'point of sale' promotion of their goods for a few days. They can learn from the shopkeeper what customers think of their products and the packaging, so that, if necessary, they can try to alter them to meet the demands of consumers.

Before **starting a new shop**, the retailer should make certain that he has enough money or capital to carry on the business. He must discover how many shops selling the same kind of goods as he does are already in the neighbourhood and decide if there is enough trade to support another shop. He must consider the kinds of customers that are available. If he deals in expensive goods, they will not sell well in a poor quarter. If his customers want credit, he will need more capital because he will have to buy goods to replace those sold but for which he has not yet been paid. To obtain customers, he may have to deliver goods and incur more expenses. He should inquire about plans for building houses and roads, or for closing down factories and decide what effect they are likely to have on business.

If he decides that the prospects are good, he will look for premises conveniently situated for customers and determine whether he will buy or rent. He may prefer to rent for a short period with, if possible, the chance of buying later. In this way he can discover if it is worth while continuing with the business before he buys the premises. If he buys, he will need more capital but will be certain that if the business succeeds he cannot be made to pay more rent or be forced to leave and start elsewhere.

The retailer is the last link in the **chain of production** which connects the maker or grower with the consumer. The American cotton-grower links up with a merchant who buys the crops from many farms before selling to an exporter who collects supplies from many merchants. The exporter forms a link with a British importer who gets in touch with factories making the raw cotton into thread and cloth which is sold to other factories to be made into dresses, etc. The factories make links with the wholesalers and these with the retailers who form the last link with the consumer. To forge each link the traders need the help of transport and the other aids to trade.

Retail businesses are of different kinds. They vary in size from hawking to huge department stores selling all kinds of goods. Most of them own just one shop, but the multiple or chain businesses may possess hundreds of branches. Some have only one owner while the ownership of others may be shared between partners, or shareholders, or the members of a cooperative society. These various types will be discussed in Chapters 22–26.

Questions

1. What services do customers expect from a shopkeeper? Do all shopkeepers give all these services? Which three services do you consider the most important?

2. Why do retailers weigh and package less than they used to do?

3. From whom does the retailer obtain goods? Why do we buy from the retailer instead of from his suppliers?

4. Show by means of a diagram how goods from a factory reach the consumers. Indicate by lines of different widths the volume of goods dealt in at each stage.

5. Why are there more grocery shops than furniture shops? Are there furniture shops in small villages? What kinds of shops are found only in towns?

6. Give an account of the matters which would have to be considered by a person wishing to set up in business as a retail draper.

7. What is meant by 'credit'? Why do some retailers refuse to give credit? Why do some customers want credit?

8. Why is the situation of a shop important? Why do you find grocers in side streets, but not jewellers?

9. One of the functions of commerce is to provide a link between producer and consumer. Illustrate how this works in the case of one of the following: (*a*) vegetables, (*b*) raw cotton, (*c*) tea.   (A.E.B.)

10. Why are workers in extractive industries said to be primary producers, those in manufacturing and construction industries secondary producers and those providing commercial and direct services tertiary producers?

Chapter 3

Documents · Order · Invoice · Credit note · Value added tax

When a retailer desires to buy goods, he may write letters of **inquiry** to several wholesalers, asking for prices and terms of payment. In reply he receives **quotations** giving the information asked for. After comparing the quotations, he decides on the most favourable and sends an order for the goods.

The **order** must state quite clearly what goods he requires and in what quantities. He can say what he requires quite briefly by using catalogue, sample or pattern numbers. A carbon copy of the order is kept for reference purposes.

When suppliers send the goods, they may send an **advice note** informing the retailer that the goods have been dispatched. Very often now the advice note is not necessary because the bill can be sent as soon as the goods are ready, and when the retailer receives the bill he knows the goods are on the way.

The bill is known as the **invoice**. It gives the quantity, quality, prices and values of the goods bought on a certain date. When the buyer receives it, he checks the prices and arithmetic, checks it with the carbon copy of the order, and with the goods when they arrive. He then copies it into his purchases book and files it away. The seller, who sends the invoice, will enter the carbon copy in his sales book.

A **delivery note**, giving a list of the goods without showing their prices, may be sent to the buyer. The buyer's employees can then use this note instead of the invoice for checking the goods without learning their cost price.

In checking the invoice the retailer may find that it contains an error. In the invoice given on page 10 a mistake has been made in adding up. The total should be £90 and the trade discount should be £30, giving £60 as the amount to be charged for the goods. The error is corrected, not by altering the figures, but by using another document. When the seller is informed of the error, he sends his customer a **credit note**, usually printed in red to distinguish it from other documents. The invoice makes the buyer a debtor for £66 and the credit note makes him a creditor for £6. On balance, he is a debtor for £60 which is the correct charge for the goods.

Credit notes are also used when the buyer sends back goods because they are not what he ordered, or because they are damaged, and the seller makes him an allowance. The seller enters them in his sales returns book, and the buyer in his purchases returns book.

An error in the invoice resulting in an undercharge is corrected by means

Order 1

Teleg.:

28 Queen Street,
Stratford
1 January 19 . .

Mr A. Seller,
53 Bridge Street,
Birmingham

Please forward the following goods per B.R., as soon as possible.

125 Exercise books, list no. 24 @ £3 per 25
100 Notebooks, list no. 29 @ £9 per 100
125 Bookkeeping books, list no. 34 @ £2.40 per 10
200 Shorthand books, list no. 36 @ £9 per 50

B. Buyer

N.B. – All invoices must quote order number.

Invoice 49

Tel.:
Teleg.:

53 Bridge Street,
Birmingham
8 January 19 . .

Mr B. Buyer,
28 Queen Street,
Stratford

Bought of A. Seller

Order No. 1.

Per B.R., Carr. Pd.

List number	Description	Quantity	Price	£
24	Exercise books	125	£3 per 25	15
29	Notebooks	100	£9 per 100	9
34	Bookkeeping books	125	£2.40 per 10	30
36	Shorthand books	200	£9 per 50	36
				—
				99
			Less trade discount 33⅓%	33
				—
				66

TERMS: 3% one month, 1% two months, net three months.

E. & O.E.

Credit note 3

Tel.:
Teleg.:

53 Bridge Street,
Birmingham
12 January 19 . .

Mr B. Buyer,
28 Queen Street,
Stratford

Credited by A. Seller

Date	Particulars	£
19 . . 8 Jan.	Error in invoice no. 49, dated 8th instant	6
		—

of a **debit note** sent by the seller to the buyer. The seller enters it in the sales book, while the buyer copies it into his purchases book. A debit note is similar in form to a credit note save that the heading is 'Dr to A. Seller'.

An error on an invoice can be corrected by cancelling the invoice with a credit note for its full amount and then sending another invoice for the correct amount. An undercharge may be corrected by entering it on a second invoice instead of sending a debit note.

A trader who deals in taxable goods or services worth £5000 a year must register with Customs and Excise and use a tax invoice showing the registration number, the rate, and the amount of the tax. Credit and debit notes must also show these particulars. A **tax invoice** could be ruled as follows.

Order No. 5		v.A.T. Registration No. 834 1645 52		Per B.R., Carr. Pd.	
List no.	**Goods**	**Cost**	**V.A.T. rate**	**V.A.T. Amount**	
		£		£	
11	30 tables at £10 each	300			
	Less trade discount				
	33⅓%	100			
		200	10%	20	
	Total Goods	200			
	Total v.A.T.	20			
	Total	220			

Terms: Net.

Traders who sell taxable goods or services to the public are not bound to show the tax on their bills.

Value added tax (V.A.T.) is calculated on the selling price. Many goods are rated at a standard rate of 8 per cent, but there are higher rates for some goods, and the Government may change the rate at any time. The seller of the goods in the invoice must collect £20 tax from the buyer. Had the seller bought the goods for £150 he would owe £15 tax to his supplier. He has to collect £5 more in tax than he was charged and this £5 is equal to 10 per cent of the £50 value he added to his cost price. He must pay this £5 to Customs and Excise. Had he sold the goods for £100 he would receive £5 less tax than he had to pay and he would reclaim this £5 from Customs and Excise. Every three months each trader pays to, or claims from, Customs and Excise the difference between the tax on his purchases (input tax) and the tax on his sales (output tax) so that the total received by the Government is equal to 10 per cent of the amount by which the price has increased from the first to the last seller. The one who really pays the tax is the final buyer.

Some goods and services are **zero rated** and some are **exempt**. Books are zero rated which means the buyer does not pay any tax and the seller can reclaim any tax he paid for paper and supplies. Exempt items, like postage, are also sold free of tax but in these cases the seller cannot reclaim any tax he paid for supplies.

The documents illustrated in this and succeeding chapters are merely examples. All businesses do not use invoices like the one shown here. Whatever form the documents take, they give the same kind of information and fulfil the same purpose, serving as written records of what has taken place. Some, like the invoice and credit note, provide information required for writing up the **books of account**. The filed invoices, instead of being copied into books, may be made to serve as the purchases and sales books.

The preparation of documents and accounts is an expense which increases the cost of the goods. Anything that reduces this expense, such as the use of accounting machines, lessens the costs of distribution.

Questions

1. T. Cole orders from S. Walker the following goods:

   3 bedroom suites, catalogue no. 15, @ £100 each; 10 chairs, catalogue no. 46, @ £10 each; 5 carpets, catalogue no. 72, @ £40 each.

   The trade discount is 33⅓ per cent and the terms of payment are net one month. Make out the order and the invoice, adding any information that you think may be necessary.

2. If T. Cole in the previous question returns two chairs because they are damaged prepare the document that S. Walker sends to him.

3. If T. Cole pays within the month how much does he pay for the goods kept? How much tax does he owe if the rate is 10 per cent?

4. Why does the buyer ask the seller to quote the order number on the invoice? What do the letters E. & O.E. stand for?

5. When a retailer buys goods from a wholesaler what documents may pass between them? Why are these documents important?

6. What are credit and debit notes? When are they used?

7. In what ways can errors on invoices be corrected?

8. What is an invoice? What does it contain? When invoices are used in a business what particular records and activities are affected by them?   (A.E.B.)

9. Distinguish between (*a*) an order and an invoice, (*b*) an advice note and an invoice, (*c*) a delivery note and an advice note.

10. Write a paragraph on each of the following: (*a*) an advice note, (*b*) an invoice, (*c*) a credit note, (*d*) a statement of account.   (S.R.E.B.)

11. On 26 March, Emlyn Hughes & Co. Ltd, Ironmongers, sold the following goods to the Secretary of your local Youth Club:

    2 rolls of chain link fencing @ £7.40 per roll;
    2 boxes staples @ 30p per box;
    1 hammer @ 70p;

20 fencing posts @ 30p each.
V.A.T. @ 10 per cent must be added.

(*a*) Draw a copy of the invoice. (*b*) What are the uses of an invoice? (*c*) Name two other documents which are likely to pass between the two parties regarding this transaction.   (W.J.E.C.)

Chapter 4

Accounts · Statements · Receipts

The documents, and the books mentioned in the previous chapter, provide the information which the trader requires to write up his accounts. In order to find out how much his customers owe him and how much he owes to his suppliers, the trader must keep an account for each one with whom he deals. These **accounts are kept in the ledger**. A. Seller would have an account for B. Buyer as shown below.

Everything A. Seller has sold to B. Buyer he has entered in his sales book, and from this book he copies the items on to the debit side of the account. Anything he receives from B. Buyer, or any allowances he makes him, are entered on the credit side. The difference between the two sides shows how much B. Buyer owes on the date the account is balanced.

B. Buyer similarly keeps an account for A. Seller and it should agree with B. Buyer's account in A. Seller's ledger.

Periodically, the seller copies out the buyer's account as it appears in his ledger and sends the copy to the buyer. This copy, shown on page 15, is the **statement of account** which the buyer compares with the account he keeps under the seller's name in his own ledger. The balance at the end of this statement would be the first item in the next statement.

When the debtor pays, he is given a **receipt** stating how much was paid, when it was paid, who paid it and who received it. Copies or counterfoils of

Dr		**B. Buyer**			*Cr*
19..		£	19..		£
8 Jan.	Sales	22	12 Jan.	Returns	2
20 Jan.	Sales	10	26 Jan.	Cash	19
			26 Jan.	Discount	1
			31 Jan.	Balance c/d	10
		32			32
1 Feb.	Balance b/d	10			

The discount entered in this account is cash discount. As it is an allowance made by the seller if the debtor pays by a certain date, its amount is not known and cannot be recorded until the debtor has actually paid. Cash and trade discount will be discussed fully in Chapter 12.

Dr			A. Seller			Cr
19 ..		£	19 ..			£
12 Jan.	Returns	2	8 Jan.	Purchases		22
26 Jan.	Cash	19	20 Jan.	Purchases		10
26 Jan.	Discount	1				
31 Jan.	Balance c/d	10				
		—				—
		32				32
		—				—
			1 Feb.	Balance b/d		10

Statement of account
Tel.:
Teleg.:

53 Bridge Street,
Birmingham
1 February 19 ..

Mr B. Buyer,
28 Queen Street,
Stratford

Dr To **A. Seller**

Date 19 ..	Particulars	Debits £	Credits £	Balance £
Jan. 8	Sales	22		22
Jan. 12	Returns		2	20
Jan. 20	Sales	10		30
Jan. 26	Cash		19	11
	Discount		1	10

Subject to cash discount if paid according to terms.

receipts given for cash and cheques received are entered on the debit side of the cash book. Receipts obtained for cash and counterfoils of cheques paid to creditors are credited. The difference between the two sides of the cash book shows how much money should be left on the date of balancing.

Receipt 142

26 January 19 ..

Received from .... *Mr B. Buyer* ....

the sum of .... *Nineteen Pounds* ....

Cash   £19.00
Cheques, etc.
Discount   £1.00

Mr. B. Buyer

A. Seller

Nineteen Pounds

Besides personal accounts for debtors and creditors, the trader must keep accounts to show how much property and equipment the business possesses. He must, too, have a purchases and a sales account to show the total cost price of the goods he has bought and the total selling price of the goods sold, so that he can calculate his profit or loss. The totals of the various expenses incurred are shown in accounts headed wages, rent, advertising and so on. The documents and books already mentioned, together with any others that may be used, such as the petty cash book, provide the information required for writing up these accounts in the ledger.

With **cash sales**, when goods are sold for cash across the counter and the buyer takes them away himself, the buyer obtains a receipted bill, and it may not be necessary to use other documents or to keep an account for the buyer because he owes nothing for the goods.

A trader must credit his supplier and debit his customer with the value added tax. The opposite entries are made in a v.a.t. account whose balance shows how much the trader must pay to, or claim from, Customs and Excise.

Questions

1. K. Woods has the following account for R. Lee. What does each entry tell us?

Dr			R. Lee		Cr
19..		£	19..		£
Jan. 1	Balance	45	Jan. 27	Returns	5
,, 23	Sales	40	,, 29	Cash	76
,, 30	Sales	55		Discount	4
			,, 31	Balance	55
		140			140

2. From the above account prepare the statement that K. Woods would send to R. Lee, adding any information that a statement should give. What would be the first item in the next statement?

3. Make out the receipt for the payment in question 1. What rate of cash discount was allowed?

4. Which documents provided the information for writing up the account in question 1?

5. In what ways does a statement differ from an invoice?

6. What is a ledger? What information does it give?

7. What are (*a*) purchases books, (*b*) sales books, (*c*) cash books?

8. Prepare the account that R. Lee in question 1 would keep for K. Woods.

9. Which documents would be used for the following transactions between A. Mills and D. Marks?

> 19..
> Apr. 3 Mills bought goods for £30.
> ,, 6 Mills returned goods worth £5.
> ,, 20 Mills paid what he owed being allowed 4 per cent cash discount.

Prepare the statement that would be sent to Mills at the end of the month.

10. What important documents would be kept by a firm selling goods both for cash and credit? Give reasons why each document is kept. (A.E.B.)

Chapter 5

Settling debts · Legal tender · Postal and money orders

Debts can be settled in one of the following ways:

1. By paying in cash.
2. By set-off.
3. By means of postal orders, money orders and cheques.

By **cash** is meant coins and notes. The coins in use in this country are **token coins**. The metal in one of them is not worth the value stamped on its face. If a 5p coin were melted down into a lump of metal, it could not then be sold for 5p. The cost of making a 5p coin is much less than 5p.

Coins which are worth as much as metal as they are as coins are called **standard coins**. Our standard coins were the sovereign and the half-sovereign, but these are no longer minted, and have been replaced by bank notes and the 50p coin. A £1 note states that the Bank of England promises to pay the bearer on demand the sum of one pound. Originally, this meant that the Bank would give one gold sovereign in return for a £1 note. The Bank still promises to give gold in return for notes, although it has not done so since 1931.

If a creditor were paid a large sum in small coins, not only would it be very inconvenient, but he would not be receiving the full value of what was due to him because token coins are not worth their face value. The law therefore gives him the right to *refuse* more than a certain amount of token coins which are intended only for small payments. What a creditor cannot lawfully refuse in settlement is termed **legal tender**.

Bank of England notes are legal tender for any amount.
Cupro-nickel coins are legal tender up to £5.
Bronze coins are legal tender up to 20p.

English coins and £1 notes are legal tender throughout the United Kingdom, but the £5 and higher notes are legal tender only in England and Wales, including the Channel Islands. A small quantity of notes issued by banks in Northern Ireland and in Scotland are not legal tender anywhere. Notes issued by the Governments of the Isle of Man and Guernsey are legal tender only in their own islands and the same applies to Guernsey and Jersey coins. These notes can be accepted in England and Wales. For a small charge the banks will exchange them for English money.

Set-off is the settling of debts by setting-off, or balancing one debt against another. If A owes B £45 and B owes A £40, the debts can be settled by A paying the difference of £5 to B. In this way less cash is needed to meet the needs of business.

Payment to someone at a distance can be made by means of the Post Office. Notes can be posted in a registered envelope and insured up to a maximum of £500. Instead of sending the actual money, postal and money orders can be used.

All post offices belong to a single nationalised corporation, set up by the Government, so that it does not matter which office pays out the money so long as it has been received at some other office first. A debtor in Birmingham wishing to pay £1 to a creditor in Leeds can pay £1 to a post office in Birmingham obtaining in return a **postal order**, which is a written 'order' or command to the postmaster to pay £1. He then sends the order to his creditor who can exchange it for £1 cash at a Leeds post office. There are spaces on the order for writing in the name of the person to whom payment is to be made and the name of the office which is to pay him. It is not essential to fill in these, but if they are left blank anyone can cash the order at any office. It is safer, therefore, to fill in the order before posting it. When the order is cashed the person receiving the money must add his signature in the space provided. A counterfoil, bearing the same number as the order, is kept by the sender.

Postal orders are issued for:

5p and by 2½p steps up to 25p,
30p and by 5p steps up to 100p,
and for £2, £3, £4 and £5.

A small fee called 'poundage' is payable, varying with the value of the order.

Orders can be increased in value by affixing stamps which must not be more than two in number nor more than 4½p in value. If the sender could add stamps of any value, he might not be paying the appropriate poundage rates. To send £2.16 by postal orders two orders would be necessary, one for £2, and one for 15p to which 1p in stamps would be added.

Money orders can be obtained for any sum up to £50 excluding fractions of 1p. To obtain a money order, a form must be filled in first, stating the amount, the name of the person who is to be paid, and the name of the post office where payment is to be made. From these particulars, the post office official makes out the order, and also a card which is sent to the postmaster at the paying office requesting him to make the payment. The purchaser of the order fills in the counterfoil and keeps it while sending the order to the payee. The one cashing the order at the paying office is asked the name of the sender and if he cannot give this information payment will be refused. The name of the sender is not asked for in the case of postal orders and the paying office is not bound to be inserted. For these reasons, they are not as safe as money orders.

Money orders can also be made safer than postal orders by deferring payment. The sender can ask that payment be deferred for so many days, not exceeding ten. This gives him time to be notified that the order has been received by the right person before the cash is paid. For an extra fee, the Post Office will inform the sender of the date the order was cashed.

Money can be sent quickly from one place to another by means of telegraphic money orders. In this case the receiving office wires the paying office to pay as requested, the sender paying the cost of the telegram and a small fee as well as the poundage.

For sending a sum of a few pence only, **stamps** can be used. A person who receives a large number of stamps can sell them back to the post office at a slight discount.

Denominations of orders and poundage rates may alter. They can always be found in the *Post Office Guide*.

Postal orders, money orders and stamps are not legal tender and a creditor can refuse them if he likes: they are used mainly by people who have no bank accounts.

Wages of manual workers must be paid in cash unless the worker makes a written request that he wants them paid by cheque or by postal or money order and the employer agrees. When an employee is absent from work his employer has the right to send his wages by postal or money order (but not by cheque) unless the employee has stated that he does not want his wages paid in that way.

Questions

1. Explain what is meant by (*a*) cash, (*b*) standard coin, (*c*) token coin.

2. What is the meaning of the word 'tender' as used in legal tender? Why are token coins legal tender for only limited amounts?

3. When can a creditor refuse token coins? Can he refuse postal and money orders? Give reasons for your answers.

4. What is the promise on a £1 note? Who makes the promise? To whom is it made? Can you enforce it?

5. Why are postal and money orders called 'orders'? Describe how they work.

6. In what ways is a money order safer than a postal order? In what other ways do they differ?

7. Explain what is meant by 'set-off'.

8. Obtain the *Post Office Guide* from your library and read what it says about postal and money orders. If necessary, alter the figures given in this book.
   State, with reasons, whether you would make the following payments by cash, postal order, or money order:
   (*a*) £1 to your grocer;
   (*b*) £5 to someone in a distant town;

(*c*) £50 to someone in a distant town;

(*d*) £20 to your brother who wired you to send it to a certain post office because he has lost all his money;

(*e*) 1p entry fee for a newspaper competition.

9. Why do most workmen want their weekly wages in cash?

Chapter 6

Cheques

The following is one of the oldest cheques still in existence:

Mr. Thomas Ffowles,
   I desire you to pay unto Mr. Samuell Howard or order upon receipt hereof the sume of nine pounds thirteene shillings and sixepence and place to the account of

Yr. servant,
Edmond Warcupp.

14th. August, 1675.   £9   13   6*d.*

For Mr. Thomas Ffowles, Gouldsmith, at his shop betweene the two Temple Gates, Fleetstreete.

On the back Howard has written, 'Recd. in full of this bill the sume of nine pounds thirteen shillings sixepence. Saml. Howard'.

In those days the goldsmiths were the people who had strongrooms in which valuables could be safely kept, and other people paid the goldsmiths for looking after their money. When Warcupp required some money to pay to Howard, he saved himself the trouble of going to the goldsmith's to fetch it by writing the above note and giving it to Howard who then could obtain the money from the goldsmith. If Howard did not need to use the money just then he probably asked the goldsmith to keep it safely for him so that all the goldsmith had to do was to deduct £9.67½ from what he owed to Warcupp and add £9.67½ to what he owed to Howard. When they realised that only some of the money they were keeping for others was taken away from them, the goldsmiths began to use it themselves by lending it. So profitable did they find this business that instead of charging for keeping other people's money they began to pay for being allowed to keep it. In this way they became bankers.

Today the banks provide **printed cheques** to be filled in by their customers. Cheques are 'personalised' by printing on them the customer's code number, and his name (below which he adds his signature). The numbers at the bottom of a cheque are in magnetic ink so that they can be sorted very quickly by machines. Reading from left to right they are: the serial number of the cheque which also appears on the counterfoil; the number of the bank and the branch providing the cheque, which is also seen at the top right; and the customer's code number. When the bank receives the cheque, the amount can be printed on it in special type so that the machines can read the figures, and the records be prepared at great speed. The number at the top left is used in clearing cheques – this process will be described in Chapter 48.

All **cheques are** really notes ordering the banker to pay somebody a certain sum of money on demand, i.e. the banker must pay immediately he receives a cheque signed by his customer. As a rule there are **three parties** (or persons) concerned with a cheque. The person who draws out and signs the cheque is the drawer. He is B. Buyer in the following example. The second party, the one who is ordered to pay the money is the drawee – Lloyds Bank in the example. The drawee is always a banker. The third party is the one to whom the banker is ordered to pay the money. He is called the payee and is A. Seller in the example. When a drawer writes out a cheque to himself, he is the payee as well as the drawer and there are but two parties to the cheque.

By taking the cheque to Stratford, A. Seller can obtain cash for it at once. No other bank will cash it on demand because the order to pay is given to the bank at Queen Street, Stratford, where B. Buyer keeps his money. A. Seller will probably take the cheque to his own bank at Birmingham, which may be a branch of Lloyds or of any other bank. He will then have to wait a day or two before receiving the cash because his banker must now collect the money from B. Buyer's bank before he can pay it to A. Seller. Instead of taking the cheque to a bank, A. Seller can pass it on to somebody else in return for money or goods.

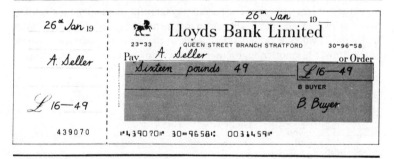

Cheques are of two kinds – bearer and order cheques. The **bearer cheque** tells the banker to pay so-and-so or bearer, i.e. he can pay anybody who brings the cheque to him. The **order cheque** tells the banker to pay so-and-so or order, i.e. he is to pay the person named on the cheque or do as that person orders him to do, such as paying the money to someone to whom the payee has passed on the cheque. If the payee passes on an order cheque, he must **endorse** it by writing his name on the back exactly as it is written on the front. If his name is incorrectly given on the front, say T. Seller instead of A. Seller, he must first endorse as T. Seller and then write his correct name underneath. If the endorsement does not correspond exactly with the payee's name as written on the front of the cheque or if the endorsement is illegible, the banker may return the cheque marked 'endorsement irregular'.

The bearer cheque does not require endorsement. Once the payee has endorsed an order cheque it acts like a bearer cheque and anyone to whom it is given can cash it without further endorsement. All who pass on the cheque can endorse it if they wish. By endorsing it, they are implying that they believe the cheque to be good for payment. In the vast majority of cases the payee does not pass on the cheque but pays it into his bank account, i.e. he does not exchange the cheque for cash, but requests the banker to add the amount to what he already has in the bank, in which case there is no need to endorse. **Order cheques must be endorsed when**

1. the payee cashes the cheque (unless it is a cheque made out to self) instead of paying it into his account;
2. the payee passes on the cheque;
3. The letter 'R' appears on the cheque. The 'R' means that the drawer wants the payee to endorse the cheque so that when it has been returned to him by his banker he can use it as a receipt. The 'R' which must be at least half an inch high and placed near the amount, warns the banker that he must see to it that this particular cheque is endorsed before he accepts it.

Anyone can write out a cheque for any sum, but unless he has enough money in the bank the cheque will be worthless. The banker would refuse to pay it and mark it 'Refer to drawer' followed by the reason for not paying, such as 'No account'. That is why cheques are not legal tender and why it is not safe to accept cheques in payment for goods from a stranger. When a person accepts a cheque in payment, he trusts the drawer and believes that when he presents the cheque at the bank the cash will be there. If the drawer has not enough money in the bank to meet the cheque, he is said to **dishonour** it.

Questions

1. What is a cheque? To which class of documents does it belong?
2. Why is a cheque not legal tender? How does it differ from a £1 note?
3. Using the following information and adding any details you think necessary make out a cheque dated 10 March 19 . .

   Drawer: F. James
   Payee: L. Smith
   Drawee: Barclays Bank
   Amount: £11.60.

4. Who are the parties to a cheque? What parts do they play in connection with a cheque?
5. What is endorsement? When must cheques be endorsed?

6. Of what use are the numbers on a cheque? Why is the letter 'R' sometimes added to a cheque?

7. Why does a bank prefer its customers to use the cheques it provides for them without charge?

8. When is a cheque 'dishonoured'? Why is such a cheque described as a 'dud' cheque, a 'rubber' cheque, and is said to 'bounce'?

9. In what ways does a cheque differ from a postal order and a money order?

10. Write an account of the different ways in which payments can be made in settlement of debts and the organisations which provide the facilities. Describe briefly the steps which must be taken to use each method and state one advantage to be gained in each case. (W.M.E.B.)

Chapter 7

Current and deposit accounts · Paying-in book · Statement

To obtain the right to use cheques, one must open a current account with a banker. Before he consents **to start a current account**, the banker will ask for references. If these are satisfactory, the customer will be asked to sign a signature card. This is necessary because by law the banker must be able to recognise the signature of every one of his customers, and if he cashes a cheque with a forged signature he must refund the money to the person whose signature was forged. If, therefore, the banker has any doubts about the genuineness of any signature, he will compare it with that on the card.

The owner of the account will now be given a paying-in book and a cheque book. The **paying-in book** is filled in by the customer himself every time he puts money into his account. The banker checks it with the money and signs it, tearing off one half page to keep at the bank and returning the other half page, which acts as a receipt, to the customer. The **cheque book** is the paying-out book. When the customer wants to pay away some of the money he has in the bank, he writes out a cheque which finally reaches the banker.

The paying-in slips and the cheques in the hands of the banker provide the information for preparing the accounts. The total of each slip is placed to the credit of the customer's account. Any cheques the banker receives and pays on behalf of his customer are put to the debit of his account, the

Paying-in book (the right-hand side is torn off and kept by the banker)

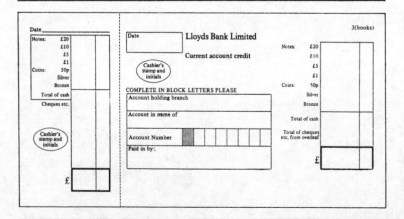

balance showing how much the customer has left in the bank. The customer debits the cash shown on his slip in the bank column (and credits it in the cash column) of his cash book, the cheques banked being debited from receipts. He credits cheques from their counterfoils.

As banker and customer write up their records of receipts and payments from the paying-in slips, cheques and their counterfoils, all of which are prepared by the customer, their records should agree. The customer can find out if they agree by asking for a **statement of account**, an example of which is given on page 32. He then compares this copy of his account in the bank's books with his own cash book. Unlike the trader's statement, it is not a request for payment.

A current account is always altering, because the customer is continually paying money in and taking it out again. When a customer opens a **deposit account**, he intends the money to stay in the bank for some time and undertakes to give the banker so many days' notice before withdrawing any of it. If he does withdraw without notice he is charged interest on the sum withdrawn for the period of notice. Cheques cannot be used to spend money in a deposit account. As the banker never knows when money in a current account will be taken away from him, he does not pay interest on it; but interest is paid on money in a deposit account.

Current accounts cause much more work for the banker than do deposit accounts. As a current account is always receiving and paying out money, it necessitates a lot of bookkeeping. Each cheque the banker handles costs him about 5p: the banker charges for this work by debiting the customer's account with the charges. Similarly, the banker credits the customer's deposit account with any interest that is owed.

Savings of small sums, such as those first collected in a savings box, can be placed in a **savings account**. Although money in a savings account earns interest, it can be withdrawn at any time upon production of the pass book.

A customer can open all kinds of accounts and transfer money from one account to another.

The **advantages of a current account** are important to a businessman. It enables him to make payments by cheque and saves him and his creditor the trouble of carrying and counting big sums of cash. It is no more trouble to write out a cheque for a big sum than for a small sum. It is also safer to carry cheques. If a cheque is lost, and the loss discovered in time, the bank can be told to stop payment.

Most cheques have counterfoils bearing the same numbers as the cheques and on which particulars should be entered when a cheque is made out. These numbers and particulars are helpful in tracing lost cheques, and together with the bank statements provide records of payment. A cheque that has passed through the bank is now accepted as evidence that the payee has received the amount stated on it, while a creditor paid by cheque is no longer obliged to give a receipt unless the debtor asks for it.

When payment has to be made to someone at a distance, a cheque can be sent easily and safely by post. Cheques can also be passed on in settlement of debts, like money. If cheques were not used, the country would require much more money than it has at present. Cheques do the work of money.

Those who have no bank account must use cash, or postal and money orders, or use bank giro credits to be described in Chapter 9.

One of the **disadvantages of cheques** as compared with cash is that they are not legal tender, and a creditor may refuse to take a cheque in payment in case it will be dishonoured upon presentation at the bank. Manual workers can demand their wages in cash, but in 1963 the payment of wages by cheque became legal, provided that the employees make a written request for it and the employers agree. It was already legal to pay employees other than manual workers by cheque. Postal and money orders may also be used for wages as explained on page 20. Postal and money orders cannot be dishonoured because their cash value must be paid to the Post Office before they are issued.

The payment of wages into workers' bank accounts would save employers a great deal of time in counting cash and placing it in pay packets. It would also make unnecessary the fetching of big sums from the banks and thus put an end to payroll robberies. Against these advantages must be set the cost of making out cheques and the extra bank charges incurred.

As yet, few workers have bank accounts and they are not accustomed to current accounts and cheques. They are usually at work when the banks close. Shopkeepers believe that their customers would ask them to cash wage cheques for which purpose they would have to keep large sums on the premises. The wage cheques would entail more entries in their current accounts and higher bank charges.

A disadvantage of paying a debt by cheque without obtaining a receipt stating for what the money was paid, or a receipt attached to an invoice or a statement, is that there may be uncertainty as to which particular debt has been paid. A debtor may have bought goods for £50 three months ago and another lot for £30 one month ago. If he now sends a cheque for £20, for which lot is he paying? The debtor, if he cares to do so, has the right to say for which lot he is paying. If he pays for the second lot, he may, for example, be entitled to cash discount, but not if he is paying for the first lot.

Unless a cheque is carefully drawn, it may be altered by a dishonest person. Six pounds, for instance, may be altered to sixty pounds. There is, too, the possibility of the drawer's signature being forged and large sums being drawn from his account without his knowledge. In such a case the banker must bear the loss because he has a specimen of the drawer's signature in his signature file and should have recognised the forgery. If the drawer alters his style of writing, he should ask the banker to let him sign the card again, for otherwise the banker may not be responsible for money paid out of his account on a forged cheque. How to guard against these and other risks connected with cheques will be explained in Chapter 10.

A cheque for a big sum is of the same dimensions as a cheque for a small sum and can be just as easily mislaid or lost without the loss being noticed immediately. The loss of a bundle of 100 £1 notes is much more likely to be noticed at once than the loss of one £1 note or of a cheque for £100. The risks involved in the use of cheques make it necessary to handle them with great care.

To be paid by cheque may be inconvenient for those who have no banking account. In order to obtain the cash for it, they may have to ask someone who has a banking account to cash it for them, as for example, when they do not live near the drawer's bank.

When more money is kept in a current account than is required to meet the cheques drawn on it, the banker is being given the use of the credit balance without having to pay interest on it. In return, if the balance is big enough, he may not charge the customer anything for the work connected with the current account. Accounts which do not maintain a sufficient credit balance will be debited with **bank charges**; these depend largely on the number of entries in the account, and numerous cheques for small amounts may be rather expensive. A cheque for £1 costs as much to handle as a cheque for £1000.

A customer who has drawn 100 cheques in a certain period may find that the bank's charges for his current account are £5. The cost of each cheque then amounts to £5 ÷ 100 = 5p. To pay 50p by cheque is, in such a case, much dearer than using a postal order. But the poundage on postal and money orders increases with the amount of the orders. If the charge for a cheque for £50 were 10p it would be still much cheaper than the poundage on a £50 money order, and postal orders for £50.

Although the charges may in some cases be heavy, and in spite of the other disadvantages mentioned, cheques are such a convenient means of payment that they are more widely used than ever.

Cheques are not the only means of payment provided by the banks. Other ways will be dealt with in Chapter 9.

Questions

1. What does a bank manager require before opening a current account for a customer? Give reasons for your answers.

2. What is a paying-in book? What purposes does it serve?

3. Describe five ways in which a current account differs from a deposit account.

4. Distinguish between a bank statement and a bank paying-in book.

5. What are the advantages of cheques to a businessman?

6. What are the advantages and disadvantages of paying wages by cheque to (*a*) workmen, (*b*) employers? Why is an employer not allowed to pay wages by cheque to a workman who is absent, but can send postal or money orders?

7. What are bank charges? Why are they charged? How are they determined?

8. From what documents does a banker obtain the information for writing up a customer's account? From what documents does a customer prepare his bank account?

9. Describe three kinds of bank accounts.

10. Distinguish between a bank deposit account and a bank current account. Explain why a bank current account is essential to a trader, while a bank deposit account, although useful, is not necessarily essential.   (W.J.E.C.)

11. An acquaintance of yours has asked your advice about the desirability of opening a current banking account. Outline the procedure involved in opening an account, and state what in your opinion are the main advantages of being a bank's customer.   (S.R.E.B.)

Chapter 8

Commercial banks · Overdrafts and loans

The banker's chief work is **to borrow and to lend** money. He borrows small sums from a large number of people and pays interest for the use of it. When he lends money, he charges borrowers a higher rate. He buys the use of money at one price and sells the use of it at a higher price, the difference between the two rates of interest being his gross profit.

The main borrowers are businessmen. **Before lending** to a business, the banker wants to know for what purpose the money is required. He will lend only if he thinks it will be spent on something that will help the business make profits and enable it to repay the loan quickly. He may also want to see the accounts of the business in order to make sure that it is well managed and in a sound financial position.

When the banker lends, he usually asks for security to place alongside the borrower's promise to repay. Such security is known as **collateral security**. If the borrower fails to repay the loan, the banker can sell the security and get his money back from the proceeds. Documents showing that the borrower is the owner of land or buildings, or stocks and shares, will be accepted as security.

There are two ways in which the banker is prepared to lend – by means of an **overdraft** and by means of a loan. Normally, no more money can be drawn out of an account than has been paid into it, but the banker may agree to allow a customer to overdraw his account up to a certain limit. The customer can then write out cheques for more money than he has in the bank and the banker will pay these cheques. The balance of the customer's account then becomes a debit balance showing that he is a debtor to the bank for the amount he has overdrawn.

Consider B. Buyer's statement shown overleaf. On 1 May B. Buyer has £200 in the bank, but he knows that during the next few weeks he will have to pay bills amounting to much more than £200, and that he is not likely to be able to pay much into the bank during that time. He then consults his banker and it is agreed that he should be allowed to overdraw up to £500. On 5 May he pays £80 by cheque which still leaves him a credit balance of £120. On 10 May he pays £140, £20 more than he has in his account. Now his overdraft is £20. On 21 May he draws a cheque for £240 which increases the overdraft to £260, and on 5 June another cheque for £180 brings the debit balance to £440. On 10 June he is able to pay £160 into the bank and this reduces the overdraft to £280. On 20 June he pays in another £330 which wipes out the overdraft and gives him a credit balance of £50.

B. Buyer must pay interest on each debit balance for as long as it remains in the account. He thus has to pay interest on:

£20 for 11 days;
£260 for 15 days;
£440 for 5 days;
£280 for 10 days.

At 8 per cent per annum the interest on these sums equals £2, and this amount will be placed to the debit of Buyer's account. If the charges for running the current account amount to £1, this sum will also be debited to him. On 20 June he therefore has £47 in the bank.

Had Buyer, on 10 May, borrowed by means of a **loan** the banker would enter it in the receipts column of his account, and add it to the £120 already there. Interest would be charged on all the loan until it was repaid. Even if Buyer did not use any of it, he would still have to pay interest, because if it

Statement of Account (To find to whom he paid the cheques, Buyer can refer to the cheque counterfoils, the numbers of which are given in the particulars column)

STATEMENT OF ACCOUNT WITH

Lloyds Bank Limited

QUEEN STREET STRATFORD

SHEET No.

71

DESCRIPTION
OF ENTRIES

BGC Bank Giro Credit
D/D Direct Debit
DIV Dividend
S/O Standing Order
Cheques are designated
by the Serial Number

MR B BUYER
28 QUEEN STREET
STRATFORD

Account No.

0031459

BUYER B

DATE	PARTICULARS		PAYMENTS	RECEIPTS	BALANCES When overdrawn marked OD.	
19	Opening Balance				200 : 00	*
5 MAY		634081	80 : 00		120 : 00	*
10 MAY		634080	140 : 00		20 : 00	OD
21 MAY		634083	240 : 00		260 : 00	OD
5 JUN		634082	180 : 00		440 : 00	OD
10 JUN	SUNDRY CREDIT			160 : 00	280 : 00	OD
20 JUN	SUNDRY CREDIT			330 : 00		
	INTEREST		2 : 00			
	SERVICE CHARGE		1 : 00		47 : 00	*

The items and balance shown on this statement should be verified and the Bank notified promptly of any discrepancy.

had not been set aside for him it could have been lent to someone else, in the same way as a man who rents a house must pay rent for it even though he has not lived in it. Any money paid into the account does not reduce the loan at once as it does in the case of the overdraft, the sums paid in being entered in the same column as the loan. A borrower can arrange to repay a loan either in one sum or by agreed instalments, each instalment including some of the loan and some of the interest.

The advantage of obtaining a loan instead of an overdraft is that the *rate* of interest is lower, because when the banker grants a loan of a fixed amount he knows where he stands, but in the case of an overdraft he does not know how much he will be called upon to provide.

Buyer's account has been overdrawn for 41 days, the biggest debit balance being £440. If Buyer had thought that he would need £440 for 41 days, he would have asked for a loan. At 7 per cent per annum the interest would have been £3.46, compared with £3.95 if he had overdrawn £440 for 41 days at 8 per cent per annum. As Buyer was not certain how much he needed nor for how long, he arranged to overdraw up to the agreed limit, if necessary. As it happened, he needed £440 for only 5 days and the total interest on all sums overdrawn was only £2. Had someone unexpectedly paid him £440 on 10 May he could have managed without overdrawing at all and no interest would have been charged, but he would have had to pay interest if he had obtained a loan.

Personal loans are made without security to people wishing to buy cars, furniture and household goods. The loan and the interest are repayable in equal instalments over an agreed period. About £1000 is the most that can be borrowed as a personal loan. A small retailer may be permitted to borrow in this way, but this kind of loan is not intended for the use of businesses.

Besides dealing with their cheques and lending to customers, a banker offers them many **other services**. He will collect money due to his customers, such as interest and dividends from investments, and place it to the credit of their accounts. He will arrange for cash to be paid in or withdrawn at any branch. He can provide open credits by means of which cash can be obtained at any branch of any bank. To enable customers to obtain cash at any time cash dispensers are being placed at suitable points. When a special card is inserted in these machines they deliver a bundle of notes and record the customer's code number so that the amount can be charged to his account.

A customer who has valuable documents or jewellery can give them to his banker for safe custody in the bank's strongrooms. Some of the big branches provide safes which customers can rent for their own use. Retailers and others who receive money after the banks have closed can make sure that it will be safe by placing it in a wallet which can be dropped into the bank through the night safes fixed in the walls of the banks. Keys are provided for the safes and wallets. If the customer uses a black wallet it will be opened by the bank next morning and the money checked with the enclosed paying-in slip and credited to his account. A brown wallet cannot be opened until its owner arrives with the key. A charge is made for the use of night safes.

The banker gives advice on financial matters. He arranges for his customers to buy or sell stocks and shares, and is prepared to manage their investments. Some prepare payrolls, deal with customers' income tax, and write up the register of shareholders for limited companies.

Banks act as trustees of funds, and documents deposited with them are dealt with according to the customer's instructions. A person making a will can arrange for a bank to act as an executor for carrying out (or executing) the provisions made in the will as to the disposal of his money and property after his death.

Banks also deal with bills of exchange. These will be dealt with in Chapters 45 and 52.

To summarise, we can say that the banker's **most important work** is (*a*) borrowing and lending, (*b*) dealing with cheques and other means of payment, and (*c*) keeping money and valuables safely.

Questions

1. What is collateral security? When and why does a banker ask for it? What kind of things will be accepted as security?

2. What is an overdraft? How is an overdraft shown on the statement?

3. What is a loan? How does it differ from an overdraft?

4. How is the interest on (*a*) an overdraft, (*b*) a loan calculated?

5. I want to borrow £100 for not more than one month. Which would you advise me to have, a loan or an overdraft? Give reasons for your answer.

6. What are personal loans?

7. What services, besides lending, does a banker give to holders of current accounts? Which services are likely to be most useful to a small shopkeeper?

8. Show how the following transactions would appear on a bank statement.

19..		£
Mar. 1	Credit balance	50
,, 2	Cheque paid to A. Wills	780
,, 17	Cheque paid to R. Grey	1190
Apr. 6	Cash paid in	1460
,, 16	Cash paid in	2000
,, 30	Charges	5

Calculate the interest due at 5 per cent per annum and enter it on the statement.

9. Describe the three most important functions of a bank.

10. To whom do banks lend and, excluding the private individual, for what purposes do customers borrow money? (M.R.E.B.)

11. Explain the procedure to open a current account at a commercial bank. What other services are available to a customer at such a bank?

12. Explain the difference between (a) a bank overdraft and a bank loan, (b) deposit and current accounts, (c) open and crossed cheques, (d) night safe and automatic cash dispenser. (L.C.C. & I.)

13. (a) Discuss the various methods by which individuals and firms borrow from commercial banks. (b) Briefly describe a situation in which each method would be most suitable. (A.E.B.)

14. (a) Distinguish between a bank overdraft and a bank loan. (b) Explain what a bank manager would require to know when considering an application for an overdraft from one of his customers. (W.J.E.C.)

15. (a) Why do banks pay interest on deposit accounts and not usually on current accounts? (b) How does a bank current account facilitate receipts and payments? (c) Why do banks usually require security for loans and overdrafts? (d) Why might a prosperous trader require an overdraft? (U.C.L.E.S.)

Chapter 9

Commercial banks · Money transfer and giro services

Chapter 6 described the cheque system. In this chapter we shall discuss the other money transfer services provided by commercial banks.

For fixed amounts due on fixed dates, such as insurance premiums and hire purchase instalments, the customer can fill in a **standing** or **banker's order** which requests the banker to make the payments when they fall due, unless the order has been withdrawn in the meantime. Payments made under a standing order will affect the bank charges, but it saves the cost of posting cheques every time the payments falls due, and the payee receives prompt payment without having to send renewal notices.

Bills for gas, rates, phones, etc., that come regularly but vary in amount can be averaged over the year by means of **budget accounts**. The customer estimates the yearly total of such bills and gives a standing order to transfer each month one-twelfth of the total from his ordinary current account to his budget account. He pays the bills by drawing cheques on his budget account or by bank giro as explained below and he can overdraw when necessary. He pays the bank a fixed charge per year as well as interest on any overdrafts.

Bank giro credit (or credit transfer) forms are most useful when several payments are made at the same time. Bank giro means the circulation of funds from debtors to creditors through the banks. Giro credits enable funds to be sent to a creditor's account at any bank in the country. The

Date	Lloyds Bank Limited 🔷 Bank Giro Credit		Notes: £20	5
			£10	
		Code Number	£5	
			£1	
Cashier's stamp and initials	Bank		Coins: 50p silver bronze	
			Total of cash	
	Branch		Cheques POs etc	
	Account in the name of			
Paid in by	Payee's account number			
Address/Ref.			£	

debtor can obtain the forms from his bank or he may receive them from his creditor with the invoices and statements. He fills in a form for each payment and retains the counterfoils signed by the banker. His bank forwards the forms to the banks named on them which, after crediting the payees' accounts, sends them to the payees who then know which payments have been received.

The number of giro credits used is taken into account in deciding bank charges, but a customer may save more than the charges because he avoids the expense of posting cheques. The creditor is spared the work of dealing with a large number of letters, cheques, postal and money orders, sorting them and paying them into his bank. The credits can be used for paying salaries, rents, gas and electric bills, etc.

To pay by cheque the payer must have a current account. He can give a cheque to anyone anywhere at any time, the payee then taking it to a bank or passing it on. The payee need not have a bank account. Anyone, whether he has a bank account or not, can pay by giro credits, but only payees with bank accounts can be paid in this way. The credit must first be taken to a bank which sends it, not to the payee, but to his bank, and it cannot be passed on. Unlike cheques, these credits cannot be dishonoured because the payer gives his own bank a cheque or cash for the total amount. Payers who have no bank accounts can use the service without any charge instead of sending postal and money orders.

When the amount and the date of the payment vary, **direct debiting** can be used. For example, a wholesaler can ask his retail customer to authorise his bank to pay when it receives a direct debit form from the wholesaler, unless the retailer has queried the invoices or statements within so many days of receiving them. The retailer saves the cost of posting cheques for each separate payment; moreover, he has less to pay in bank charges. The wholesaler gets prompt settlement without having to send further statements and reminders.

Many banks have agreed to issue a common form of **cheque card** to their customers. Cheque cards are numbered and show the bank's code number, a specimen signature of the customer and the date when the card ceases to be valid. The cardholder can give cheques of up to the figure shown on the card anywhere in this country. The shopkeeper makes sure that the card is still valid, compares the signature and code number on the card with those on the cheque, and writes the number of the card on the back of the cheque. He is certain of payment because the bank guarantees payment, even if the cardholder has no money in his account. He may gain more customers because the banks advertise the cards.

A cardholder can draw cash up to the figure shown from any branch of the bank taking part in the scheme including foreign banks which are members of the Eurocheque scheme. A card makes it unnecessary to carry around a lot of cash. It costs nothing to the holder nor to those who accept cheques on the strength of it. The banks gain because more cheques will be used and they will earn more in bank charges. A card must be renewed before it expires on the date shown on it.

Bank **credit cards** enable the holder to buy goods and services without having to pay for them at the time of purchase. Barclays Bank issues the Barclaycard through its card Centre at Northampton, and Lloyds, Midland and National Westminster Banks issue jointly the Access card through their card Centre at Southend-on-Sea. Anyone, whether he has a bank account or not, can apply to the Centre for a card. The amount of credit allowed depends on the cardholder's financial position. Transactions affecting the credit are reported to the Centre where all card accounts are kept.

When making a purchase the buyer hands his card to the trader who makes out a sales slip. The card and the slip are placed in an imprinter which records the card's details on the slip. The buyer signs the slip and the trader, having checked that the signatures agree, returns the card along with a copy of the slip. The trader pays the slips into a branch of the bank concerned which then pays him the total sum due. He is certain that he will be paid.

Every month the Centre sends the cardholder a statement of purchases together with copies of the sales slips sent in by the traders. If he pays the full amount within twenty-five days of the statement date no extra charges are incurred. If, however, he pays off only part of the debt he will be charged interest on the unpaid balance.

Any credit cardholder can, at any branch of a bank concerned with his card and at some foreign banks, draw on demand cash which will be deducted from his credit. There is a charge for this service and the amount advanced bears interest from the date it was given.

A cardholder who has a personal account with the bank issuing his card can, without charge, at almost any bank in the British Isles and at some European banks cash cheques of up to £50 a time. These withdrawals do not affect his credit and card account and will be debited to his personal account by the bank which keeps it.

There is no charge for the card. The holder is spared the trouble of carrying cash and cheques and has to make out only one cheque per month to the Centre instead of several to different traders, thus saving bank charges and having more time to pay. Shopkeepers pay a service charge on sales made to cardholders, the banks claiming that the charge is covered by free advertising of the card and credit scheme, increased sales and guaranteed payment. Credit cards, like cheque cards, can be used by businesses but both are intended mainly for the ordinary shopper. Cheque cards can be used anywhere but credit cards can be used only with businesses that have joined the scheme and display the Barclaycard or the Access sign.

Questions

1. What is a banker's order? When is it used?

2. Describe how a budget account works and its advantages and disadvantages to a householder.

3. What advantages do giro credits have for (*a*) the payer, (*b*) the payee, (*c*) the banks?

4. What is a giro credit transfer? For what kind of transactions is it particularly useful? Why is a cheque often more useful? (A.E.B.)

5. Explain how a direct debit differs from a banker's order. What do the payer and the payee gain by using direct debiting?

6. State, with reasons, which method of payment you would use in the following cases:

    (*a*) An insurance premium due on every 1 January.
    (*b*) Several bills paid to different people on the same day.
    (*c*) Rent, gas, electric and phone bills that come every quarter.
    (*d*) A retailer's bills from the same wholesaler.
    (*e*) Weekly wages to a factory worker.
    (*f*) Monthly salary to a teacher.
    (*g*) A week's wages to a workman sent to work in a distant town.

7. What are cheque cards? What advantages do they offer (*a*) shoppers, (*b*) retailers, (*c*) banks?

8. Describe how Barclaycards work. What are their advantages and disadvantages to (*a*) shoppers, (*b*) shopkeepers, (*c*)) banks?

9. What would be the cost of paying a bill of £5 and another of £50 by each of the following methods?

    (*a*) Posting money orders, or postal orders, or cheques.
    (*b*) Posting bank notes in a registered envelope.
    (*c*) By bank giro credits.

10. 'You get more than a cheque book when you open a bank account.' What more do you get?

11. Describe in detail the services rendered by commercial banks to their clients under the following headings: (*a*) safety, (*b*) cheques, (*c*) methods of payments other than cheques, (*d*) loans, (*e*) other services. (A.L.S.E.B.)

12. Explain how the services of a bank are used by a commercial trader in the following activities.

    (*a*) Making regular monthly payments on equipment purchased on H.P. terms.
    (*b*) Raising temporary additional cash to pay for stock.
    (*c*) Paying weekly wages to employees.
    (*d*) Accepting cheques from customers in the shop. (R.S.A.)

13. Describe the uses of a cheque card (e.g. Midland Bank cheque card), and a credit card (Barclaycard, Access). (R.S.A.)

14. State, with your reasons, the form of payment you would recommend in each of the following cases:

    (*a*) payment of £396 by a wholesaler to a manufacturer;
    (*b*) urgent remittance of £50 by a business man in South Wales to his daughter on holiday in Scotland to reach her the same day;
    (*c*) payment on the first of each month of a life insurance premium of £5;
    (*d*) monthly payment by a local authority of the salaries of those of its staff who have banking accounts;
    (*e*) purchase of a couple of sticks of sealing wax from a local stationer;
    (*f*) payment by post of £2 for an article to be sent by post. (W.J.E.C.)

Chapter 10

Crossed cheques

A cheque, being payable on demand, may be stolen and cashed before the bank is informed of the loss. This risk can be lessened by cancelling the order to pay the payee on demand. To do this two parallel lines are drawn across the cheque, **crossing** out as it were the words 'on demand', which, although they do not appear on the cheque, are implied after the word 'pay'.

Pay (on demand) *A. Seller* or Order

The lines tell the banker that he is not to give A. Seller cash at once, but must make him wait for it. The banker must first demand the money for himself and then transfer it to A. Seller. The cheque is still payable on demand to a banker but not to A. Seller.

Because the banker has first to collect the money, the payee must leave the cheque with him, obtaining a receipt for it. The banker's receipt for money left with him is the paying-in book possessed only by those who have accounts at the bank. The result is that a crossed cheque can be cashed only by a person who has a banking account. The cheque must be entered in the paying-in book and in the customer's account. In this way the banker always knows who paid in a crossed cheque. When open or uncrossed cheques are not paid into an account but cashed over the counter, the banker has no record of those to whom he paid the cash, except what appears on the cheque itself.

A payee who has no banking account must ask someone who has to cash the cheque for him, or ask the drawer to 'open' the crossing by writing on it 'pay cash' and adding his signature.

If there are only two parallel lines across the cheque, the crossing is a **general crossing** and the cheque can be paid into any bank where the owner happens to keep an account. When the name of a bank is written between the lines, the crossing is a **special crossing** and the cheque must be taken to the special bank named between the lines. As this might be inconvenient for the payee, the practice developed of just writing in the words with

General crossings

& Co.

Not Negotiable

& Co.

A/c payee only
Not Negotiable

which the names of all banks at one time ended, the words '& Co.', so that anyone could turn a general crossing into a special crossing by adding in front of '& Co.' the name of the bank he wished to use. Unless this has already been done when the banker receives the cheque, he writes in his own name as the banker who is to collect and transfer the cash to the payee.

Cheques are negotiable like cash. Anyone who takes a cheque honestly and gives something for it has the right to demand payment, even though it is found that the person who passed it on to him had stolen it. The owner of a cheque can protect himself against this danger by writing on it the

Special crossings

Lloyds Bank & Co.

Midland Bank & Co.
A/c payee only

Barclays Bank & Co.
Not Negotiable

words **'Not negotiable'**. Anyone accepting a cheque marked 'Not negotiable' should realise that he might have to give it back to the true owner should it be discovered that the cheque had been stolen.

Sometimes the words **'Account Payee Only'** are added to the cheque. The banker will then enter the cheque only in the account of the one named as payee who must pay it into the bank instead of passing it on to somebody else. The words 'or order' and 'or bearer' can be crossed out and the word 'only' written instead, so that the cheque then reads 'Pay A. Seller only'. The banker is then bound to pay A. Seller and no one else, but, in this case, unless the cheque is crossed, it need not be paid into an account.

If A. Seller passes on the cheque to L. Smith and just writes his name on the back, he is said to **endorse** in blank as

A. Seller.

Smith can then pass on the cheque without endorsing it. If Smith does endorse it before giving it to S. Brown, he is telling Brown that he believes the cheque to be good and in the event of dishonour by the drawer he himself will pay Brown. Everyone who endorses the cheque can be called upon to pay if the drawer fails to do so.

A. Seller, the payee, can compel Smith to endorse the cheque by means of a special endorsement as follows:

Pay L. Smith
  A. Seller.

Smith cannot then pass on the cheque without endorsing it.

An endorsement that prevents the cheque being transferred is a restrictive endorsement, such as:

Pay S. Brown only
  A. Seller.

S. Brown must now pay the cheque into the bank.

A **postdated cheque** bears a date later than that on which it is actually made out. As the cheque cannot be cashed before the date shown on it, the drawer is given time to pay money into the bank to meet it or to see that the payee has fulfilled his obligations before it is paid, such as delivering goods by a certain date. If the goods are not delivered as promised, the drawer of the postdated cheque can request his banker to refuse to cash the cheque.

Cheques are usually paid into the bank within a few days of being drawn, 95 per cent being paid into the payee's account without being passed on. When a cheque bears a date several months earlier than the date of presentation, the banker may require confirmation by the drawer before he pays it. Cheques which are about six months old are known as **stale cheques**, and are marked 'out of date' before being returned for confirmation.

Money orders and postal orders are not negotiable and these words are always printed on them. They can be crossed just like cheques and in that case must be paid into a banking account instead of being cashed at a post office. They can be paid into accounts at savings banks as well as into accounts at commercial banks.

Another danger in using cheques is that a dishonest person may alter the words and figures. To make **alteration** more difficult no spaces should be left between the words: 'nine pounds' could easily be altered to 'ninety pounds' if enough space were left between the two words. A further safeguard would be to write as well 'under ten pounds (£10)' on the cheque. This is always done when the payee is given a blank cheque on which he himself is to fill in the sum payable. When the cheque is made out, the exact sum may not be known, but it may be known that it will not be as much as £10.

Where large numbers of cheques are made out, special cheque-writing machines are used. It is very difficult to make alterations on these cheques that cannot be noticed at once. When it is necessary to alter a cheque, the drawer should confirm the alteration by adding his signature.

Questions

1. How is a cheque crossed? What difference does the crossing make?

2. Why is a crossed cheque safer than an open cheque?

3. Explain the difference between a general crossing and a special crossing. Give examples.

4. What is the difference between 'negotiable' and 'not negotiable'? Which of these are negotiable: £1 notes, coins, postal orders, money orders, stamps, cheques?

5. Why are the words 'not negotiable' written on cheques? Can cheques marked 'not negotiable' be passed on?

6. Distinguish between (*a*) a blank cheque and an open cheque, (*b*) a postdated cheque and a stale cheque, (*c*) an order cheque and a bearer cheque.

7. What is endorsement? When must an order cheque be endorsed?

8. Give examples of a blank endorsement, a special endorsement and a restrictive endorsement. What is the effect of each kind of endorsement on the transferability of a cheque?

9. Why may a person who passes on a cheque refuse to endorse it?

10. In what ways can a cheque be made not transferable? What is the difference between 'not transferable' and 'not negotiable'?

11. What precautions should be taken against a cheque being altered? If a drawer alters a cheque, what should he do?

12. What is the difference between a cheque crossed 'A/c payee only' and an open cheque made payable to 'A. Payee only'?

13. If a postal or money order is crossed, what difference does it make to the payee? Why should the sender of the order cross it?

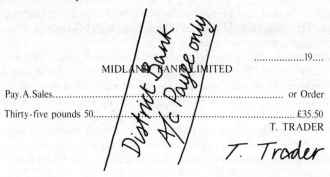

MIDLAND BANK LIMITED ....19....

Pay. A. Sales... or Order

Thirty-five pounds 50..£35.50

T. TRADER

T. Trader

(a) Copy the above cheque adding any details that are shown on a printed cheque.
(b) Name the drawee, the payee, and the drawer.
(c) What kind of crossing is on the cheque?
(d) Can the payee pass on the cheque?
(e) How must A. Sales deal with the cheque?
(f) Must the cheque be endorsed?
(g) How could the cheque be turned into an open cheque?
(h) If '& Co.' had been added to the crossing, what difference would this make? Why were these words used on a cheque in the first place?
(i) If T. Trader wanted to use the cheque as a receipt, how would this be shown on the cheque? What would A. Sales then have to do when paying the cheque into his account?

15. (a) What is a cheque and what information is necessary to be written on a printed cheque form? You may illustrate your answer if you wish.
(b) If a cheque is said to be crossed what does this mean and what effect does this have on the payment of it?
(c) Draw an example of a General Crossing and of a Special Crossing.

(S.R.E.B.)

Chapter 11

Savings banks · National Giro

The banks we have so far discussed are commercial or joint stock banks. Another kind of bank is the deposit or savings bank, such as the trustee banks.

Trustee savings banks are run for the benefit of the customers and not for the profit of the trustees. They are governed by Acts of Parliament which limit the deposit of a customer to £10 000 and state how the trustees must invest the funds. They are meant for the use of small savers. They take money on deposit and pay interest on it. A few pounds can be withdrawn on demand from a savings account, but notice is required for the withdrawal of larger sums. Some of these banks will make certain payments on behalf of their customers, such as paying their rates, electric and gas bills, and they take charge of valuables. They provide current accounts (but not for businesses) and issue cheque cards to customers who satisfy their requirements. Their charges are known beforehand. They open investment accounts which earn a higher rate of interest than deposit accounts but demand more notice of withdrawal.

As these banks **do not lend**, overdrafts are not allowed. They sell savings certificates and arrange to buy and sell stocks and shares. They provide travellers cheques and giro credits. The Birmingham Municipal Bank is a savings bank, but not a trustee bank. It offers the same services as trustee banks and also lends for house purchase.

The Post Office Savings Bank (now known as the **National Savings Bank**) has a long history of service to the small saver. A child of seven may open an account with as little as 25p, the money deposited earns interest, and it may be withdrawn on demand subject to certain limitations. Up to £10 000 may be held in one person's account. Investment accounts earning varying rates of interest may also be opened.

National Development Bonds may also be bought at post offices. These securities earn interest and there is a small appreciation in value after a period of years.

Premium savings bonds were introduced in 1956. No interest is paid on them, the interest being accumulated in a prize fund and distributed among bond holders by regular monthly (and weekly) draws. These draws are made by Electronic Random Number Indicator Equipment (ERNIE).

The **National Giro** was started by the Post Office in 1968 as a means of providing a cheap and convenient banking service for the millions of wage-earners in Britain who traditionally do not use accounts with the commercial banks. Two features of the system make an immediate appeal to would-be members: ordinary cheque transactions between account holders are free of charge, and National Giro banking business may be done at any post office (except very small sub-offices).

References are required when a Giro account is opened, and a small deposit (not less than £1) must be paid in. All accounts are kept at the National Giro Centre in Bootle, Lancashire. Deposits do not earn interest as the scheme is designed to act like a current account at a commercial bank. Giro cheques, postage-paid addressed envelopes, and transfer/-deposit forms (used for transferring money from the holder's account to the account of another Giro account-holder, and also for paying money in to the holder's account) are supplied at nominal charges.

Girocheques have no stubs, but the account holder keeps a record of his drawings and deposits on his Transaction Record Sheet. Girocheques are not sent direct to the payee as bank cheques are: they are drawn in favour of the payee and sent to the Giro Centre. If the payee is a Giro account-holder, the Centre debits the drawer's account, after verifying that the account is in funds, and credits the payee's account, advising the payee that this has been done. If the payee is not a Giro account-holder, the Centre debits the drawer's account, 'authenticates' the cheque, and sends it to the payee. The payee may then cash it at any post office, pay it into his bank account, or endorse it and pass it on to somebody else. Authenticated Girocheques are absolutely safe from being dishonoured, and are therefore acceptable to any creditor; they can therefore serve as 'traveller's cheques' within Britain.

Traveller's cheques for use abroad can be supplied by National Giro to account-holders and non-account-holders alike, through an arrangement existing between the Giro and a leading travel agency. Where Giro links exist with other countries, money can be sent to and received from those countries through Giro.

Since all transactions take place at the Giro Centre, and the solvency of accounts is verified before payees are credited or cheques are 'authenticated', **no overdrafts** are possible. However, arrangements exist with a finance company for personal loans to be made available to account holders approved by the finance company. The amount of the loan is credited to the Giro customer's account, and the loan plus interest is paid back by regular monthly transfers to the finance company's Giro account.

An account-holder draws cash by making out a Girocheque to 'Self'. Withdrawals are made from one of the two post offices specified by the account-holder when opening his account. A Giro card and Withdrawal Record sheet must be produced by the account-holder. Withdrawals are limited to £20 every other working day. More than this amount may be drawn, and a different post office can be specified, but in this case the Girocheque must first be authenticated by the Giro Centre.

A limited number of **standing orders** are accepted for payment on behalf of account-holders. They are paid by direct debit to the Giro accounts or bank accounts of the payees.

Business firms and other organisations (mail order firms, hire-purchase companies, telephone, electricity and gas authorities, etc.) that have many accounts with wage-earning members of the public may enclose a Giro form with their invoices or statements. Customers who are Giro account-holders can then pass this on to Giro and have their accounts debited with the due amount. Non-account-holders can also pay such accounts over the counter of a post office, a small charge being payable on each transaction. **In-payment forms** for this purpose can be obtained at post offices. Firms may have special forms printed carrying their own messages to customers, and as the form is returned to the payee as evidence of payment, the customer is invited to use the back of the form as an order form, or to convey a message.

Inpayment form

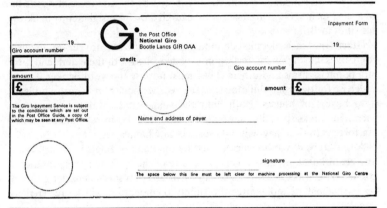

The National Giro provides a simple, quick and cheap current account. Wage-earners have made little use of the commercial banks. Now that they can have a current account at a post office which they already use, many are expected to open accounts for the receipt of wages and for paying bills, and their employers may encourage them to do so by agreeing to pay some of the charges. From the account-holder's point of view, the advantages and drawbacks of National Giro compared with the services offered by the commercial banks may be summarised as follows:

Advantages: Giro service charges (particularly between account-holders) are cheap – ordinary transactions are free of charge; and all charges are known beforehand.
(*Note:* It is fair to say here that the commercial banks nowadays also offer cheap, and sometimes free, banking facilities to private customers, as already mentioned; bank charges, too, are now well known and largely standardised and there is a tariff of charges for private accounts.)
Giro business can be transacted at any post office that handles savings business. These offices are more numerous than the branches of banks and their hours of business are far longer.

Once a Giro cheque has been authenticated, its value is in no doubt; it cannot be dishonoured.

Drawbacks: The limits on personal cash drawings can be inconvenient.
The delay involved in sending Girocheques for authentication.
The lack of overdraft facilities.
The lack of the personal relationship that exists between a bank customer and his branch manager, and the valuable advice that frequently results from this relationship.

Explanatory booklets fully describing all the services offered by the National Giro are available from the Post Office. Specimens of Girocheques and other documents are illustrated. A study of this literature, together with similar publications distributed by the commercial banks to advertise their services to customers, can give useful insights into banking activities in Britain today.

Other types of banks include industrial banks. These are run by finance companies which pay interest on money deposited with them and lend it to hire purchase firms and others. They must not use the word banker if they advertise for deposits. Building societies receive money on deposit and lend it to buyers of houses. Both limit the sums withdrawable on demand. Merchant banks specialise in obtaining capital for businesses and in financing foreign trade. They will be discussed in Chapter 52.

A sixth type of bank is represented by the Bank of England. It is known as a **central bank** because it is in the centre of the banking system, and as a **chartered bank** because it was set up by means of a special charter granted by Parliament. It looks after the supply of money. It will be referred to later.

Questions

1. Write an account of the facilities available at a post office for the saving of money.   (S.R.E.B.)

2. What services are common to trustee savings banks and commercial banks? What services can one obtain at a commercial bank but not at a savings bank?

3. What services does the National Giro provide? Which people and which businesses are likely to make most use of it?

4. Compare a National Giro account with a current account at a joint stock bank under the following headings: (*a*) deposits, (*b*) withdrawals, (*c*) methods of making payments, (*d*) charges, (*e*) other services available.

5. Obtain National Giro booklets from the post office and study the examples of Girocheques and other documents shown in them.

Chapter 12

Cash and trade discount · Terms of payment

Every trader likes to be paid quickly, and, in order to encourage his debtors to pay quickly, he will give a cash discount. If the terms of payment are 3 per cent one month the seller will accept £97 instead of £100 if the payment is made within one month.

It pays the creditor to give this discount. In letting the buyer have the goods without being bound to pay for them for, say, three months, he runs the risk that he will never receive some of the money due to him. He would rather have £97 for certain now than the promise of £100 in two months' time. Besides, the loss is not as much as it seems at first sight. The £97 can be invested to earn interest. At 5 per cent per annum it will grow to £97.80 in two months. But the trader would not invest it but use it in his own business. He may need it to pay his own creditors and earn the cash discount allowed by them, or he may buy more goods with it and sell them at a profit greater than the cash discount. If he needs £97 to buy goods which he can sell for £120, it pays him to accept only £97 for a debt of £100. He gains £23 on the goods and loses £3 on the discount, leaving him with a net gain of £20.

Another reason for giving cash discount is that prompt payment saves the trader some clerical work. When he is paid in small sums at intervals, he has to keep a record of these payments, and he may have to write frequently to the debtor to remind him that it is time that he settled the debt. Payment of all the sum due at once saves him this trouble.

Quick payment also brings **advantages to the debtor**. Suppose that the invoice is for £100 and the terms are 3 per cent one month, 1 per cent two months, net three months. By paying at the end of the first month he is giving the money to the seller two months before he need do and deprives himself of the use of it for that time. He loses the use of £97 for one-sixth of a year and saves £3 by so doing. Had he kept the money in a bank for another two months at 5 per cent per annum it would have earned only 80p as compared with £3 earned by using it to pay quickly for the goods. The cash discount is equivalent to a rate of $(3 \div 97) \times 6 \times 100 = 18.5$ per cent per annum. By waiting two months before paying he loses the use of £99 for one month and gains £1, which is $(1 \div 99) \times 12 \times 100 = 12.1$ per cent per annum. At the end of three months he will have to pay the £100 in full. The quicker the debtor pays the more he earns in cash discount. It may pay him to borrow in order to pay his debts quickly.

The prompt settlement of debts means a good name for the trader.

Suppliers will be anxious to please and to give him good service. When goods are scarce, the good payer will be given preference and the slow payer will have to wait for supplies or will be refused credit and will have to pay before the goods will be delivered.

In spite of these advantages gained by quick payment, many small traders take the full term of credit allowed. They may be short of money because they give too much credit and must sell a second lot of goods before paying for the first lot. Or it may be that they can use the money to buy goods that can be sold at a good profit: £95 spent on goods that can be sold in two months at a profit of £20 earns more than £95 paid to settle a debt of £100 two months before it is due.

The **terms of payment** do not always provide for the granting of cash discount. When no deduction is to be made from the invoice price, the terms are 'net' and payment is expected within a few days. When goods are ordered by a customer whose ability to pay is being questioned by the seller, cash may be demanded with the order (c.w.o.), or when the goods are delivered (c.o.d.). 'Spot' cash means that the buyer must pay for the goods when he takes possession of them, wherever they happen to be at that time. 'Prompt' cash allows two or three days to examine and check the goods and invoices before paying.

Three per cent one month is not the same as 3 per cent monthly. In the first case the buyer can pay within one month of the date of the invoice and earn the discount. In the second case a monthly statement of account is prepared and all invoices sent during the month must be paid by the end of the month in order to earn the discount. Thus, goods bought towards the end of the month must be paid for almost immediately if the discount is to be obtained. The terms may provide for interest to be added to debts that are overdue.

Cash discount when earned is shown on the statement of account. The invoice may show another kind of discount, trade discount, which must not be confused with cash discount.

Anybody who pays quickly can earn cash discount, but **trade discount** is given by one trader to another. It is a percentage of the catalogue or recommended retail prices. If these prices are entered on the invoice, the trade discount must be taken away in order to arrive at the price to be charged to the retailer. The retailer's account is debited with the amount left after deducting the discount. Trade discount, unlike cash discount, does not depend on the time of payment. It is granted to a retailer who asks for several months' credit as well as to the retailer who pays ready cash.

In some trades, special discounts are allowed to certain categories of customers – those who hold stocks, perhaps, and distribute to smaller customers, or those who manufacture the goods into other articles; and trade discount is sometimes granted to those who buy in bulk.

The wholesaler can afford to sell the goods cheaper to the retailer than to the public. He sells big quantities to the retailer and this is much easier than weighing and packing a large number of small parcels, receiving cash and giving change for a large number of transactions. It is much cheaper, for example, for the wholesaler to fill a truck with 10 tonnes of coal, weigh it once, and send it to the retailer on one invoice, than it is for the latter to place the 10 tonnes of coal in 200 bags, each of which must weigh exactly 50 kilograms, and then deliver them possibly to 200 houses situated in many streets, make out the same number of delivery notes, take money and give change perhaps 200 times. The retailer sometimes allows his customers a similar discount when they buy a large quantity. He may sell potatoes by the kilogram, but may allow a customer 11 kilograms for the price of 10, because it is less trouble to serve one customer with 11 kilograms than ten customers with 1 kilogram each.

The rate of trade discount, like that for cash discount, may alter from time to time. Suppliers often prepare expensive catalogues which they send to their customers. If prices change, they need not print new catalogues, but can adjust the prices by increasing or decreasing the rate of trade discount, customers being notified of the change by letter or by affixing labels showing the new rates on further catalogues sent out. An article listed at £100 and subject to 20 per cent trade discount costs the retailer £80. If wholesale prices now rise by 5 per cent, the wholesaler requires £84 for the article and must alter the trade discount to 16 per cent of the catalogue or list price which remains at £100.

The percentage allowed for trade discount is not the same in all trades. Different wholesalers in the same trade give different trade discounts and a wholesaler may give more trade discount to some customers than to others who only buy small lots at long intervals and for whom he may have to incur heavy delivery costs. Customers whose purchases during a period total a certain amount may be given an extra discount known as 'quantity discount'.

Trade discount is not in general use. In many cases the price shown and quoted on the invoice is the price charged to the retailer. Instead of showing the price as £100 less trade discount £20 = £80, the invoice just shows the £80 which, in either case, is the actual price charged.

Trade discount, if any, must be deducted before charging value added tax. Cash discount at the highest rate offered must also be deducted. If goods are invoiced at £200 and the terms are 5 per cent one month, 2 per cent two months, net three months, the tax is found on £200 less 5 per cent = £190. If the rate is 10 per cent the tax is then £19 as compared with £20 when no cash discount is allowed. The seller must pay the tax even if the customer never pays him.

Questions

Note: In the grocery trade the credit usually starts from the date of the invoice. In the book trade payment is expected within ten days of the receipt of the statement and in the textile trade by a customary date in the month following that in which the statement is received. Count from the invoice date in these exercises.

1. Give five reasons for the giving of cash discount.

2. What is meant by spot cash, prompt cash, net, 5 per cent one month, 2 per cent monthly account, C.W.O., C.O.D.?

3. An article is advertised at £10 cash down or £12 in monthly instalments of £1. Give reasons for the difference in the prices.

4. (*a*) How does cash discount differ from trade discount?
    (*b*) Explain the benefits of cash discount to (i) creditors and (ii) debtors.
    (*c*) Why do debtors sometimes not take advantage of cash discount?

    (A.E.B.)

5. Why do makers charge less to retailers than to us?

6. Goods cost £800 less a trade discount of 25 per cent and a cash discount of 4 per cent. How much is charged on the invoice? How much is paid for them? Which document shows the cash discount earned?

7. Five per cent cash discount was allowed on a debt of £240. The cash was spent on goods which sold for £285. How much per cent was earned on the cost of the goods?

8. The terms of payment are 5 per cent 1 month, 3 per cent 2 months, 1 per cent 3 months, net 4 months. Express these rates as percentages per annum.

9. Five per cent C.O.D., 3 per cent 1 month, 1 per cent 2 months, net 3 months. Which is the best rate per annum?

10. Why do many small traders take the full term of credit allowed?

Chapter 13

Quotations · Price lists · Prices current

When a business receives an inquiry from a customer the reply it sends is known as a quotation. The quotation should provide, besides the **price and terms** of payment, all the information required by the customer.

The goods are named and their **quality** or kind given by description, such as best Welsh steam coal, or by reference to the sample, pattern or catalogue number. The **price** is stated per unit used for reckoning quantities, such as 50p per metre or per kilogram or per ten. A lower price or a bigger discount may be allowed if a large quantity is purchased. If so, the quotation should include this information. A clause is usually added stating that the prices quoted may be increased if the cost of materials and of labour rise.

The buyer should be familiar with the **customs** of the trade. The unit of measurement may mean something different from what it means in everyday speech and the same word may mean different quantities in different trades. Booksellers may give thirteen copies for every twelve ordered, and cloth manufacturers may allow more than one hundred centimetres to the metre, for instance. In certain trades an allowance is made for errors in weighing and for loss in weight after the goods have been packed, e.g. ullage is an allowance for leakage from casks.

When goods are sold by **weight** it is necessary to know how the weight is determined. Packed goods may be weighed with the packing to give the gross weight. The weight of the packing or container, known as the 'tare', must be deducted from the gross weight in order to find the actual weight of the goods:

Net weight = gross weight − tare.

The tare may be the average weight of a few containers that were weighed as samples so that the net weight may not be the actual weight of the goods delivered.

The quotation should also say when **delivery** will take place. If the seller has plenty of the goods in stock he can quote delivery as 'ready', i.e. the goods will be dispatched as soon as the order is received. If the goods have to be packed before being forwarded, or obtained from elsewhere first, and this can be done in a short time, delivery will be given as 'prompt', meaning that delivery will take place within a few days of receiving the order. Where goods are not in stock and cannot be obtained in a short time the seller will quote 'forward delivery', the actual date being communicated later. If he knows the goods can be obtained in three months he will quote 'delivery 3 months'.

The quotation should make clear who bears the cost of **packing** and delivery. If packing is to be charged on the invoice, credit notes may be sent for returned empties. Unless anything is said to the contrary, delivery takes place at the seller's place of business and the buyer is responsible for taking the goods away. As a rule, however, the seller undertakes to send the goods to the buyer. The method of quoting the price indicates how much he is prepared to do and pay for, as shown in the following examples, some of which are used only in connection with imports and exports.

£100 carr. pd.	The cost of the carriage is included in the £100. The seller pays for transporting the goods to the buyer.
carr. fwd.	The buyer has to pay the carrier as well as paying £100 to the seller.
carr. extra	The seller will pay the carrier, but will add the cost to the £100 quoted for the goods alone.
f.a.t. f.a.s. f.o.q.	Free alongside truck, free at station, free alongside ship, and free on quay. Expenses of loading and any further transport charges must be paid by the buyer. Free alongside ship may not be the same as free on quay because in some harbours a big ship may be unable to come right up to the quay and has to stay in midstream, the goods being taken to the ship by barges or lighters, thus causing extra expense.
f.o.t. f.o.r.	Free on truck and free on rail. The seller sees that the goods are loaded on to a truck or are ready to move by rail. Any further expenses must be borne by the buyer.
f.o.b.	Free on board. The seller is responsible for all expenses incurred until the goods have been placed on board a ship or an aeroplane.
c.i.f.	Cost, insurance and freight. In this case, the seller insures the goods and pays the shipping company's charges for carrying the goods.
ex works or ex warehouse	The buyer must pay the cost of removing the goods from the factory or warehouse.
loco	The buyer is to take charge of the goods wherever they happen to be and be responsible for any expenses incurred in moving them and perhaps for packing them.
franco	The seller undertakes to deliver the goods and to pay all costs, including customs duties, to the buyer's place of business.

Quotations for work such as building or road construction are known as **tenders**. The term is sometimes used in connection with goods. Traders, for instance, may be asked to tender for supplying school kitchens with meat and goods for a term or for a year. To enable traders to estimate the cost and to tender a price, a 'specification' may be sent to them, giving a detailed account of the work to be done and the goods to be supplied.

A retailer need not send an inquiry for every lot of goods he buys. Catalogues, prices current and price lists are sent to him, and travellers visit him to show samples and to give information. A **prices current** is merely a list of prices of the goods mentioned on it for a certain date. The sender of the prices current is informing his customer of the prices charged in the markets and by dealers in general, and he is not saying that he himself is prepared to sell at those prices. His customers can compare his prices with those shown in the prices current. Prices current are published in newspapers and trade journals. A **price list** gives the same information as a quotation but may include other goods as well as those mentioned in the letter of inquiry. It differs from a prices current in that it gives the prices at which the sender is prepared to sell, providing that he has any goods left when he receives the order. Some price lists can be used as order forms.

Sometimes an inquiry is answered by sending a **pro forma invoice**. This is exactly the same as an ordinary invoice except that the words 'pro forma', which mean 'as a matter of form', are stamped on it. It tells the retailer what the actual invoice would be like if he decides to order the goods. A pro forma invoice is also used when a copy of the original invoice is required for some purpose, e.g. to show the customs officers what goods have been exported. When goods are sent to an agent, a pro forma invoice may be used to inform him of the prices at which he must sell the goods. It is used when goods are sent on approval and is sometimes sent as a reminder that payment is expected before the goods are dispatched.

Questions

1. What is (*a*) a letter of inquiry; (*b*) a quotation?

2. What, besides the cost of the goods, may be included in the price quoted?

3. Explain gross weight, tare and net weight. Why should a trader know the differences between them?

4. What do the following mean? C.O.D., C.W.O., spot cash, prompt cash, ready delivery.

5. What do the following mean? £20 f.o.t. Cardiff; £500 f.a.s. Liverpool; £100 f.o.b. Hull; £60 loco Birmingham.

6. What information does a retailer need about delivery of the goods he is buying? Give reasons for your answer.

7. Explain the difference between a price list and a prices current.

8. What are estimates, specifications and tenders? When are they used?

9. How does a pro forma invoice differ from other invoices? When is a pro forma invoice used?

10. Why may a retailer decide to buy from a maker whose quotation is the highest he has received? What would he consider besides the actual figure quoted?

11. Mr Trader, a shopkeeper, wishing to restock a particular commodity, considers the following quotations:

Quotation	Quantity	Price per unit	Trade discount	Cash discount	Delivery time
A	200	50p	25%	5% (2 weeks)	14 days
B	300	50p	$33\frac{1}{3}$%	$2\frac{1}{2}$% (2 weeks)	1 month
C	200	45p	20%	5% (1 month)	14 days

What considerations would determine Mr Trader's choice?   (A.E.B.)

12. What kind of information does a wholesaler usually supply to a retailer in reply
     to a letter of inquiry? Explain any four terms of abbreviation that he might
     use.   (J.M.B.)

Chapter 14

Profit and loss · Gross and net profit · Overhead expenses · Percentages

The object of every trader is to make a profit by buying at one price and selling at a higher price, the difference being called the 'gross profit'. The profit is usually found at the end of each year's trading and in order to be able to determine it proper books and accounts must be kept.

In Chapter 4 we saw that the purchases account gives the cost of the goods bought in the year and the sales account gives the amount of the goods sold in the year. If all the goods bought were sold by the end of the year all that would be necessary to find the gross profit would be to deduct the purchases from the sales. But some of the goods will be unsold at the end of the year and the trader has then to find what the goods sold cost him to buy. The profit must be reckoned only on the goods that have been sold.

To find the cost price of the goods he has sold in the year, the trader has to **take stock** and count up what the goods left at the end of the year cost him. By taking the value of this stock away from the total purchases he arrives at the cost of the goods sold. For example, a shopkeeper who started with no stock and bought £2000 worth of goods during the year has £300 (cost price) worth left unsold at the end of the year. Then the cost price of the goods sold must have been £2000 − £300 = £1700. Next year he begins with £300 stock on to which is added what he buys during the year, say, £2200. During the second year he has had £300 + £2200 = £2500 worth of goods in his shop and if his stock unsold at the end cost him £400 the cost price of the goods sold during the year was £2500 − £400 = £2100. This is what is done in the Trading and Profit and Loss Account as shown overleaf.

The **gross profit or mark-up or margin** is merely the difference between the selling price and the cost price of the goods sold. It does not represent the amount the business has earned during the year because the trader has to pay for other things as well as for the goods in which he deals. He may have to pay for rent, for cleaning, advertising, delivery, etc. When he has allowed for these other expenses and substracted them from the gross profit he knows how much the business has really earned. This final profit is known as the **net profit**. It does not mean that the trader has that much cash because he may not have been paid for some of the goods yet, just the same as he may not have paid for some of his purchases. It shows how much profit has been earned in the year whether it has been received in cash or not. Later he may discover that some of his customers will never

Trading and profit and loss account for the year ending 31 Dec., 19..

	£		£
Opening stock	1000	Sales	5600
Purchases	4000		
Cost price of all goods left			
if none had been sold	5000		
Less closing stock (goods			
actually left unsold)	800		
Cost price of goods sold	4200		
Gross profit c/d	1400		
	5600		5600
Rent	150	Gross Profit b/d	1400
Rates	60		
Salaries	450		
Lighting and heating	35		
Repairs	50		
Discount	10		
Advertising	25		
Postage and telephones	12		
Bad debts	38		
Insurance	10		
Total expenses	840		
Net profit	560		
	1400		1400

(Instead of deducting the closing stock on the debit side the same gross profit is obtained by adding it on to sales.)

pay him, and that therefore the net profit shown in the previous year's account was not correct. When preparing the accounts an allowance is made for this possibility of 'bad debts' by taking a percentage of the total debts due away from the gross profit.

The expenses, other than the cost of the goods, are known as **overhead expenses** or the cost of doing business. The cost price of the goods varies in the same way as the sales. If sales double, the cost price of these goods will also be about double, but rent, for instance, will be the same year after year, no matter how much is sold. Rent, rates, expenses of cleaning and lighting, are examples of **fixed overheads**. Rates may increase although sales have decreased, and vice versa.

Some expenses will increase or decrease with the sales but not at the same rate. If sales this year are twice as much as they were last year, it will cost more to deliver goods to customers, but it will not cost twice as much. The same applies to postage and telephone expenses, cash discount, bad debts, etc. They are **variable overheads**. It is important to remember also that when sales go down by 50 per cent these variable overheads will not go down 50 per cent. Consider the table below showing the results of selling varying quantities of an article whose cost price is 5p and selling price 10p.

Number sold	Gross profit	Overhead expenses	Net profit
100	£5	£3	£2
120	£6	£3	£3
140	£7	£3	£4
160	£8	£4	£4
180	£9	£4	£5
200	£10	£4	£6
400	£20	£7	£13

Comparison between the sales and gross profit shows that they both vary in the same way. When, for instance, the sales increase by one-fifth, from 100 to 120, the gross profit also increases by one-fifth, from £5 to £6. The overheads and the net profit, however, do not alter at the same rate as the sales. When sales are 120 the overheads are the same as for sales of 100 and the net profit is £3, an increase of, not one-fifth, but one-half. **When the sales double**, the gross profit doubles but the net profit more than doubles, if cost price and selling price remain the same.

By using the figures given in the account on page 58, it can be seen that:

S.P. $\qquad\qquad$ = C.P. of the goods sold + G.P.
G.P. $\qquad\qquad$ = S.P. − C.P. of the goods sold.
C.P. of the goods sold = S.P. − G.P.
N.P. $\qquad\qquad$ = G.P. − Overheads.
G.P. $\qquad\qquad$ = N.P. + Overheads.
Overheads $\qquad$ = G.P. − N.P.

Having found the gross and net profits the trader will want to compare the results with those of previous years. For purposes of comparison it is useful to express the **profits as a percentage of the sales** or turnover. Selling price is usually used rather than cost price because the total selling price is always known, whereas the cost price cannot be accurately determined until stock has been taken. The gross and net profits shown by the accounts on page 58 expressed as percentages of sales would be:

$$\frac{\text{Gross profit}}{\text{Sales}} \times 100 = \frac{1400}{5600} \times 100 = 25 \text{ per cent,}$$

$$\frac{\text{Net profit}}{\text{Sales}} \times 100 = \frac{560}{5600} \times 100 = 10 \text{ per cent.}$$

These figures mean that for every £100 worth of goods sold the trader makes £25 gross profit and £10 net profit. For every £100 received for goods sold he has £25 left after paying for those goods, and out of this £25 he has £10 left after paying for wages and all other expenses. To make £10 clear profit the trader must incur £90 in expenses, £75 being the cost of the goods sold and £15 being the expenses of doing business or the overhead expenses.

Profit as a percentage of sales is not enough to form a judgment: it must be taken in conjunction with other figures. Sometimes some of the chief expenses, such as wages, are expressed as percentages of sales in order to compare results. If these percentages, known as 'operating' or 'expense ratios', appear less favourable, the trader must discover the reason for it and try to improve matters. If, for instance, wages last year were 10 per cent of sales and this year they are 12 per cent, the reason may be that wage rates have been increased and nothing can be done about it, but it may mean that there is lack of supervision and that the employees are not working as well as in the previous year.

Let us **compare the results** of two businesses, A and B.

	A	B
Turnover	£2400	£3000
Gross profit	£800	£900
Net profit	£240	£300
Gross profit as percentage of sales	33⅓	30
Net profit as percentage of sales	10	10

In order to make £33⅓ gross profit A has to take £100, but B, to make the same gross profit, has to take $\dfrac{£100}{30} \times 33\frac{1}{3} = £111$. Assuming that A and B buy similar goods at the same price, B must be selling at a lower price than A. Because B charges less he can sell more and his total gross profit is greater than A's by one-eighth.

A's overheads are £800 − £240 = £560 = 23.3 per cent of sales; B's are £900 − £300 = £600 = 20 per cent of sales. B's total overheads are £40 more than A's, but for every £100 of sales they are £3.30 less. In both cases the percentages give

$$\text{G.P.\%} - \text{overheads \%} = 10\% \text{ N.P.}$$

With his greater sales, B. makes £60 more than A. His net profit is greater than A's by one-quarter, although his gross profit is greater by only one-eighth.

When comparing two businesses with a view to purchasing one of them, the prospective buyer should inquire into the profits for several years in order to ascertain the trend of the profits, whether they are steadily increasing or diminishing, and he should try to discover the reason for any decrease. It may be that the district has suffered from unemployment and that people are leaving for places where work is available. In such a case there are no good prospects. But if the district is being developed and new factories are being built there the prospects are good. Inquiries should also be made as to the amount of credit that has to be granted and whether the neighbourhood is wealthy or poor. Giving credit means waiting for the money and the use of more capital.

The items in the profit and loss account should be examined in order to see that due allowance has been made for everything. The accounts may show that a trader has made £300 net profit in a year but he might have earned this sum by working for somebody else and unless he has deducted £300 wages for himself from the gross profit he really has not gained anything financially through being in business. If £300 wages for himself has been included in the expenses, then he has gained £300 more than he could have earned through working for somebody else. An allowance should also be made for the interest lost on the money that is being used in the business instead of being invested in some other way. This point will be referred to again in Chapter 27.

Questions

(Sales are always given at selling price and stock at cost price unless otherwise stated. The 'mark-up' is the profit on cost price and the 'margin' the profit on selling price.)

1. What is gross profit? How is it found? Why must stock be taken before finding gross profit?

2. Complete the following table.

Cost price	Selling price	Gross profit	Gross profit cost price	Gross profit selling price
£1	£2	£1	$\frac{1}{1}$	$\frac{1}{2}$
2	3			
3	4			
5	8			
7	11			
10	18			

How can the fraction G.P./C.P. be turned into the fraction G.P./S.P., and vice versa? (Keep the numerator the same and add it to, or deduct it from, the denominator to get a new denominator.)

Can G.P./S.P. be 1/1 or 100 per cent?

Can G.P./C.P. be 2/1 or 200 per cent?

3. Convert the following percentage rates of gross profit on cost price into the equivalent rates on selling price:

   20; 25; 30; 33⅓; 40; 50.

4. Convert the following percentage rates of gross profit on selling price into the equivalent rates on cost price:

   12½; 24; 35; 45; 66⅔; 75.

5. Why is the rate of gross profit on selling price less than the rate on cost price?

6. A trader begins the year with stock worth £3000. During the year he buys goods worth £7500 and sells goods for £12 000. The stock unsold cost £2500. Find his gross profit and express it as a percentage of selling price and of cost price.

7. What is an overhead expense? State, with reasons, which of these are overhead expenses to a retail draper: rates, cloth for making suits, tailor's wages at so much per suit, window dressing, wages of a shop assistant, packing material, suits bought from a factory, decorating the shop, wages paid to an errand boy, postage.

8. Which of the expenses in question 7 are fixed and which variable?

9. (*a*) Opening stock £2000, (*b*) closing stock £1800, (*c*) purchases £8000, (*d*) sales £10 250, (*e*) expenses £1025. Find (i) the cost price of the goods sold, (ii) the gross and net profits, (iii) express both profits as percentages of cost price and of turnover.

10. Why are profits expressed as percentages of turnover? Why is selling price rather than cost price used?

    The gross profit is 30 per cent and the net profit 10 per cent of sales. For every £100 worth of goods sold, what is (*a*) the cost price of the goods sold, (*b*) the gross and net profit, (*c*) the expenses?

11. If prices remain the same and sales increase by 50 per cent, what will be the result on (*a*) gross profit, (*b*) net profit and (*c*) expenses?

12. The principal divisions of operating expenses in retail business are frequently set out as general administration, occupancy, publicity, buying and selling, delivery. If the sales (turnover) are increasing from year to year, how do these several categories of expenses vary in respect to one another?   (R.S.A.)

13. The account on page 58 shows a net profit of £560. What should be deducted from this figure in order to see if it pays the owner to run his own business? If you were considering buying this business, what else would you want to know?

14. The table shows the cost price and selling price of a number of commodities in a supermarket.

    (*a*) Calculate, for each commodity, the profit or loss as a percentage of sales.
    (*b*) Calculate the average profit as a percentages of sales.
    (*c*) Give reasons for the differences in the profit or loss margins for the different commodities.

    All calculations to be made to the nearest whole number.

Commodity	Cost (£)	Sales (£)	Profit or loss margin (%)
Fruit and vegetables	250	375	
Butter	170	175	
Cosmetics	50	80	
Sugar	183	180	
Frozen foods	83	100	
Others	964	1090	
Total			

(A.E.B.)

Chapter 15

Increasing the profits · Prices · Competition · Trading stamps

Every business is out to make a profit, and as much profit as possible. A trader makes his profit by selling and his object is therefore to sell as much as he can in order to increase his profit. There are many ways in which traders try to obtain more customers and sell more goods and make more profit. Here are some of the most important.

1. Reduce the prices.
2. Use trading stamps.
3. Give credit as well as selling for cash.
4. Advertise in various ways.
5. Employ self-service methods.
6. Give services, such as free delivery of the goods.
7. Big businesses may provide facilities like lifts.
8. Open branches.
9. Sell different kinds of goods.
10. Give a wider choice of the same kind of goods.
11. Win customers by using the Post Office, travelling shops and slot machines.

The best way of increasing sales is to **lower the price**. It is better to sell two articles at a profit of 20p each, yielding a total profit of 40p, than to sell only one at a profit of 25p. Of course, the trader will not reduce the price unless he feels certain that more will be sold at the lower price. If 100 articles can be sold now at a profit of 25p each, there is a total profit of £25. If the price is reduced by 5p per article so that the profit on each article is only 20p, the shopkeeper must sell 125 (= £25 ÷ 20p) in order to make the same profit as before. If he can sell more than 125 as a result of reducing the price by 5p, it will pay him to do so. By selling 130 at the lower price he would make £26 profit instead of the £25 he made at the higher price.

The greater the sales the lower the price at which a trader can afford to sell. Suppose a trader can sell in one week 100 articles which cost him 10p each to buy. His selling price must therefore be 10p + something to cover overheads + something for profit. If the overheads are £5 per week, they equal £5 ÷ 100 = 5p per article sold. To avoid a loss the trader must sell the articles for at least 15p each. If his sales increase to 125 per week, the minimum selling price to escape a loss need be only 10p + (£5 ÷ 125) = 14p each. Doubling the sales would enable the trader to reduce the price to 10p + (£5 ÷ 200) = 12½p. Even if the overheads increase, they should not increase as fast as sales. Suppose that in order to double his sales the trader has spent £3 on advertising, etc., and the overheads have increased to £8 per week. He can now afford to sell for 10p + (£8 ÷ 200) = 14p per article, which is 1p less than the price at which he can afford to sell 100. The greater the sales, the more the **overheads are spread** and the smaller they become for each article sold.

Selling more means buying more. In purchasing big quantities the retailer may be able to obtain his goods at a smaller cost per article, enabling him to reduce his price lower still.

We can say that

$$\textbf{S.P. each} = \text{C.P. each} + \left(\frac{\text{Total expenses} + \text{Total profit}}{\text{Sales}} \right)$$

and that the greater the sales the smaller need the profit per article be in order to give the same total profit. The bigger the divisor (sales) the smaller is the answer to the division sum.

The trader does not know exactly how much he will sell if he lowers the price. He will be guided by his experience of what has happened on former occasions. When a new product is introduced, the makers try by various means to obtain an idea of how many they will be able to sell before deciding on the price. In the case of a very expensive motor car, for example, they can discover from statistics about earnings how many at most can afford to buy the car.

Before he decides to reduce the price the trader will consider, not only how much more he is likely to sell at the new price, but also what his competitors are likely to do. When these see their customers leaving them for the cheaper shop, they will try to win them back by reducing their prices, possibly below those of the shop that began the reduction. In this way cut-throat **competition** may be started which will end only when some traders have been put out of business. While this price war is in progress customers gain from the low prices, but the traders lose. When the struggle is over, those still left in business will have the field to themselves for a while and will make up for what they lost when competition was keen.

For many years retailers were not free to charge what they liked because the retail prices of many goods were fixed by the makers. This **resale price maintenance** was made illegal in 1965. Makers who wished to continue it had to justify it to a Restrictive Practices Court which was to decide in the best interest of consumers: so far only book and map publishers and makers of medicinal products have been able to do so. Every time the Court ruled against it, many retailers reduced the prices of the goods concerned. Makers may still 'recommend' retail prices, but retailers are now free to charge what they like.

If one firm buys up other firms so that it can then supply one-quarter of the market, there will be less competition and prices may rise. Such cases are referred to the Monopolies Commission, whose report is placed before Parliament which decides whether or not to allow the amalgamation.

Trading stamps have been widely adopted as a means of increasing sales. Stamp companies sell the stamps to traders who issue them to their customers at so many per pound spent. The customers exchange the stamps for 'gifts' from the stamp company. The company makes a profit by buying the gifts cheaply in bulk and exchanging them for stamps equal to the retail price of the gifts, and by having the use of the money paid by the trader before the customers have collected enough stamps to exchange for gifts. A company does not sell stamps to traders in close competition with one who already uses its stamps, but all traders can get stamps from some company.

In favour of stamps, it is claimed that the company advertises the stamps and the trader more than recovers the cost from increased sales. They may turn occasional customers into regular customers. As we cannot use coins of less than a halfpenny stamps may be regarded as a means of reducing prices by a fraction of a halfpenny. Many people like collecting stamps.

Against stamps, it can be said that if all traders used them no trader would have an advantage, unless some gave more stamps than others. They cause more expense and work for the trader, so, unless sales increase enough, traders do not benefit and may increase prices to pay for them. Each stamp is of very small value: the shopper may have to spend £80 and collect thousands of stamps to obtain a gift worth £1. Before enough have been collected the company may increase the number required for a particular gift. The value of the stamps exchanged may be more than the retail price of the gift. Some stamps are never exchanged and add to the profit of the company which has been paid for them by the retailer. The law requires stamps to show their value, and a collector with stamps worth 25p has the right to exchange them for cash.

Questions

1. Complete the following table. What can be learned from it?

Number sold	Cost price each	Total overheads	Selling price each	Gross profit	Net profit
100	50p	£20	75p		
120	50p	£20	72½p		
160	50p	£20	70p		
200	50p	£22	67½p		
300	50p	£25	65p		
500	45p	£30	60p		

2. In a week 300 articles costing 25p each are sold for 30p each and the overheads are £10. Find the net profit.

   If 400 per week were sold and the overheads were £11, at what price could the articles be sold to make the same total profit as before?

3. A retailer about to open a new shop thinks he can sell 1000 articles per week.

The cost price is 75p each and he reckons that his fixed overheads will be £20, and the variable overheads £15 per week. If he wants to make a net profit of £15 per week, what must the selling price be?

If his sales increased to 1500 and the variable overheads to £20, what must the selling price be to give a profit of £20?

4. What are the advantages and disadvantages of trading stamps to retailers and their customers?

5. A trader making 20 per cent gross profit on sales adopts stamps at a cost of 2½ per cent of sales. What percentage increase in sales is required to recover the cost of the stamps?

6. What is the purpose of competition? Name six ways in which traders can compete.

7. Would it be advisable for a new shop to sell its goods at prices below those charged by similar shops in the neighbourhood? Give reasons for your answer.

Chapter 16

Deferred payments · Credit sale · Hire purchase

Some traders try to increase their sales and profits by giving credit. They allow the customers to have the goods now and to pay for them afterwards, i.e. payment is deferred. Sometimes the buyer is allowed to pay when he can, without signing an agreement. This method is used mainly by the small retailers who know their customers well. In the case of the more expensive articles, such as furniture, the buyer must agree to pay a definite sum on definite dates.

There are two kinds of agreements for deferred payments: **hire purchase and credit sale** (or instalment) agreements. Under the credit sale system the buyer becomes the owner of the goods as soon as the agreement is made. He can do as he pleases with them, and if he fails to pay the seller can sue him for the money due. Under the hire purchase system the buyer only hires or rents the goods until he has finished paying for them. He does not become the owner until all the instalments have been paid.

All goods are not suitable for hire purchase and credit sale trading. **Goods bought in these ways** are usually fairly expensive and should last at least as long as they are being paid for. Perishable goods, such as flowers, are obviously not suitable. Goods that are made specially for a customer and which cannot be taken back and sold again, such as clothes, are more suitable for credit sale than for hire purchase. The goods that are most suitable are necessary goods like cookers, goods that reduce expenses like washing machines that save laundry bills, and goods that earn and help to pay for themselves like buses.

If it costs me £1 a month to travel to work, it might pay me to buy a cycle. If I bought one for £12 to be paid at the rate of £1 per month, the instalments would be no more than my bus fares per month, and at the end of the year I should have paid for the cycle out of the money saved on fares and I should still have the cycle.

Hire purchase has **advantages and disadvantages for the seller**. He can sell more than when he sells only for cash and so make more total profit. He can also charge more, although the extra charge is not all profit. The article sold is a security for the debt, and, if the buyer fails to keep up the instalments, it may be taken back and sold again, the trader keeping the instalments already paid.

The hire purchase trader runs the risk that he will not be paid for some of the goods sold, and that the article when taken back will be so damaged as to be almost worthless. He has also to incur more expenses for the extra bookkeeping necessary for recording and collecting the instalments.

The trader who sells on credit needs more capital than the one who sells for cash. As the goods are sold they must be replaced by new stock. The cash trader who sells goods that cost him £80 can replace them out of the cash received for them as soon as they are sold. The hire purchase trader who sells every month goods that cost him £80 for £120, to be paid at the rate of £5 per month, receives in the first month only £5 towards the cost of replacing them and must find another £75. At the end of the second month he receives £10 in instalments and must find another £70, and so on. He has to wait sixteen months before one month's instalments total £80. During the first fifteen months he buys goods worth £1200 but receives only £600 cash. He has to find and lose interest on £600 more capital than the cash trader who, after the first month, can pay for his purchases from his receipts.

To meet this demand for extra capital and other needs of hire purchase trading, **finance companies** have been formed. After inquiring into the financial position of the trader the company is prepared to pay him the full price of the goods less an allowance for its expenses and profit. It is really buying the goods for cash from the trader who has merely found the customer to whom the goods are to be sold. The hire purchase agreement is made between the customer and the company which may relieve the trader of all further responsibility and the risk of bad debts. Some companies make the trader their agent for collecting the instalments, while others bind him to buy back from them any article returned by customers who fail to keep up the instalments. In this way the hire purchase trader receives ready cash and capital and avoids some of the expenses and risks of allowing credit, but he does not receive the full price paid by the customer. He has to share the profit with the finance company.

Hire purchase has its **advantages and disadvantages to the buyer** who cannot pay cash. It enables him to obtain the goods when he needs them instead of having to do without them until he has saved enough to pay all the price at once. He may need the goods to earn his living. A furniture remover must have vans and from what the vans earn he can pay the instalments. It would take some people several years to acquire all the furniture they need if they had to pay cash for everything. The buyer can obtain articles of better quality when given time to pay the higher price. He has, too, time to test the goods before he has finished paying for them, and if there is anything seriously wrong with them he can refuse to pay any more until they have been put right or replaced. In many cases the seller agrees to do minor repairs free of charge for a certain time.

In buying on hire purchase terms the buyer runs the risk that he will not be able to keep up the payments and so will lose the article and some of his money. He has to pay more than the buyer for cash, because the price must include an addition to cover the interest on the money outstanding. the cost of the extra clerical work and the risk of bad debts. As he can go only to traders who are willing to sell on credit, he has less choice and may have to take an article not exactly suitable or of inferior quality. Hire purchase encourages some people to save in order to pay the instalments regularly, but it causes others to buy recklessly and to pile up debts which they can never pay.

Although they account for only about 7 per cent of the total trade, hire purchase and credit sale agreements are **important for** motor vehicles and cycles, furniture, cookers, washing machines, vacuum cleaners, refrigerators and radio and television sets. They help to keep down the prices of these goods because they enable more to be sold and therefore more to be made, and the more that are made the cheaper they are to make.

In the past buyers who were persuaded to sign agreements which they did not understand, for goods which they could not afford, often found that when they missed an instalment the goods were taken back and the trader kept all the money they had paid. Trader's rights have now been limited by law.

The **Hire Purchase Act**, 1964, deals with goods that do not cost more than £2000. It states that there must be written agreements giving prices, amounts and dates of instalments, etc. Separate transactions must be given separate agreements so that one lot that has been paid for cannot be taken back because an instalment has been missed on another lot. A buyer who signs an agreement at home or anywhere other than the trader's premises will later receive a second copy which must state in red print that he can, if he likes, cancel it within four days of receiving it (but this right does not apply to credit sale agreements for goods costing £30 or less). Once the agreement has come into force, the buyer who wishes to cancel must return the goods and pay half the price. A seller who wants to recover the goods must give notice that unless the buyer pays within seven days he will take back the goods. The Act protects individuals but not companies.

When one-third of the price has been paid, the seller cannot take back the goods without first of all obtaining permission to do so from a court which may allow the buyer to keep some of the goods. If he does take away the goods without obtaining the consent of a court, the buyer can claim back everything he has already paid. Goods sold on credit sale become the property of the buyer immediately and he has no right to return them, while the seller sues for the debt and not for the goods.

In some stores a customer can open a **budget account**. He pays an agreed sum per month and is allowed to buy, on credit, goods worth several times that sum. He pays interest on the balance owing at the end of each month.

Another form of budget account is known as an **option account**. The customer arranges with the retailer a 'ceiling' above which his total purchases will not rise without mutual consultation. Each month the retailer sends the customer a statement showing the amount owing. The customer may then pay whatever amount he chooses to reduce his indebtedness. Interest is charged on amounts that remain unpaid.

Many shops, mainly clothing shops, accept trading company **checks** and club vouchers. Those who issue the checks and vouchers collect the money from their members and pay the trader for goods he has supplied in return for the checks and vouchers. Their profit consists of the discount allowed them by the trader on the selling price of the goods sold to the members, and of a poundage, usually 5 per cent, they collect from their members.

So important is hire purchase that the Government, when it thinks too much is being spent for the good of the country, tries to restrict it by increasing the deposit, limiting the period over which the balance must be paid, raising the rate of interest on borrowed money, and increasing the tax.

Goods sold by shops which grant hire purchase and other forms of credit equal to ten per cent or more of sales are shown below.

Kind of shop	Credit as percentage of total sales
1 Electricity showrooms	56
2 Radio and television hire	53
3 Gas showrooms	39
4 Furniture	31
5 Radio and electrical	26
6 Cycles and perambulators	14
7 Clothing and footwear	10
All Goods	9

Questions

1. What is the difference between discount and credit? Explain the purpose of each. Describe two kinds of discount and two kinds of credit. (J.M.B.)

2. What is the difference between hire purchase and credit sale buying? Which is the more suitable method for the following articles? Are there any articles not suitable for either method? Give reasons for your answers.

   Dresses, cigarette machines, houses, flowers, cycles, pianos, sewing machines, cricket bats, lorries, typewriters, hats.

3. Indicate the salient features of hire purchase. State, with your reasons, whether or not you would be prepared to use hire purchase to furnish your own home. (U.C.L.E.S.)

4. A large percentage of motor car sales are on hire purchase. Describe the advantages and disadvantages of this system of buying from the point of view of (a) the buyer, (b) the car retail dealer, (c) the motor car industry in general. (W.M.E.B.)

5. (a) What safeguards does the law provide for customers making a hire purchase agreement?
   (b) From whom can they get free expert advice on matters connected with hire purchase agreements? (W.M.E.B.)

6. How is credit obtained by means of budget accounts? Compare store budget accounts with bank budget accounts.

7. Describe the principal methods by which goods can be bought on credit. How does the law protect the customer in these transactions?   (S.R.E.B.)

8. Set out the arguments for and against the giving and acceptance of credit by a sole trader starting a new business.   (R.S.A.)

9. Refer to the table on page 70 and explain why some goods receive much more credit than others. State, with reasons, which of the goods are sold mainly under hire purchase and which under credit sale agreements.

10. In March a young married couple, John and Janet Jones, are considering the purchase of a television set. The cash price of the set is £208. Alternatively hire purchase terms are available. A deposit of £70 is required and repayments are either £2.20 a week over eighteen months or £1.80 a week over two years. The Jones's have savings of £250 in a building society account. Neither of them knows very much about hire purchase.
    What advice would you offer them? Provide sound reasons for the advice you are offering.   (R.S.A.)

11. Describe: (*a*) the advantages of hire purchase to (i) buyers and (ii) sellers;
    (*b*) the part played by finance houses in hire purchase sales.   (L.C.C. & I.)

12. A customer may obtain credit from a retailer by

    (*a*) Hire purchase agreement
    (*b*) Credit sale agreement.

    Explain (i) the distinctive advantages and (ii) the disadvantages to the customer of each form of agreement.   (A.E.B.)

Chapter 17

Advertising · Trade marks · Market Research · Self-service

A most important method of competition is advertising, the aid to trade that deals with the problem of giving **information** about goods and services and helps to put buyers and sellers in touch with one another. By means of advertisements a supplier tells us what goods he has for sale and emphasises their good points in the hope that we shall buy them. If I want to buy a car, I can compare advertisements by various suppliers to see what **choice** there is and then choose the model that suits me best.

The **methods** employed vary from sandwich-boards to television. The local grocer will advertise in the local newspapers and the local cinema only, for he cannot expect customers to travel more than a certain distance to his shop. A grocery firm with branches all over the country will advertise in the national newspapers and on commercial television, because all who read or hear the advertisements live near one of its branches and are possible customers.

Over £600 million is spent on advertising in a year. About 60 per cent of this sum is devoted to newspapers and periodicals, 28 per cent to television, and the rest to leaflets, catalogues, posters, free samples, coupons to be exchanged for gifts, etc. Cinema advertising accounts for only 1 per cent of the total.

Advertising to all and sundry, as by posters, is **indirect** advertising. Advertising to individuals, as by door-to-door canvassing, is **direct** advertising. When a product appeals only to a limited number, direct advertising may be the only method employed. The people likely to buy this book are teachers and students of commerce: it will be brought to their notice by sending letters directly to teachers and by representatives calling at schools, as well as by advertisements in educational journals. It will not be advertised in newspapers and on television because very few of the people who would see the advertisements would be interested in the book.

Although advertising is an expense to be deducted from gross profit it is claimed that it **need not raise prices**. The increased sales following an advertising campaign may cause gross profit to increase by more than the cost of advertising. Suppose the net profit was £10 per week. Then £1 per week is spent on advertising as a result of which the gross profit increases by £3. The extra gross profit is enough to cover the cost of advertising and leave £2 to bring the net profit up to £12.

When the advertising expense is divided by the greater sales, it may work out to a very small sum per article. In addition all the other overheads are spread. The reduction per article in these may be greater than the amount per article to be added for advertising. More goods will be bought and obtained at lower prices. More goods will be manufactured and the more goods a factory makes the cheaper they are to make.

A boy starts a school newspaper. The school provides everything except stencils which he must buy at 10p each and he must spend 60p on postage. In the first week he obtains orders for 10 copies and duplicates that number. His selling price per copy is then made up of 1p for the stencil + 6p for postage = 7p. In the second week he spends 10p on posters to place on the notice boards and receives orders for 20 copies. His selling price per copy can now be $\frac{1}{2}$p for the stencil + 3p for postage + $\frac{1}{2}$p for advertising = 4p. Advertising has caused an addition of $\frac{1}{2}$p per copy to the cost, but this is more than balanced by the reductions of 3p per copy for postage and $\frac{1}{2}$p per copy for the stencil. Advertising, by increasing sales, has led to lower prices.

A rival editor, also paying 10p each for stencils and 60p for postage, and who has been selling at 7p, may now be forced to advertise and to lower prices in order to keep readers. If his sales continue to fall, the cost per paper sold rises making it more and more difficult to reduce prices. If he were a poor typist wasting two stencils per edition, he could not, even with 20 readers, afford to sell at 4p, and he would be driven out of business by the more efficient editor.

Makers give their goods **tradenames**, **trademarks and brands**, which are registered to prevent their being used by competitors. The brands can be easily recognised and distinguished from others, particularly when the goods are pre-packaged. Extensive advertising of branded goods brings them to the notice of the public. 'Don't ask for bread. Ask for "Sunbread"', says an advertisement by Baker. Without prepackaging and branding, all loaves in a shop would look alike, neither the retailer nor the customer being able to distinguish the various makes. Baker, however, wants us to ask for a definite make instead of being vague and accepting any loaf. By packaging and branding his loaves, he gives them individuality so that the retailer can pick them out from others, and the customer is certain that he is being given the make for which he asked.

To keep new customers, makers must give them the same quality every time they buy. Branded goods are standardised so that all with the same brand are the same and it does not matter which one is taken. To compete with other makes, a constant effort must be made to improve their quality.

Without advertising manufacturers could not make their goods known everywhere, particularly new goods, and there would be less competition. The less efficient makers and retailers would run less risk of losing customers and could charge higher prices. Had our new school editor not advertised many pupils might not know that a cheaper paper was available and the less efficient typist could continue to charge 3p for some time yet. Modern advertising makes possible mass distribution.

A business may be forced to advertise, not so much to increase sales, as to prevent sales from falling and to keep customers from turning to other advertised goods. It may also have to advertise for staff, tenders for building and other work, and for supplies.

Advertising plays such an important part in modern commerce that special businesses have been formed to undertake the work. Instead of arranging the advertising himself the seller of goods can employ one of these advertising agencies to do the work.

An **advertising agency** looks after much detailed work for its clients, and also offers them the expert services of its artists and copywriters. Advice and recommendations are available free of charge, since the agency collects commission from the media with which advertising space is booked for its clients.

Market research is a part of the advertising function that is frequently undertaken by advertising and market research agencies. These specialist firms have built up information and statistics over the years which enable them to give expert advice and service to clients. Market research may be carried out to determine:

(*a*) If a new product is likely to find a market.
(*b*) Whether an established product is likely to meet with a good demand in a new market.
(*c*) Why sales of a product have declined, either generally or in a certain area.

Direct information is gathered from trained market research investigators who actually question consumers in an area and record their replies on questionnaire forms. Other information is obtained from field salesmen, from replies to advertisements, from the response to 'sampling' campaigns and from statistics gathered from trade journals and trade associations.

The importance of market research before a product is manufactured and launched is plain. If no research is done, the manufacturer is working 'in the dark'; he can only surmise that his product will appeal to consumers and will be bought by them in preference to the products of his competitors. Subsequent events may prove his surmise to be wrong. A market research campaign does not guarantee that a product will be successful, but from it the manufacturer can learn what the attitudes of potential customers are, how some of them would react to this product if it were on sale at such-and-such a price and what competition already exists in his field.

In selling overseas, market research is even more important, and much valuable information can be passed on to the exporter by agents in the overseas territories. This aspect of market research, including the services offered by the Government, is dealt with in Chapter 50 of this book.

Branding, standardisation, prepackaging and advertising have assisted the development of **self-service** shops which began to spread rapidly when labour was scarce after the war ended in 1945. The goods being already packaged and well known to shoppers there is no need for the retailer to give advice or service. He does not require as many assistants because customers serve themselves. He can, too, sell other types of goods beside his main lines. Grocers now sell patent medicines, toothpaste and aspirins, goods which at one time were sold only by chemists.

With counter service, selling is limited to the counters and to the number of customers that can be served by the staff on duty. In a self-service shop selling can take place anywhere and there is no time wasted in fetching goods to show to customers. In a self-service store customers can see the prices and inspect all the goods they can buy at that store, and they often buy, on impulse, items which are not on their shopping lists. The use of adding machines at the exit points enables bills to be made up quickly and accurately. Sales per assistant and sales per square foot are higher than in counter shops. Sales per person employed in a grocery self-service store are greater by one-third than in a grocery counter shop.

Customers have the advantage of obtaining what they want quickly without having to queue at the counter, or they can take their time to examine and compare the goods and their prices which are clearly marked. They know that they will not be pressed to buy goods which they do not want in the presence of others waiting to be served. Prices on the whole may be lower than in other types of shop.

Self-service is not suitable for all types of goods. Groceries are the main goods sold in this way. The goods must be such as can be packaged in containers that can easily be picked up and placed in a basket provided by the shop. If they are standardised and branded, the shopper knows what the packet contains without seeing the contents. The packets are interchangeable and it does not matter which one is taken. The use of transparent material for packaging, and of refrigerator display cases, has made it possible to use self-service for selling goods like meat and potatoes, which are not standardised, and which customers want to see before they buy.

Self-service shops as a rule do not give personal attention, do not allow credit and do not deliver. Customers who desire these and other services from the retailer will go elsewhere. The shopkeeper who turns his shop into a self-service shop must find more capital for the necessary equipment.

Shops where the counter assistants merely wrap articles handed to them by customers and take payment are termed **self-selection** stores. Where self-service is used but no baskets are provided customers take goods to a '**cash and wrap**' unit or counter. The same store may use one method in one department and a different method in another department.

Questions

1. Large sums of money are spent by firms on advertising. Name five ways in which advertising is done. Choose one of these methods and state which products you think would be advertised in this way and why.   (M.R.E.B.)

2. Describe the main methods of sales promotion which might be used in each of the following situations.

   (*a*) An improved version of a nationally-known breakfast cereal.

(*b*) A new British sports car to be sold in both home and overseas markets.

(*c*) A new do-it-yourself method of building furniture based simply on inter-locking parts.

(*d*) A new pocket-sized calculating machine to be sold to school pupils.

(W.M.E.B.)

3. What is the purpose of advertising? Why is it that:

(*a*) manufacturers of detergents advertise on television but oil tanker builders do not;

(*b*) a laundry might advertise by distributing leaflets from door to door but a tourist agency would not;

(*c*) a department store advertises by posting catalogues to its customers and multiple shops do not? (W.J.E.C. modified)

4. What is the main purpose of branding an article? Explain what trademarks are. Give examples and show how they help the sale of branded goods. (R.S.A.)

5. The proportion of advertising done on television is increasing. What are the advantages and disadvantages of television advertising as compared with press advertising?

6. Explain by means of an example how advertising can lead to lower prices.

7. What are the advantages and disadvantages of brands and tradenames to (*a*) makers, (*b*) consumers and (*c*) retailers?

8. By means of an example, show how mass production can produce cheaper per article than small-scale production. Why is mass distribution or selling neces-sary for mass production? What is one important way of obtaining mass distribution?

9. What made the development of self-service shops possible? Why is this method of selling much more important for groceries than for furniture and jewellery?

10. What are the advantages and disadvantages of self-service shops to (*a*) retailers, (*b*) customers?

11. A big manufacturer of soaps and margarine said, 'No packaging, no brands; no brands, no trade'. What does this statement mean and how true do you think it is?

12. (*a*) What are the purposes of advertising?

(*b*) Why is it that we see on television advertisements by manufacturers of car tyres but not those of manufacturers of car engines and gears?

(*c*) What is emphasised in advertisements of (i) beer, (ii) milk, (iii) banks?

(W.J.E.C.)

13. A company manufacturing colour TV sets wishes to expand its production. In what practical manner could market research assist with this objec-tive? (L.C.C. & I.)

Chapter 18

Advertising · Consumer protection · Standardisation

Advertising has two purposes. **Informative advertising** tells us what goods are available and gives the facts about them so that a consumer can choose the article that suits him best. **Competitive advertising** tries to persuade us to buy the goods, whether or not we want them. Both purposes may be seen in the same advertisement. It is competitive advertising that attracts criticism and against which the consumer needs protection.

One **criticism of advertising** is that much of it is unnecessary, especially when it deals with similar goods. In some cases this objection is met by cooperative advertising, the cost being shared by a group of traders. 'There is no substitute for wool' is an example, no particular maker being mentioned.

Some products are so similar that it does not really matter to the purchaser which make he buys, but advertisements try to turn people from one make to another. The total quantity sold may be no greater. We eat the same amount of bread each week no matter how much it is advertised. All that may happen is that one maker gains customers and others lose them. Consumers do not gain unless the maker who wins trade gives better quality or service or, like the school editor, reduces prices.

If two businesses advertise at the same time, neither may gain more trade. In such a case the expense of advertising decreases the profits of both and both might increase prices in order to pay for the advertising. It is usually the big business that can find vast sums for advertising that wins, the smaller businesses being driven out or having to come to terms with the big business. In this way advertising may lead to less competition.

The two school editors might decide that instead of prolonging the life and death struggle, intensified by advertising, and exerting themselves to give better value to customers it would be easier and more profitable for them to work together and to amalgamate the papers. The less efficient editor might then feel safe and make no effort to improve his typing. He might even become careless and waste more stencils. Readers might then have to pay for his inefficiency by being charged 8p for a paper. In the same way the successful editor might relax his effort if he had driven out his rival and obtained a monopoly.

In the past the rule was **let the buyer beware**, and if he had been deceived by a seller or by an advertisement he might have been unable to do anything about it or have to face the trouble and expense of a lawsuit. Recently, the consumer has been given more protection against the increasing pressure of advertising and doubtful practices in three ways.

First, the consumer is protected by the Government. Laws dealing with resale price maintenance, monopoly and trading stamps were mentioned on pages 64 and 65, and the Hire Purchase Act was dealt with on page 69.

The **Sale of Goods Acts** give the buyer the right to refuse the goods or to claim damages from the seller when

(*a*) the name or description of the goods delivered is not the description of the goods ordered, e.g. beans delivered but peas ordered;

(*b*) most of the goods sold by sample differ from the sample, e.g. good apples shown as samples but most of those delivered rotten;

(*c*) the article cannot do the work for which it is usually used, e.g. a hot waterbottle that bursts when first filled.

The Government can, on the advice of the Food Standards Committee, lay down regulations about the quality of foods, such as forbidding the use of harmful chemicals. It can forbid the sale of dangerous goods, like flammable children's nightdresses, and ban television advertising of goods it considers to be harmful, such as cigarettes. Inspectors check on weights and measures and hygiene. Packages can be made to deceive by giving the impression that they contain much more than they do. In 1965 it became compulsory to state on the containers the weight or volume of many prepackaged goods. Some goods can be sold only in certain weights. Large loaves, for example, must be sold in units of 397 grams or multiples thereof. This makes it easier to compare prices charged by different shops.

Most people who buy a television set do not know whether it is well or badly made. When one set costs more than another, the reason is not always obvious. Buyers rely on the descriptions and explanations of the makers and the retailers. A serious criticism of advertising is that so much of it is misleading, deceiving, and even false in these matters, and that many of the advertised guarantees are worthless at law.

The **Trade Descriptions Act**, 1968, makes false and misleading statements about goods and services and the use of a trademark registered by another firm illegal. It is an offence, for example, to describe foreign goods as English. It is also an offence to pretend to lower prices by crossing out high prices which were not charged for at least twenty-eight consecutive days during the previous six months and replacing them by lower prices. The Department of Trade can, when it thinks it advisable in the interests of consumers, order advertisements about some goods to give certain information or order the information to be given on labels affixed to them. It can also give exact meanings to words, such as ruling that a garment must contain at least a certain percentage of wool before it can be described as a woollen garment. The weights and measures inspectors are responsible for seeing that the Act is observed.

The Director-General of Fair Trading now looks after consumer affairs. It is his duty to protect the interests of consumers. Some pre-packed foods will not be fit to eat after a certain period. It is now compulsory for all makers of pre-packed foods to show on the packets the date of manufacture or the date by which they should be sold, so that the consumer can judge whether or not the goods are safe to use.

Consumers can obtain help and advice on hire purchase and other problems from the Citizens Advice Bureaux, and some local authorities provide a consumers' protection service to help consumers whose complaints seem justified.

Second, there is more protection by business people who form associations for the purpose. Some associations of professional people, like doctors, lawyers, accountants and stockbrokers, forbid their members to advertise.

The **Retail Trading-Standards Association** is a voluntary trade organisation comprising retailers, manufacturers, advertising agencies, newspapers and others who are prepared to pay the necessary subscriptions for membership. It is 'concerned with promoting satisfactory standards of quality of consumer goods – and textiles in particular – as well as with the maintenance of high standards of advertising and trading practice'. It seeks to have goods correctly labelled and described. It describes what terms like 'waterproof', 'preshrunk', 'non-iron', etc., mean and which goods should be so described. It has a laboratory where goods can be tested for these and other qualities. Advertisements are scrutinised and, when possible, legal action is taken against offenders. It publishes reports of its work and issues bulletins for the guidance of its members.

The standardisation of goods is the aim of the **British Standards Institution**, a voluntary organisation of business people. Standardised goods are interchangeable. We can buy an electric bulb anywhere, knowing that it will fit any socket in the house because bulbs and sockets are made in standard sizes. There is no need to try them first nor to have them specially made.

When it has been decided to standardise an article, the Institution draws up a document, known as a 'Standard', setting forth details of the dimensions, the materials to be used, the tests to be employed, the service the article should give, and the way it should be used. Manufacturers are not compelled to adopt these standards, but if they do they can make the goods more cheaply because they can then make a large number of the same model instead of making small batches of many models. Once the school editor had cut the stencil he could roll off any number of identical copies. Had he, however, given readers a choice of small type and large type he would require two typewriters and two stencils and would roll off a few of each kind, which would add considerably to the cost. It is also easier to handle, to store and to pack identical articles. Women's hats would be much cheaper if they would all wear the same standardised model. Standardisation gives us lower prices and convenience at the expense of variety.

Makers who adopt the standards can use the Institution's trademark, a kite, which is a guarantee to the consumer that the article, e.g. an electric iron, is suitable for the purpose for which it is intended, is safe to use, will give good service, and that spare parts which will fit can be obtained easily.

The kite is a **seal of approval**. Other examples are the seal of the British Electrical Approvals Board for the safety of domestic electric equipment, the Lux seal for textiles, and that of the Design Centre for such things as furniture, china, cutlery and various other domestic items. While these seals show that the goods sent by the makers for testing are satisfactory, they do not usually guarantee that the goods sent to the shops are of the same standard. Some makers prefer to use their own trademarks because the seals may guarantee only minimum standards.

Some traders, such as housebuilders and garage-owners, have formed associations to deal with complaints from consumers. It is, however, only complaints against traders who are members that can be settled in this way. The worst offenders are not likely to join the association. In 1962 the advertising businesses formed the Advertising Standards Authority to promote observance of the 'Code' which had been drawn up by the Department of Trade in conjunction with the Press in order to ban the worst type of advertisement.

Third, consumers can protect themselves. In 1957 the **Consumers' Association** was formed. This is a voluntary body which is not connected with any trade or industry. Anyone can join by paying the necessary subscription. The Association buys goods in the shops and tests and compares them. It publishes its findings in its magazine called *Which?* In this it states which article it considers to be the best value for money. As well as being a guide for shoppers, *Which?* is useful to traders who want to stock goods that will give good value to their customers. Makers, knowing that their products may be examined and reported upon, will be more careful to maintain and improve their quality. *Which?* and other publications by the Association have caused newspapers, magazines and television programmes to mention and discuss its reports and to consider the merits and faults of various goods and services. *Which?* does not sell advertising space so that there is no danger of its reports being biased in favour of advertisers.

The Consumers' Association has been very successful, and in 1964 the Research Institute for Consumer Affairs was formed to examine services, such as services provided by house agents, in the same way as the Association deals with goods. It publishes *Consumer News*. Consumer groups to consider local shopping and prices now exist in so many towns that they have formed a National Federation of Consumer Groups.

Questions

1. Distinguish between (*a*) informative and competitive advertising, (*b*) direct and indirect advertising.

2. 'The purpose of advertising is to enable consumers to make a choice.' Give reasons in support of this statement.

3. Should advertising be abolished? Justify your answer.   (R.S.A.)

4. What are the objections to advertising? Give examples of advertisements that are misleading.

5. What is the purpose of consumer protection? In what ways does the Government provide for the protection of the consumer?   (A.E.B.)

6. Describe the various ways in which the public is legally protected against unfair trading, particularly with regard to the quantity and quality of the goods sold.   (A.L.S.E.B.)

7. What was the Consumers' Council? How did it help the consumer? Should a new Council with more powers be set up?

8. Describe the work of the Retail Trading-Standards Association and of the British Standards Institution.

9. What are seals of approval? Give examples and show how they help makers and consumers.

10. How do associations of traders protect consumers?

11. Describe the work of the Consumers' Association. What effects has it had on consumers, manufacturers, retailers and the Press?

12. What protection is given to consumers by the Sale of Goods Act and the Trade Descriptions Act?

13. 'The costs of product advertising are borne by the consumer, so if the Government banned advertising, goods would be cheaper and the consumer would benefit.'
   'Advertising can help to reduce the cost of goods to the consumer.' Discuss the apparent contradiction in these two statements.   (R.S.A.)

14. What is meant by (i) collective advertising, (ii) competitive advertising? Give **two** examples of each. What are the advantages of collective advertising to producers and consumers? Why do those who pay for collective advertising also often engage in competitive advertising?   (U.C.L.E.S.)

15. Write an essay on advertising describing the purposes, types, methods, advantages and disadvantages to both consumers and industry. You may also mention governmental and other restrictions imposed on advertisers.   (A.L.S.E.B.)

Chapter 19

Channels of distribution · Manufactured goods

The other ways of increasing profits mentioned on page 63, selling all kinds of goods in one store and opening branches, have led to the growth of big businesses, the department and multiple stores. These have an advantage in being able to buy straight from the maker instead of from the wholesaler. Before dealing with them we shall first see in what ways the maker can dispose of his goods or through what channels the goods can be distributed from the producers to the consumers.

One channel leads **directly from the manufacturer to the final consumer** without anybody intervening. The maker himself takes his goods straight to the homes of the consumers as is done by the local baker. In this way he knows exactly what is happening to the goods and is in a better position to discover the consumers' likes and dislikes. He may also save time, important in the case of perishable goods. The baker obtains more for his goods in this way than by selling to shopkeepers, but on the other hand he has to find more capital for buying vans and has to employ salesmen and incur expenses in doing the work of a retailer.

The method is not suitable for all kinds of goods. The local baker can rely on a steady demand throughout the year for bread and a large number of customers within a small area to keep down his delivery costs. A maker of footballs could not expect to sell many by taking them around from door to door. No one would buy footballs in the summer and his vans and salesmen would be idle. Household cleaning materials and brushes are required at all times and one firm sells its goods only through its own salesmen who call regularly at the homes of customers. Another firm does so for cosmetics. Neither can the maker of one kind of sweets rely on sufficient regular sales. As tastes vary widely a choice of many makes must be offered. The same is true of fashionable goods like hats, handbags, jewellery, clothing, etc. All people want bread every day, but these goods are bought occasionally and to many they are special purchases.

Low-priced goods, not in universal and steady demand, may take as much time and effort to sell as expensive goods. A salesman who sells in one week 200 books for 30p each at a gross profit of $33\frac{1}{3}$ per cent, has made a total gross profit of £20 out of which must be paid his wages and all other expenses. Another salesman who sells in one week one encyclopaedia for £100 at the same rate of gross profit has made over £33 available for his wages and expenses.

Direct dealing between maker and consumer takes place when the goods have to be made to suit the customer's special requirements. The tailor waits for an order to measure a customer before he makes a suit for him and sells it direct to that customer. The same is generally true for costly engines, ships and machinery. Office equipment, such as accounting machines, is also sold direct to firms that need it. In such cases the number of possible customers is limited, and they are known beforehand to the salesmen who need call only on those firms who could use the product. The makers of such machines may undertake to overhaul them periodically and to keep them in repair. This is sometimes done for household equipment, such as vacuum cleaners, and is referred to as 'after-sales service'.

Heavy goods like furniture cannot be taken around the streets by salesmen. The maker who decides on direct dealing with the public must use **showrooms** where the goods can be displayed and demonstrations given. Such showrooms are opened for sewing machines, vacuum cleaners, refrigerators, washing machines, etc.

Before deciding to sell direct to consumers the maker will have to consider whether his product is cheap or expensive, whether the demand for it is regular or seasonal, whether the likely customers are few and far between or are concentrated in certain areas, and whether an after-sales service is desirable or not. In addition he may have to be prepared to grant credit for expensive goods, and to find more capital.

Some goods are sold direct to the consumer through the Post Office as will be shown on page 116.

If a maker can sell his goods in sufficient quantities it may pay him to **open his own retail shops** where the goods can be better displayed and a wider selection given than is possible with travelling salesmen. Men's clothing, boots and shoes, drugs and stationery are the main goods distributed in this way. They are goods that last and are not bought frequently. A man may buy boots and clothes once or twice a year only. The shops selling them need not be so close together as shops selling goods in daily demand, and the maker has to find less capital and open fewer shops than would be required for other types of goods. There are, for instance, twenty times as many grocery shops as bookshops.

The goods are also those about which the buyer requires advice or direct service, such as advice about medicine from the chemist and about fittings from clothiers. By opening his own shops the maker is certain that his salesmen know what varieties he has to offer and that they will sell his own goods and not other makes. The maker's desire to make sure that every effort is made to sell his goods is one of the main reasons for direct trading. Some makers have set up a chain of retail branches, or multiple shops, throughout the country.

The method is not suitable for goods for which the demand is seasonal or enough of which cannot be sold to make a shop worth while. A baker can sell enough of his own bread and confectionery to make a shop pay, but the maker of cricket bats or fountain pens would have to sell other goods as well in order to make a retail shop show a profit. Only 4 per cent of the shops selling sweets rely entirely on sweets.

Instead of setting up a chain of retail shops, the maker can **sell to independent retailers**. This saves him a lot of work and the necessity for finding the extra capital required for opening shops. One disadvantage is that the maker is not in touch with the final buyer, and if sales decrease he may not know the reason for it. Another disadvantage is that an independent retailer sells similar goods from competing makers and will tend to push those makes which give him the biggest profit. To compel the retailer to stock his goods, the maker may have to advertise widely to make his products well known to the public. To overcome these difficulties, some makers allow one retailer in a district to sell their goods, binding that retailer not to sell competing makes.

Familiar examples of **tied retailers** are the owners of petrol stations, the great majority of whom sell only one brand. By confining his station to one brand, the retailer requires less capital for pumps and equipment and reduces repair and other expenses. In return the manufacturers are prepared to help with finance and advice for improving the equipment and the layout of the station. They undertake the advertising of the petrol leaving the retailer more of his own resources to advertise anything else that he provides. Although he may receive training and advice on how to run his station he is free to manage it as he thinks best.

The makers gain in that they are certain that only their brand will be sold and that it will be sold with good service to the customers. They save transport costs because they can deliver bigger loads to tied stations than to free stations selling several brands. Tied stations may give the consumer better service and they may help to keep prices down, but they offer less choice. The retailer loses customers who prefer other brands. Car manufacturers may allow their cars to be sold only by 'authorised' or 'approved' garages with the necessary showrooms and equipment.

A manufacturer producing goods on a large scale likes to get rid of them in big lots. A large number of retailers have small businesses, and their orders for a few pounds' worth of goods may take as much time and trouble to handle as an order worth thousands of pounds given by a department or chain business.

A maker, employing a large number of men, must have ready cash for paying wages each week, and he therefore likes to sell his goods for cash. On the other hand, the small retailer does not want to pay for goods until he has sold some of them. A maker selling direct to small retailers must be prepared to grant credit and to handle a large number of small accounts. One firm of tea merchants trading directly with the retailers delivers to 135 000 shops throughout the country. Newspapers, books, tobacco, chocolate, sweets, tea, biscuits, boots and coal are some of the goods which are sold direct to retailers.

Whether he sells direct to the consumer or to the retailer, the maker will have to hold sufficient stocks to meet variations in demand and from which orders can be executed quickly. To do this he will need a lot of storage space, and may open depots at suitable points for serving the surrounding regions. The tea firm mentioned above, for instance, had seven packing and blending factories. Goods are taken in bulk to these depots where they are packed into small lots for delivery to customers. The handling and transporting of small lots is more expensive per tonne than for big lots. These and other disadvantages of direct trading can be lessened by dealing with **the wholesalers**; these are discussed in Chapter 21.

A seller may employ all channels of distribution in order to dispose of his goods to the best advantage. Out of £1 spent by the consumer, 25p go to the retailer to cover his expenses and net profit, 10p to the wholesaler and about 5p to the maker, the cost of making the goods being 60p. The cost of distribution thus accounts for over one-third of the retail price, so the selection of the best channel for getting the goods into the hands of the consumers as easily and as cheaply as possible is of the greatest importance.

Questions

1. Give two examples of goods that you buy straight from the maker. Explain why the goods are sold in this way rather than through retail shops.

2. What are the factors which influence a manufacturer in his choice of the channel of distribution for his product? Illustrate your answer by reference to the following goods: fashion goods, prepackaged and branded groceries, refrigerators, television sets.   (R.S.A.)

3. What are the advantages and disadvantages to a maker of selling to small retailers?

4. Why do makers of men's clothing set up their own retail shops to a much greater extent than makers of women's clothing?

5. In what way may a manufacturer of shirts distribute his product to consumers in this country? Give the advantages and disadvantages of the method you suggest.   (R.S.A.)

6. Under what circumstances and in what trades is it possible to combine manufacturing and direct sales to: (*a*) the general public; (*b*) retailers? Give examples.   (J.M.B.)

7. 'Mass production entails mass distribution.' In what ways do manufacturers seek to achieve mass distribution in the home market?   (R.S.A.)

8. Explain why selection of the channel of distribution is important to (*a*) the manufacturer, (*b*) the consumer.

9. Trace the various stages through which a packet of breakfast cereal has passed before it reaches the consumer.   (W.J.E.C.)

Chapter 20

Channels of distribution · Farm products · Produce markets · Marketing Boards

Agricultural products can be, and are, marketed through the same channels as manufactured goods. The farmer, however, encounters **difficulties** not experienced by the manufacturer. The manufacturer can regulate his output. If he needs 100 articles, he can turn out that number exactly in a given time, but the farmer does not know how much his crop will be. The crop may be good or bad according to the weather and other factors beyond the farmer's control. The seed must be planted long before harvest, and farm production cannot be stopped or modified suddenly like factory production. It takes several years to rear cattle and crops may vary considerably from year to year.

The manufacturer can turn out a given number of articles all of the same dimensions and quality, but a farmer cannot guarantee that his wheat, potatoes and eggs will be of the same quality and size. To obtain a given quantity of the same quality or size, farm products must be sorted and graded.

When a farmer has difficulty in selling his goods, he cannot store them as easily as factory goods. Some, like strawberries, are highly perishable and must be sold almost as soon as they are picked. If there happens to be a glut, they must be sold at very low prices. A factory can spread output all through the year but a crop must be harvested during a few weeks. All the wheat grown in this country must be harvested in August and September, the whole year's crop being ready for the market at the same time. The period between ploughing and reaping is a long time for the farmer to wait for his money, and very often he cannot afford to wait for better prices, even if the product can be stored. Output and prices of farm products vary more than those of manufactured goods. In three years the price of sugar rose from £30 to £90 and then fell to almost £10 per tonne. Total receipts may be greater from a small crop than from a big crop.

To secure a more even flow of cereals to the market and steadier prices, a Cereals Marketing Council was set up in 1965. The Council may advance money to farmers who are prepared to store their crops instead of selling them as soon as possible. When supplies are plentiful, it may buy cereals which it will store for a while and release later in the year when supplies become scarcer.

Farmers near towns **can retail** milk and vegetables from door to door or sell direct to retailers. They can also sell butter, poultry, eggs and vegetables at the local market where they may have a stall, while livestock can be auctioned at markets and fairs. A large number of farms, however, are situated in remote districts far from populous centres and sell very little locally. These sell eggs, butter and poultry to **wholesale dealers** who assemble or collect supplies from the farms into big lots to take to the towns; or they send them to salesmen who will find buyers for them, charging a commission for their services. Crops like wheat and barley if not sold direct to millers and brewers are sold by sample to dealers who may make the round of the markets and farms to see the quality before buying. Some farmers agree to grow crops of peas, beans, etc., to meet the requirements of a canning and preserving factory which then buys the whole crop.

Most large towns have **wholesale produce markets** for vegetables, fruits, flowers and poultry, like London's Nine Elms. Such markets are necessary because the goods in which they deal are perishable, and supplies must be received frequently, sometimes daily, if they are to be fresh and in good condition, and the buyer, unlike the buyer of manufactured goods, wants to see and sample each lot he purchases. A central market enables the buyer to see and choose the goods he wants. Retailers can always find sellers in these markets and obtain a choice. Without these markets they would have to spend more time travelling from one place to another in search of what they wanted. The sellers are the wholesalers who have collected supplies from the farms, and the commission salesmen employed by farmers to sell their goods. Competition among them keeps prices down.

In the big markets the buyers include, besides local retailers, wholesalers who require supplies to send to wholesalers and retailers serving outlying districts. For the same reason similar markets exist for buying and selling fish. Such markets are not necessary for manufactured goods.

Farmers who must dispose of their products in bulk receive lower prices than those who can sell retail. They may, too, have to bear heavy transport costs, especially if, as is frequently the case, they send small lots. Broccoli and flowers, for instance, are sent from Cornwall to London. Some of these difficulties could be overcome by **cooperation** between farmers as in Denmark. In this country, however, cooperation has made very little progress. It is not easy for the 320 000 farmers in Great Britain, mostly small farmers with varied interests, to reach agreement. There are no big producers dominating the trade corresponding to the manufacturers of tobacco, sugar, or chemicals.

Many farmers, however, do cooperate to buy in bulk fertilisers, seeds, etc., and to purchase expensive machinery which would not be profitable if used only on one small farm, as well as cooperating to sell vegetables, fruit, etc., and to form marketing boards.

During the years following the First World War prices of agricultural products fell to very low levels and farm workers were leaving the land to seek employment elsewhere. To check this movement and to encourage the production of more food at home, the Government in 1931–3 passed Acts to help farmers market their goods by allowing the formation of **marketing boards**. After a scheme had been prepared it had to be approved by a majority of the producers, who then elected members of the Board to be responsible for carrying out the scheme. Any producer can apply to be registered with the Board and registered producers must contribute towards the costs of working the scheme. Unless a producer is registered, or is exempted from registration, the Board has authority to prohibit him from selling the product, and it can fine producers breaking its regulations. Small producers, such as those planting less than an acre of potatoes, are exempt.

A board may, like the Wool, Milk and Hop Boards, buy all the product and sell it itself, or it may make other arrangements. It may fix the prices and terms of sale, make provisions for grading and testing, packaging and transport. Potatoes are graded by riddling, the smaller ones that fall through the mesh being used as animal food. They are sold through merchants licensed by the Board. When supplies are plentiful the Board itself may buy surplus stocks in order to prevent prices from falling. The wool clip is sold at auctions arranged by the Board.

Auctions are used for selling products that vary a great deal in quality and cannot be graded, or are perishable, or seasonal, like wool, tea, fruit and animals. Buyers want to see or to sample such products before bidding for them. Auctions save time and work by bringing many buyers and sellers together in one place instead of each buyer having to visit and deal with each farmer separately. The buyers have more choice and the sellers gain from greater competition among buyers.

A marketing board has the power to control production. The output of potatoes can be increased or decreased by fixing the acreage to be planted by each producer. The quantity coming on to the market can be regulated by altering the size of the mesh used for riddling. Enlarging the mesh reduces the supply because it allows bigger potatoes to fall through for use as animal food. At the same time the Government may control the quantity of potatoes imported.

Marketing boards exist for milk, hops, wool and potatoes. In 1971 the former Egg Marketing Board was replaced by the Eggs Authority which will, when necessary, buy eggs in order to prevent the price falling below a certain level. There is also a Fatstock Marketing Corporation which collects stock from the farms, arranges the slaughter, the grading and the distribution of the meat to the shops, and pays the farmers.

As the boards are formed for the sake of the producers, the interests of consumers are looked after by Consumers' Councils; the Minister of Agriculture also appoints two members to the Board, and any plans that would raise the price or alter the quantity produced must be approved by the minister.

An account of the **Milk Marketing Board** will serve as an example of the work done to help farmers sell their products. Formed in 1933, it now has over 88 000 registered producers in England and Wales, Scotland having its own Board. The Board must take all milk offered to it and find buyers for it. Ninety-five per cent is sold direct to the Board. A small number of farmers are producer retailers, selling the milk themselves. These must send returns to the Board and sell at the same price as other retailers who receive their supplies from the Board.

The retail price is now fixed by the Government, but the price of milk sold to factories is settled between the Board and the buyers, and varies according to the use to be made of the milk. All buyers pay the Board which then pools the receipts and, after deducting expenses, calculates the average price per litre for each region. Regions far away from big cities receive slightly less than others because of the heavier transport costs involved. All farmers in the same region receive the same price for the same quality. A farmer whose milk was sold at low prices to a factory gets the same price per litre as one whose milk was sold at higher prices for liquid consumption. Every month a cheque or giro transfer is sent to each farmer for the amount due to him. Some of the higher price received by producer retailers must be paid to the Board.

The Board is now responsible for the transport of milk from the farms. It pays outside contractors to do this work, but undertakes some itself in order to check prices charged by the hauliers. The transport is planned so that one lorry collects from a group of farms. This is cheaper than for each farmer to find his own transport. Many farms provide only small amounts, the average per farm being less than 300 litres per day. The milk is taken, whenever possible, straight to the retail dairymen or factories, again saving time and expenses.

The Board promotes the wider use of milk by advertising, opening milk bars, and providing milk at low prices to schools. As the Board buys all the milk and supplies vary with the seasons, it has set up a few factories to deal with any surplus and to provide a check on manufacturers' prices.

The breeding of better cattle and the production of better milk have been fostered by the Board. For these purposes it has set up laboratories and experimental stations and distributed information and advice. Producers of the best grades of milk are given a higher price. Statistics relating to herds and milk production are recorded by the Board.

The Board consists of eighteen members. The country is divided into eleven regions. The big North-Western region elects two members and the rest one each. Three others are elected by all dairy farmers and the Minister of Agriculture appoints another three. Being the only buyer from the farmers and the only seller the Board has a monopoly for its huge wholesale milk business.

The Board has brought **benefits to farmers**, particularly small farmers in remote areas who could not sell at the higher retail price but had to sell a perishable product quickly and cheaply to factories, and bear high transport costs on small lots. They now have an assured market and do not have to seek buyers. They know beforehand how much they will receive and that they will receive their money regularly and they have been relieved of transport and other difficulties. They have more time and money to devote to their farming, the Board, again, helping by giving advice and information.

Activities of the Milk Marketing Board

EXECUTIVE
Experienced and qualified
staff carry out the Board's
policies.

Milk collected from farms
at agreed prices; payment
by monthly cheque to
farmers.

Surplus milk processed
into milk products at
the Board's 'Creameries'.

Cattle Breeding stations
for improvement of dairy
and beef cattle strains;
A.I. service for farmers.

Advisory service for
dairy and beef farmers.

Collective advertising of
milk schemes to increase
consumption of milk
products.

For milk and many other farm products, the Government guarantees **minimum prices** to the farmers in order to encourage the production of more food at home and to enable the farmers to make long-term plans. The guarantees are arranged each year by the Minister of Agriculture after consultations with the National Farmers' Union. Milk is the only product whose price is fixed by the Government. Some products are sold at prices fixed by the marketing boards while others are sold for what they will fetch, the Government compensating the farmers if they receive less than a certain amount. By 1978 this policy will have been replaced by that of the Common Market.

Questions

1. What difficulties are there in the marketing of farm products as compared with factory products?

2. Why are milk and vegetables sometimes sold directly to consumers, but not wool and hops?

3. Describe an auction. Which farm products are sold by auction? Why are auctions suitable methods for selling such products? What other products are sold by auction?

4. What are wholesale produce markets? Why are they necessary and where are they found? Give some examples.

5. What are the advantages to (*a*) the buyer, (*b*) the seller, of dealing in a public wholesale market? Can you put forward reasons why certain goods are normally sold in these markets while others are usually not so marketed? (R.S.A.)

6. Each day the wholesale fish and vegetable trade supplies retail outlets with many kinds of fresh produce. Explain how both home and overseas produce reach the housewife.   (M.R.E.B.)

7. What is a marketing board? Why were such boards set up? How are they formed? What protection is there for consumers?

8. For which products do marketing boards exist? Give an account of the powers and work of any one of them.

9. Give four reasons why the channels of distribution of some foodstuffs are different from others. Illustrate your answer with reference to relevant commodities in each case.   (J.M.B.)

10. Why does the Government guarantee minimum prices for certain farm goods, but not for manufactured goods?

11. The channels of distribution for raw materials and manufactured goods are basically different. Explain clearly why this is so, illustrating your answer as fully as possible.   (A.E.B.)

12. Suppose you are a farmer **or** a fisherman. Describe the way in which you would make use of the services of commerce.   (W.J.E.C.)

Chapter 21

The wholesaler and warehousing · Direct trade

Many of the difficulties encountered by makers in direct trading can be avoided by employing the wholesaler as a channel of distribution. The maker may turn out enough goods to supply millions of people. It is cheaper and quicker to pack and transport these goods in big parcels than to make them up into the comparatively small lots required by individual retailers. The wholesaler buys 'wholes' from the maker. One order from the wholesaler is equivalent to many orders from small retailers. He saves the maker time and work by buying in bulk.

The wholesaler **buys in bulk from many makers**. He breaks down his purchases and repacks them into lots suitable for his retail customers. The retailer can obtain in one parcel from the wholesaler different kinds of goods and similar goods of different makes. A wholesaler may carry thousands of lines from which the retailer can choose the goods that suit his customers best. Without the wholesaler, the retailer would have to deal with many makers in order to obtain a variety of goods. As compared with the maker, the wholesaler serves a small area and he knows his retailers and their needs much better than the maker. He saves time and work for the retailer as well as for the maker.

By buying direct from the maker, the retailer may obtain his goods cheaper, but he may have to buy a big quantity which will take a long time to sell. The disadvantages of keeping goods in stock for a long time may easily outweigh the saving in price as will be explained in Chapter 27 which deals with the rate of turnover.

Mass production has been made possible by modern machinery, which is costly and takes up a lot of capital. We learned from the example of the school newspaper that the bigger the output of a machine the less each article costs to produce. To make expensive factories and machinery pay they must be kept working as long as possible. Otherwise the costs per article will increase. Although goods may be required only at certain times, they are being made throughout the year. Makers of Christmas cards do not wait until people begin to ask for them in the shops. They are making them a long time before Christmas. Manufacturers prefer to work regularly throughout the year rather than put their factories on overtime for some months and on short time during slack periods. They often work to a 'budget'. From past experience and information about economic conditions and the trends of trade, they prepare figures of the probable sales for the next year, the amount of raw materials that will be required, how much will be spent on wages and other items, and then, as far as possible, work to the programme that has been planned. This is what is meant by budgetary control.

In producing goods in advance of demand there is a **risk** that the demand will not materialise or will be much less than was expected, involving the makers in heavy loss. The wholesaler frequently takes this risk instead of the maker. He is in touch with the retailer all the time and may be better able to judge what will be demanded. He **orders the goods in advance of demand** from the shops, and may even supply the maker with the funds required for making them.

If the wholesaler did not take the goods from the maker before they were actually required, the maker would have to find storage space for his output and incur expenses in looking after it. The wholesaler relieves him of this work and **stores the goods** in his warehouses until demanded by the retailer, who is also able to do with less storage space because the wholesaler is usually not far away from him and can send him goods quickly when he runs out of stock. Besides having to meet the expenses of storing the goods the wholesaler **loses interest on capital** locked up in the goods. £1000 on deposit in the bank earns interest, but if the money is spent on goods it earns nothing during the time the goods are being stored. We shall refer to this point again in Chapter 27. Both the maker and the retailer are spared some of the expenses of storage through the work of the wholesaler.

As a rule the maker is not ready to give credit. He employs large numbers of workers and must find big sums in cash to pay their wages every week. He therefore likes to sell his goods for cash. On the other hand, the retailer often wants time to pay for the goods. He wants to sell some of them first before beginning to pay. Both can obtain what they want from the wholesaler who will **pay cash to the maker and grant credit to the retailer**. Even when a maker obtains an order direct from a retailer he may, if he is not prepared to give credit, pass it on to a wholesaler.

Retailers like ironmongers or chemists may stock a large number of items made by different makers. If the retailer buys direct from a maker he can obtain only one make of goods from that maker. By going to the wholesaler, he has a **choice of makes**, the wholesaler being able to buy big quantities from several makers. The retailer can visit the warehouse and inspect the goods before he buys them. The wholesaler also sends him catalogues describing the goods and giving their prices. His **travellers** call on the retailer to show samples and take orders. When two makers deal direct with one hundred retailers, two hundred transactions take place involving two hundred orders, two hundred invoices, etc. By using the wholesaler, the makers have one transaction each with the wholesaler who then sells both makes of goods to the retailers in one hundred transactions, giving a total of one hundred and two as compared with two hundred when no middleman was employed, thus **reducing clerical work**.

All wholesalers do not buy big quantities from factories. Some collect up small supplies, such as the dealer who buys eggs and dairy produce in country districts and takes them to retailers in the towns. It is part of the wholesaler's work to collect supplies in areas where goods are plentiful and take them to regions where they are scarce. It is also part of his work to **sort and pack** goods when necessary, and to **transport** them to retailers.

Some wholesalers deal only with raw materials. They import them or buy them from big importers and then sell to the factory owners. Others deal only with the manufactured goods that leave the factories, selling them sometimes to other wholesalers who may export them. Goods may pass through the hands of several wholesalers before they finally reach the consumers. One of the complaints against wholesalers is that in some cases there are too many of them, each one adding his profit to the price of the goods. In trades where supplies are provided by a large number of small, scattered producers, one wholesaler may concentrate in collecting supplies for selling to other wholesalers who make it their business to keep in touch with numerous retailers.

Compared with a retailer, the wholesaler invests less of his capital in fixed assets. In proportion to the size of the business, a retailer has to spend more on acquiring suitable premises, equipping them, and making them attractive to customers. The capital so spent is fixed, i.e. so long as the business continues it cannot be turned back into cash. The wholesaler's warehouse can be in a back street so long as it is well placed for serving the surrounding district. Many of his retail customers never visit it, and those who do are not attracted by luxurious premises. The wholesaler puts relatively more of his capital into stock which is sold and replaced by debts due to him, and these debts are in due course replaced by the cash paid in settlement. Cash, debts and stock are current capital, changing from one form into the other, the cash coming in all the time. This process is most important to the wholesaler who buys goods in advance of demand, pays cash for them and gives credit to the retailer. His capital is largely in the form of current assets.

The turnover of a wholesale warehouse is, on the average, 27 times as great as that of a retail shop, and sales per person engaged are 4 times as much as in retailing. His bigger sales enable the wholesaler to spread his expenses and profit to a much greater extent than is possible for small retailers. The average rate of gross profit in wholesaling is only about half that in retailing. The wholesaler can sell to the retailer at less cost per £100 of sales than the retailer can sell to his customers.

Compared with the maker, the wholesaler may have a much bigger business. Although it is the big concerns that produce the greater part of the output, most factories and farms are small. Great Britain has, including retail tailors' workshops, over 11 000 establishments making clothing, but the total employed by 40 per cent of these equals only 4 per establishment. If we exclude mountain and rough pasture land, 60 per cent of Great Britain's agricultural holdings are less than 0.2 square kilometres (25 times the area of a football pitch). A wholesaler may buy from hundreds of small suppliers and have a much bigger business than any one of them. If these small concerns sold small lots direct to retailers, they could not do so as cheaply as the wholesaler who can spread his expenses over a big turnover.

Suppose that three makers can make an article for £10 which they sell to wholesalers for £12. When a wholesaler's traveller calls on a retailer, he may obtain an order for the three articles. If we assume that the traveller's salary and other expenses of getting the order total £3, this sum can be shared between the three articles. Only £1 need be added to the cost price of each in order to recover the expenses. The wholesaler can afford to sell each article for £12 + £1 = £13, plus profit.

Had a maker's traveller called on the retailer he would take an order for one article only, the one made by his firm. As this traveller's salary and expenses would also probably total £3, the whole of this sum would have to be borne by the one article. The maker would have to sell at £10 + £3 = £13, plus profit. Unless he makes less profit than the wholesaler, his selling price will be the same as the wholesaler's.

This example shows how it is possible for the wholesaler to sell for the same price, or even for less, than the maker. If we add a fourth maker to our example, the wholesaler could sell for £12.75, which is **less than the maker's price**. In addition to spreading the selling expenses between different makes, the wholesaler can spread transport costs by combining small lots ordered by one retailer into a big parcel; whereas the maker would have to send a small parcel containing only his own goods and pay higher rates. The maker can sell at less cost to the wholesaler who buys in bulk than to the retailer who buys in small quantities. Some makers will not sell direct to retailers unless they order at least a certain amount. If there were no wholesalers, makers and retailers would have to do the work now done by wholesalers, and unless they could do it at less cost it pays to deal with the wholesaler.

The wholesaler, then, is particularly **useful in dealing with** small retailers and small producers. His position is strongest in goods which are unstandardised and supplied by a large number of small producers scattered over a wide area and where production is seasonal, as in confectionery, clothing, hardware, fish, vegetables and fruit. Where manufacturing is carried on by big businesses like oil companies, he is much less important as the table on p. 96 shows.

Chapters 22–24 deal with multiple, department and cooperative society stores. Among these are some big businesses made possible by the adoption of limited liability and the development of quicker and better transport. It is these large retail concerns, dealing in big quantities, that can best **bypass the wholesaler**. Nowadays, too, the retailer is not so dependent upon the wholesaler for replenishing his stocks quickly because better transport and communications make it possible to obtain supplies quickly from a factory at a distance.

Manufacturing businesses have also increased in size for the same reasons and the invention of suitable machinery has enabled makers to package their own goods instead of leaving it to the wholesalers and retailers. By packaging the goods ready for the consumer, the makers ensure that they will not be mixed with other makes, and the consumer can

Number of wholesale business units per £ million sales

Kind of business	Business units
Chocolate and sugar confectionery	8
Fish	7
Clothing and textiles	7
Hardware and electrical goods	6
Vegetables and fruit	6
Coal merchants	5
Boots and shoes	5
Chemists' wares	3
Stationery and books	3
Cigarettes and tobacco	2
Beer, wines and spirits	2
Meat	1
Tea and coffee	1
Grocery and provisions	1
Petroleum products	0.2

see from the advertisements on the wrappers that he is getting the make he wants. Mass production turns out such large quantities that makers, particularly of new goods that must fight against well-established goods, have feared to leave marketing to wholesalers who sell other makes as well. They have therefore given brands and tradenames to their goods, and advertised on such a scale that the products have become well known and the retailer is forced to stock them, whether the wholesaler pushes them or not, because the retailer's customers ask for them. Standardisation of the quality and the package makes it possible for the retailer to order straight from the maker knowing exactly what he will receive. He need not rely so much upon the wholesaler for advice about the goods nor as to where they can be obtained.

For these reasons, as well as for those given in the two preceding chapters, there has been an increase in direct trading during recent years. How wholesalers are trying to check this tendency will be described in Chapter 25.

All wholesale **warehouses** are not run in the same way, but usually the different kinds of goods are placed in different departments, e.g. cotton and wool departments, each department being in the charge of a buyer. When an order is received, copies are made and sent to the departments which can provide the goods required. Each department sends the goods to the packing and dispatch department, where they are collected together into one lot, and after having been checked with a copy of the order, are suitably packed and sent off to the retailer.

As the wholesaler gives credit to retailers, he must keep a strict watch on the amounts due from his customers. Before an order is fulfilled, a copy is sent to the accounts department in order to see that its amount does not exceed the credit allowed that particular retailer. When a new customer desires to buy on credit, the wholesaler may ask for references first. The retailer may give the names of other wholesalers with whom he has done business, or the name of his banker. Letters are then sent to the referees asking them if they think it safe to give credit to the person named. The wholesaler can also obtain information about his customers from agencies that specialise in this kind of work.

The wholesaler uses his warehouse for his own goods and he tries to sell them and get them out of the warehouse as soon as possible. Other kinds of warehouses merely store other people's goods and charge for the space occupied. Warehouses are an essential aid to trade, storing goods until such time as they are required by consumers, and aiding in their distribution.

Without warehousing, huge quantities of goods would waste. Potatoes lifted in the autumn must last until the next crop. Unless they could be stored they would be ruined by frost and there would be a scarcity in the winter. By preserving surplus potatoes, warehousing evens out the price. Buying for storage helps to keep up the price when there are more than people need, and releasing supplies when they are scarce helps to keep the price down. The same is true of manufactured goods made in advance of demand. Storage enables trade to continue all through the year.

Warehouses act as reservoirs. In the rainy season the reservoirs hold the water instead of letting it run to waste so that we are certain of enough water in the dry season. Warehouses help to keep supplies coming to us in a steady stream. They hold reserves of goods which can be drawn upon when there is an increased demand or when supplies fall off owing to bad crops or some other cause.

Goods arriving in bulk at the docks may have to be stored until they are weighed, sampled, sorted, graded and packed for transport to various parts of the country. Warehouse-owners are prepared to do this work as well as to collect and deliver. The faster this work can be performed and the goods sent on their way to the consumers the better. Every day the goods lie in the warehouse means more interest lost on the capital they represent, and in the case of perishable goods the quality deteriorates. To do their work efficiently warehouses must be suitably equipped with machinery such as lifting trucks and conveyors.

Warehouses must be adapted to the goods which they handle. Goods like coal and builders' materials may be kept in the open, but others like salt and flour must be under cover. Many warehouses are specialised to deal with wool, tea, fruit, etc. Meat and fish must be kept in cold stores. Liquids like petrol require tanks with safety precautions. Bonded warehouses store goods upon which duty has to be paid: they will be referred to again in Chapter 49.

Questions

1. In what ways does wholesale trade differ from retail trade in (*a*) suppliers and customers, (*b*) time of purchasing and size of purchases, (*c*) size of stock kept and variety of stock, (*d*) payment and credit, (*e*) risk, (*f*) turnover, (*g*) method of selling, (*h*) premises and capital?

2. What services does the wholesaler offer (*a*) the maker, (*b*) the retailer?

3. Describe the functions of the wholesale merchant. How far is it true to say that he is no longer essential?   (U.C.L.E.S.)

4. Some manufacturers sell their goods direct to retailers whereas others prefer to market their goods through wholesalers. Discuss the advantages and disadvantages of the two methods.   (J.M.B.)

5. Describe the pattern and importance of credit facilities in (*a*) the wholesale trade, and (*b*) the retail trade. Why are there fewer wholesalers than retailers?
                                              (J.M.B.)

6. What do you understand by the term 'seasonal fluctuations in trade'? Give two examples to illustrate your answer and suggest how the wholesaler can often help to lessen its effects on the production and price of goods in these cases.   (R.S.A.)

7. In what ways does a wholesaler keep in touch with his retail customers?

8. Explain by means of an example how a wholesaler may be able to sell as cheaply to the retailer as the maker can.

9. 'Although the wholesaler is less important today than formerly his functions have still to be carried out.' What are these functions and who carries them out?   (R.S.A.)

10. Describe the developments in trade that have made the wholesaler less important than he used to be.

11. Examine the table on page 96 and state in which trades the wholesaler is most important. Why is he more important in fish than in chemists' wares, and more important in chemists' wares than in groceries and provisions?

12. Visit a wholesale warehouse and describe its work. How does it differ from a small retail shop?

13. Describe the part played by warehouses in commerce. Distinguish between different types of warehouses.

14. Show how warehousing (or storage) is connected with trade, transport and insurance.   (W.J.E.C.)

15. (*a*) Why are wholesale warehouses needed? (*b*) Describe the organisation of a typical wholesale warehouse.   (L.C.C. & I.)

16. (*a*) What is the meaning of production?
    (*b*) Describe the part played by warehousing in production.   (L.C.C. & I.)

Chapter 22

Multiple shops

By using the methods mentioned in Chapter 15 sales can be increased. But there is a limit to the area one shop can serve. Customers will not come a long distance to obtain goods like groceries which they need constantly, when they can buy them near home, even if they have to pay a little more for them at the more convenient shop. The area served can be increased by accepting orders to be fulfilled through the Post Office, but this method is suitable for certain kinds of goods only.

A more important way is the opening of other shops or branches in other parts of the town and even all over the country. Some multiple businesses now own a chain of over 2000 branches. A business with **ten or more branches** is classed as a multiple or chain business. Traders owning less than ten branches are referred to as independent traders. Cooperative societies are dealt with separately.

Chain businesses have many **advantages over unit shops**. Many of the branches may be small shops, but their total sales and their total profit are very much more than the sales and profit of a single shop. A single shop cannot carry on for long if it does not make a reasonable profit, but the multiple shops can stand a loss at a few branches so long as the group as a whole is making a profit. This places them in a strong position when it comes to competition with a single shop. They can afford to run a branch at a loss until the single shop is forced to close down.

When branches are scattered all over the country, they are not likely to suffer at the same time from bad trade. If there is serious unemployment in one area, the traders with one shop suffer, but the multiple shops are making profits in areas where business is good and do not feel the results of the local unemployment as much as the traders whose shops are confined to the unemployment area. When people move away from a district, the single shop in that district loses their custom, but if they buy from a multiple shop their custom is merely transferred to another branch, which sells the same goods at the same prices.

Branches are often built alike so that people recognise them easily and the shops become well known. They advertise themselves. The multiple firms can afford to advertise in a big way, one advertisement serving for all branches. The total cost may be great but when divided by the number of branches the cost per branch may be small. £1000 spent on an advertisement covering 2000 branches is only 50p per branch. They can also spread the cost of the experts they can employ for buying, accounting, architecture, etc.

Selling great quantities means buying great quantities also. The chain stores can buy goods and equipment straight from the maker. As they buy as much as and even more than one wholesaler, they obtain them at the wholesale price. They are their own wholesalers cutting out the middleman, and the profit that he would make on the transaction they obtain for themselves. Some of them go further than this and cut out the maker as well. They set up their own factories to make the goods they sell. In this way they try to obtain the profits of the maker, the wholesaler and the retailer. Makers, too, have the same idea and instead of selling their goods to wholesalers they have decided to sell direct to the consumers by opening their own chain of retail shops.

Another advantage enjoyed by chain stores is that they can transfer staff and stock from one branch to another. If certain goods do not sell well in one area they may be sent to another where they may sell easily.

Multiple businesses have **difficulties** as well as advantages. In the first place they need a lot of capital and must make big profits in order to pay a return on it. As the branches increase in number they become more difficult to control. A manager is in charge of each branch, but each manager cannot be allowed to run the branch exactly as he pleases. All branches must be run on the same lines as decided by head office, and the managers must do as they are told. A manager may not be allowed, for instance, to buy stock, even although he may be able to get it cheaper than through head office. In order to see that branches are properly managed, inspectors must be employed to visit them and report to head office.

At one time multiple firms sold only for cash. The branch managers do not know their customers as well as the small trader does and they would deal with the matter in different ways. With so many customers credit sales would involve a great deal of clerical work. It was easier to have all branches selling for cash only. With the growth of hire purchase trading, however, they have become readier to grant terms, particularly for durable consumer goods which can be reclaimed if the customer fails to continue the instalments. Most of their sales of furniture, radio and television sets, electrical goods, cycles and perambulators are now made on hire purchase and other credit terms.

Although big quantities of goods are bought, some of the advantages thus gained are lost again. The multiple business buying in bulk must do the work of the wholesaler. Depots must be provided for storing the goods and then the goods must be transported to the various branches. It might have been cheaper to employ the wholesaler who specialises in this kind of work. Their gross profit may be bigger than that of the small trader, but out of it they must pay expenses which are included in the cost price of the small trader's purchases.

A chain business specialises in selling one main line of goods, e.g. only clothing or only groceries, and when it manufactures its own goods it will tend to push these and may offer less choice to customers than the single shop. It provides a delivery service only when it is necessary, as in the case of furniture.

The Census of Distribution shows that on the average the total value of **sales** each year is 4 per cent greater than in the previous year, but most of the increase is due to rising prices. Sales by multiple shops, however, have increased by 8 per cent each year. By comparing the table below with the one on p. 114, it can be seen that in each group their share of the trade is greater than their share of the shops. The differences are most marked in men's clothing and footwear, groceries, books and stationery, chemist's goods, and radio and television hire shops. All these are goods which are standardised and for which fashion is not important. The chains own 15 per cent of the shops but have 35 per cent of the trade. They sell more than 3 times as much per shop as do the independent traders.

Approximate percentages of shops owned by different types of businesses are shown in the table below.

	Percentage owned by		
Kind of shop	*Cooperatives*	*Independents*	*Multiples*
Groceries and provisions	10	78	12
Other foods	8	74	18
Confectioners, tobacconists, newsagents	—	90	10
Clothing and footwear	3	76	21
Furniture	3	85	12
Radio, electrical goods, cycles, perambulators	1	84	15
Radio and television hire shops	—	19	81
Ironmongery, hardware	1	89	10
Booksellers, stationers	—	87	13
Chemists	6	79	15
Jewellery, leather and sports goods	—	94	6
Other non-food shops	—	97	3
Total	5	80	15

Questions

1. When is a business described as a chain or multiple business? What advantages do the owners gain by having a large number of shops?

2. What are the advantages and disadvantages of chain businesses to the customers?

3. Show how a chain business can cut out the middlemen. What are the advantages and disadvantages of doing so?

4. Why can a chain business often sell more cheaply than the owner of a single small shop?

5. Using the tables on pages 101 and 114, state
   (a) how much of the total retail trade is done by chains;
   (b) in which goods are they most important;
   (c) why do they deal mainly in these goods;
   (d) why are they more important in men's clothing than in women's clothing?

6. It is said that the multiple shop system in retail trade leads to standardisation, simplification and specialisation in the details of the business carried on accompanied by a limitation of choice of goods to the consumer. Give a sufficient survey of the system to confirm or refute this assertion.   (R.S.A.)

Chapter 23

Department stores · Variety chains · Supermarkets

Instead of increasing sales by opening branches to sell the same kind of goods, a business can sell different kinds of goods in the same building. Many small shops are general stores selling all kinds of goods. **A department store** is one that employs at least twenty-five people and sells clothing and a wide range of other goods. Each department is really a shop on its own and must pay its share of the total expenses.

Certain **advantages** are common to multiple shops and to department stores. The department stores have big sales and big profits. They can advertise on a big scale, one advertisement advertising all departments. As they buy in big quantities they are their own wholesalers, able to buy straight from the makers and so obtain the goods at a lower price. They do not place all their eggs in one basket. If one department makes a loss, it is more than balanced by the profits of other departments. If a department attracts people into the store, it may pay to keep it going even although it makes very little profit. These stores, too, can afford to pay experts. Each department is in the charge of a buyer who is responsible, not merely for buying the goods, but for the running and the success of his department.

In addition the big department stores can afford to arrange exhibitions and displays such as fashion parades. They can provide expensive decorations and lifts and post offices for the convenience of customers. These overhead expenses in total are big, but when divided by the sales they may be quite small. They are spread over the large number of articles sold and make very little difference to the price.

By selling all kinds of goods in one building, these businesses enable a customer to obtain all he needs in one store and save him the trouble of going from one shop to another. People are encouraged to visit the stores and to walk around without being asked to buy anything. This helps to advertise the business and enables it to earn some rent by letting space to firms wishing to display and sell their goods to the crowds who visit the stores. Some new stores have leased most of the departments to be run by specialist traders. As departments are placed on different floors, land and rent are saved as compared with an equal number of shops owned by separate traders.

There are **disadvantages**, of course, for department stores as well as for chain stores. When they are very big, they become difficult and expensive to manage and require a lot of capital. Sufficient customers can be found only in the centre of big cities and towns where land is most expensive. The chain stores take their goods out to branches in the suburbs, but the department stores must attract people from long distances and to do this they must spend a lot on advertising and facilities. It would have been impossible to run big department stores when transport was slow and costly. The cheaper and quicker travelling becomes the greater the area from which customers can be drawn and within which goods can be delivered.

Because the department stores have to spend so much in attracting customers their profits diminish very quickly when sales begin to decrease. It would not help matters if, for example, the management decided to reduce expenses by stopping the lifts and expecting customers to walk to the top of the building. The overhead expenses remain high, even although sales have fallen sharply. They do not fall at the same rate as sales as was explained in Chapter 14.

As they do not know their customers well, and to avoid clerical work, department stores do not grant much credit, only 12 per cent of their sales being allowed terms and budget accounts.

Over 40 per cent of their **sales** consists of clothing, especially women's and children's wear, and another 20 per cent is made up of household textiles, furniture and bedding. Their sales have been increasing at the average rate for all retail sales, namely, 4 per cent per annum, and have remained at 6 per cent of the total trade, although department stores form less than 0.2 per cent of the number of shops.

Dealing in so many kinds of goods, they cannot make bulk purchases on the same scale as the multiples. To overcome this disadvantage they are combining into groups which buy in bulk and distribute the goods to the stores. Traffic congestion is causing more people to shop in the suburbs where the chains and the supermarkets are improving their premises and service, and to turn to mail order trading. Women who are out at work every day have less time to go on shopping expeditions to the towns. In city centres it is difficult and costly to find room for extending the premises and for parking customers' cars, and there is now a tendency for new stores to be built away from congested areas.

Some businesses, known as **variety chain stores**, are both departmental and multiple. A few, like Woolworth's, with branches in the suburbs and smaller towns and selling only cheap goods that are below a certain price and which are soon sold, have become very well known and have to spend little on advertising. They use self-selection and self-service methods and need not employ experienced sales staff with a sound knowledge of the goods. They dispense with the facilities and costly fittings of the more fashionable stores; they do not give credit and do not deliver.

The **supermarket** is a new kind of shop which is spreading rapidly. It is a department shop at least 186 square metres in area, using self-service with at least three check-out points to sell foods and household goods. It enjoys many of the advantages of department stores and of self-service shops. It does not provide expensive facilities, nor personal attention, does not allow credit, and does not deliver. The savings thus made, together with buying in big lots, enable it to sell some goods at lower prices than other shops. It is a 'one stop shop', where the housewife can obtain on one visit all she needs for the week. Similar shops with an area of less than 186 square metres are known as 'superettes', and the largest shops carrying a much wider range of goods are called 'superstores' and 'hyperstores'. Some firms have built up chains of supermarkets.

Discount shops specialise in buying lots of goods cheaply in bulk. They may be salvaged goods, or Government surplus stock, or manufacturers' unwanted lines. Bargains can be found at these shops, although there is no attempt to carry a complete range of goods. The proprietors keep down overheads by opening their shops in the less smart quarters of towns, by accepting only cash from their customers and by expecting them to make their own delivery arrangements.

Questions

1. Define a department store. What are its advantages and disadvantages to (*a*) the owners, (*b*) the customers?

2. What are the main goods sold by department stores? What is their share of the total trade? Why has their share not increased much in recent years?

3. What facilities and services does a city department store provide for customers? How can it provide these and yet sell as cheaply as small shops in the suburbs?

4. How does a variety chain store differ from a city department store in (*a*) situation, (*b*) premises, (*c*) sales staff, (*d*) kind of goods sold, (*e*) facilities for customers, (*f*) services given to customers?

5. How far is it true to say that department stores are chain stores and chain stores are department stores? Illustrate your answer with actual examples.
(W.J.E.C.)

6. What are (*a*) supermarkets, (*b*) superettes, (*c*) superstores, (*d*) hyperstores? What do they have in common?

7. Account for the rapid development of supermarkets by describing the advantages they have over other types of shops. What are their disadvantages to customers?

8. Distinguish between a supermarket and a department store. Explain how supermarkets can offer many goods at cut prices, but still make substantial profits.
(S.R.E.B.)

9. What is a discount house? What kinds of goods does it sell? Why can it sell at lower prices than many other shops?

10. Write about a department store, mentioning location, layout, services offered, methods of payment available, organisation and control.
(A.L.S.E.B.)

11. (*a*) Describe the functions of the wholesaler.
    (*b*) Briefly outline three examples of circumstances in which manufacturers might prefer to sell direct to retail firms.
(A.E.B.)

12. Describe the advantages of large-scale retailing both to the large-scale retailer himself and to the customer.   (W.J.E.C.)

13. What are the advantages of large scale retailing shops such as multiple, department and supermarket stores to (*a*) consumers, (*b*) retailers?   (M.R.E.B.)

14. Explain how department stores seek to attract customers.   (W.J.E.C.)

Chapter 24

Cooperative retail and wholesale societies

To increase their profits chain shops and department stores do without the middlemen. Consumers, too, have had the same idea and have opened their own retail shops in order to obtain the profits for themselves.

The first successful cooperative shop was set up in Rochdale in 1844 by a small group known as the 'Rochdale Pioneers'. They were twenty-eight in number and formed a society, each member contributing £1 capital with which they started a grocery business, later adding other goods. They were working-class consumers protecting themselves against high prices and poor quality. There are at the moment about 400 societies in Great Britain but, for reasons that will be given later, the number is becoming smaller each year. Some are quite small, but those in big cities have many branches and own department stores and supermarkets. Each society is in business on its own, and the success or failure of one does not affect the others.

A cooperative retail society is 'a voluntary non-profit making organisation engaged in retail trade and controlled by its members, who are also its customers'. **It differs from other businesses** in several ways. A society wants as many members as possible because each member must provide some capital which gives him an interest in the business so that he is more likely to be a good customer. In other types of businesses the owners may buy very little from their own business.

A society is non-profit-making because its 'profit' is not profit in the usual sense of the word but a surplus. People who buy goods wholesale and then sell them to themselves at higher prices are not really making a profit and this is what members of a society do. A society must charge more than the cost price in order to cover its expenses. It charges about the same as other shops, but anything left over (the surplus) from what members have been charged is periodically returned to them as a dividend on their purchases.

If the profit is £10 000 and sales (or purchases by members) total £200 000, the **dividend** will be

$$\frac{£10\ 000}{£200\ 000} = \frac{£1}{£20} = 5\text{p in the £.}$$

A member who bought £20 worth of goods would thus be entitled to a dividend of £1. The more a member buys, the greater will be his share of the profit. In other kinds of businesses the profits go to a relatively small number of owners in proportion to the capital they have invested.

This cash dividend system is expensive to operate because it means keeping a record of each member's purchases and calculating the dividend due to each member, and it does not attract shoppers who are not members. It has now been abandoned in favour of stamps called **dividend stamps** provided by the CWS Societies that use these stamps who will exchange them for cash or for goods or add them to a member's capital. To encourage customers to exchange them for goods the stamps are worth more in goods than in cash, and to encourage customers to become members and to invest some capital they are worth more to members than to non-members.

If the profits are enough double or more stamps may be given at certain times. When another type of business uses these stamps they are called bonus stamps.

Cooperative societies give less power to **capital** than do other types of businesses. The owners of a business usually have votes in proportion to their capital, those with the most capital arguing that as they stand to lose most in the event of failure they should have a bigger say in running the business than those who stand to lose smaller sums. In the cooperative societies the capital any one member can invest is limited to £1000, and all members have one vote each no matter how much capital they have contributed.

As capital does not receive the profits or the power, it must receive some other reward or else very few people would be willing to risk their capital in a cooperative business. The reward it gets is interest at a fixed rate, and this interest is due whether there are profits or not, in the same way that wages are due to workmen. The cooperative societies will repay capital to a member who wishes to withdraw it, but this is not always possible in other kinds of businesses.

It is plain that when a business is owned by thousands of people, they cannot all be **managing** it. A committee is elected for appointing a manager, secretary and staff for running the business, and to report periodically to the committee, who, if not satisfied, can dismiss them and appoint others in their places. This is sometimes used as an argument against cooperative societies because many elected to these committees may know nothing about business and may not be in a position to judge if the work is being done efficiently or not. They may have very little invested in the business, and will not lose much if it fails.

In 1862 the **Cooperative Wholesale Society** was formed to buy cheaply in bulk and then to sell to the retail societies. The retail societies provided the capital for this, and they share its profits according to the value of the purchases they make. Votes are also allotted to the societies according to purchases. The wholesale society is a big concern run by experts, the business being in a position to pay high salaries in order to obtain good men. Since 1862 the cooperative movement has gone a step further, and now owns many factories and farms, thus cutting out all the middlemen for certain goods. It also has an insurance business and a bank which has retail societies and their members, and trade unions among its customers.

The **societies sell** a wider range of goods than a chain business. Nearly one-half of their sales consists of groceries. Next in importance rank meat, clothing and footwear, milk, coal, bread and confectionery, furniture and chemists' goods. In 1957–66 their sales increased at just over 1 per cent per annum and their share of the total trade fell from 12 to 9 per cent. In the same period chain store sales grew at 8 per cent per annum and their share of the total trade rose from 25 to 35 per cent.

The societies were formed to provide necessities in a period when the working classes earned very low wages, most of which had to be spent on food. As earnings and the standard of living rise, the increase in wages is spent for the most part on clothing, household goods, cars and service trades like hairdressing and travel agencies. The table on page 114 shows how little of these the societies provide.

To compete with the chains the societies are now competing less with one another. They are reducing their numbers by **amalgamating** into fewer, but much bigger, businesses. The CWS wants societies in England and Wales to amalgamate into 50 big societies. Each society would then have more branches and obtain more of the advantages of a chain business. A bigger society can save on staff and equipment, can pay higher salaries for experts and place bulk orders with one of the 30 new CWS regional grocery warehouses now being planned to replace a large number of small warehouses. It can serve the same areas with fewer shops. At one time it might have been necessary for two neighbouring villages to have their own societies and a small shop each, but with present-day transport one society and one big shop might serve both villages equally well. Old shops in areas where the population has declined can be replaced by modern shops on good sites.

Unlike the branches of chain firms, the societies are free to please themselves and are not bound to take the advice of the CWS. They buy most of their goods from it, but also buy other makes to keep customers who prefer these makes, and they can fix their own selling prices.

Questions

1. What is a retail cooperative society? Describe the way it is organised or managed.

2. How does a retail cooperative society differ from other businesses in (*a*) ownership, (*b*) customers, (*c*) capital, (*d*) control, (*e*) votes, (*f*) profits?

3. Indicate four features of a cooperative retail society and explain the relationship between cooperative retail societies and the Cooperative Wholesale Society. (U.C.L.E.S.)

4. How are the cooperative societies meeting competition from the chain businesses?

5. In what ways do multiple shops and cooperative societies (*a*) resemble, (*b*) differ from each other? (R.S.A.)

6. What do the retail societies gain by amalgamating?

7. Compare the shopping facilities offered by a department store, a retail cooperative society and a multiple chain store, and in your answer show how each is trying to increase its own share of the retail trade.   (W.M.E.B.)

8. Distinguish between the Cooperative Wholesale Society and a consumers' cooperative society. Indicate the features they have in common.   (W.J.E.C.)

9. Outline the main features of a consumer cooperative society which is engaged in retailing both durable and consumable goods.

   Indicate how such a retail society would be linked with the Cooperative Wholesale Society.   (W.J.E.C.)

Chapter 25

Independent retailers · Voluntary groups

The total **number of shops**, about 500 000 at the moment, is decreasing. There has been a decrease in all groups, the decrease being most marked in the food and grocery groups. Yet the number of chain shops has increased in all groups except in the food and grocery groups. The cooperative societies have increased the number of their household goods shops, but have fewer shops of all other kinds. The **independent traders**, i.e. those owning less than ten shops, have suffered most having lost ground in all groups, especially in the food and grocery groups.

In addition to the advantages mentioned in the previous chapters, the chains and the cooperative societies have more resources than the small traders. They can find the capital to modernise their shops, to convert to self-service, to sell more of the expensive household goods on hire purchase, and to provide better service. They can pay more for good sites than the small retailers, many of whom are driven out of the main streets. The small traders are no longer protected by resale price maintenance and they have to compete with the city department stores and the growing number of supermarkets in the suburbs which can often sell for less than they can.

A reduction in the number of shops results in a loss of convenience to the public. At present there is one shop to every hundred people and a customer has a wide choice among different types of shops and services, and if not satisfied in one place he can usually find another within a short distance. Limiting the number of selling points would give him less choice and less personal attention.

While the number of shops is decreasing, the **size of shops** is increasing. Although the average sales per shop are rising, the majority of shops, particularly those owned by independent traders, are small. The department stores sell fifty times as much, the chains three times as much, and the cooperative societies more than twice as much per shop as the independent traders. The cooperative societies and the chains also sell one-third more per person employed. One-fifth of all shops are too small to have any paid employees. The bigger businesses can use their buildings, equipment and staff more efficiently than the small shops. A reduction in the number of shops would give those that were left a bigger turnover enabling them to sell more per person employed, to buy more cheaply in bulk, to spread their overheads, and thus help to keep prices down. Customers would benefit from lower prices, but lose in choice and convenience.

In spite of the popularity of the supermarkets and the tremendous growth of multiple stores, some independent retailers and wholesalers still survive and flourish.

The retailers are those that offer something special to customers, for in the last analysis it is the customers who keep a shop in business. While customers continue to patronise a shop it will remain and prosper, but if they take their business to a new supermarket and abandon the independent shop that has served them for years, that shop is forced to close. Some of the remaining small shops belong to specialised trades. A high-class pâtisserie or delicatessen, a 'do-it-yourself' shop, a sport shop, a beauty salon, a tailoring establishment, a 'garden shop' and the many women's 'boutiques' – all cater to special groups of people and will stay in business while their special services (and the specialist advice they can give to customers) are in demand.

Other independent shops of a general nature survive because they are located away from the competition of the large supermarkets. They are found in suburban and country areas.

Many small shop owners manage without paid assistants because they obtain **family help** without having to pay wages for it. This saving in wages helps them to compete with the bigger businesses which have to pay for all work done. If these small businesses had to pay wages to members of the family, and counted as losses some of the rent, rates, lighting and heating bills that they pay for the house as a whole, many would show net losses. The owners cannot live on the business so they may undertake **other work**, their wives and children looking after the shop while they are working elsewhere. They regard the little shop as a sideline.

When a small shop is owned by one man he can supervise everything himself and see that it is properly done. He does not have to pay managers and inspectors like the chains. He may not deliver goods nor provide facilities in a modern type of shop. In proportion to the size of his business he has **lower overheads**. He may not advertise, but rely on customers for whom his shop is conveniently situated. He may be able to **charge more** than shops in the main street because people living nearby prefer to pay him a little more rather than make a special journey to the main street just to get one or two items.

The small trader is free to please himself as to when he opens his shop. The big shops are restricted by trade union regulations and legal requirements and must close at certain times. The one-man business can remain **open all day** and every day including holidays. It gets a lot of trade after shops in the main street have closed. It is also free to make concessions in order to please and keep a good customer, while the managers of branch shops may have no authority to make such concessions.

The small trader knows his customers personally and is in a better position to **give credit**. He thus gets customers who can not always pay cash. He can also give them **personal attention**, important in such businesses as tailoring.

The multiple shops sometimes make the goods themselves or have them made to their specifications and try to sell these rather than other makes. They may stock only goods most in demand that sell quickly such as the most popular brands of cigarettes and the most common sizes of clothing. The small man does not care which make he sells as long as he can make a profit on it, and he may give a **better choice** of makes, sizes and qualities than the chain shops.

The multiple stores are strongest in trades selling men's clothing and footwear, groceries, books and stationery, chemists' goods, and in radio and television hire shops. These are goods which are standardised and which are not subject to sudden changes in fashion. The small retailer can compete where goods are not standardised and where **fashion** is important, such as ladies' wear. Bulk purchases of fashionable goods would involve the trader in heavy losses if the fashions suddenly changed.

In a business such as that of a tobacconist, where sales of tobacco alone would be insufficient to support the owner, and where other things, like confectionery and newspapers, have to be sold with it, the small man can also manage to survive. Many small towns and villages have only enough customers to support small **general shops**. In such cases the prepackaging of branded goods has assisted the small trader because he can add these, e.g. aspirins, formerly sold only by chemists, to his stocks without possessing special knowledge about them. He can also compete when he carries on a high-class business catering for a special class of people such as a food shop in a wealthy quarter, or when he sells different kinds of goods in different seasons, such as sports equipment.

The small trader can take full advantage of the **wholesalers' services**. The wholesaler lets him buy small lots of different makes frequently, delivers the goods to his shop, and gives credit and advice. To obtain better terms some retailers form **buying associations** to combine their orders into one bulk purchase from the wholesaler or maker. They then do some of the wholesaler's work by storing the goods in one of their shops until they are sorted, packed into small parcels and taken to the shops.

In Chapter 21 we learned that the wholesalers have also suffered from the growth of big businesses and direct dealing between makers and big retailers. It is, therefore, in the interests of wholesalers and small retailers to help one another. Many wholesalers have formed self-service **cash and carry** departments where the retailer can buy at lower prices because he serves himself, pays cash for his purchases and takes them away in his own van. In this way the wholesaler passes on some of his work to the retailer.

The most important way in which they help one another is by forming **voluntary groups** and chains. A voluntary group consists of one wholesaler and a number of retailers, whereas a voluntary chain includes several wholesalers and many retailers. Some have over twenty wholesalers and many thousands of retailers as members.

A retailer who joins a voluntary group binds himself to buy each week a certain amount from the wholesaler at agreed prices such as cost price plus a percentage, and to pay a weekly subscription. He must undertake to bring his premises and service up to the desired standard and display the group symbol.

The wholesaler is thus assured of a minimum turnover without having to spend so much on sending out travellers to obtain orders and to keep in touch with retailers. He is in a better position to plan his supplies and to arrange bulk purchases. He can arrange to transport goods to a group of retailers on the same day and save delivery costs. In return he is prepared to help the retailers with the finance necessary to modernise their shops and equipment, to brand his goods and to advertise them. A voluntary group gives its members some of the advantages of multiple firms and of tied shops, but the retailers are not bound hand and foot to the wholesaler as branches are chained to head office. Retailers can buy from other wholesalers, fix their own prices and even leave the group.

	Percentage of total trade done by		
Kind of shop	*Cooperatives*	*Independents*	*Multiples*
Grocery and provisions	17	46	37
Other foods	13	59	28
Confectioners, tobacconists, newsagents	1	85	14
Clothing and footwear	3	46	51
Furniture	5	70	25
Radio, electrical goods, cycles, perambulators	3	72	25
Radio and television hire shops	1	18	81
Ironmongery, hardware	2	86	12
Booksellers, stationers	—	66	34
Chemists	5	58	37
Jewellery, leather and sports goods	1	84	15
Other non-food shops	—	92	8
Total	9	56	35

Retail outlets or selling points include, besides shops, roundsmen's depots, yards like builders' yards, traders calling from door to door, market stalls, street traders, mail order firms, vending machines and mobile shops. Fixed shops are, however, by far the most important, selling nearly ten times as much as all the other types put together.

The sales made by different types of businesses, expressed as percentages of the totals for the country, are given above. Separate figures are not available for department stores.

Questions

1. Why is the number of small shops decreasing? What would consumers gain and lose if the small shop were driven out of business?

2. What advantage does the small shop have in competing against the big businesses?

3. In which trades is the small retailer most important? Why does he have such a high percentage of the total trade in some goods?

4. What are the main differences between shops found in the main shopping centres of a large town and the shops found in or near a housing estate? Write about (*a*) the kind of goods they sell, (*b*) the services they provide, (*c*) the way in which they are owned, (*d*) why some shops are found only in town centres, (*e*) why some shops are not found in town centres.   (A.L.S.E.B.)

5. In what ways are wholesalers and small retailers helping one another?

6. Suppose you are a small retail grocer and wish to expand your sales. What would you do?   (W.J.E.C.)

7. Compare the supermarket and the 'round the corner' shop from the customer's point of view.   (W.M.E.B.)

8. Why are some people attracted to (*a*) department stores, (*b*) cooperative retail societies, (*c*) supermarkets? In spite of these attractions some people prefer their small local shops. Why is this?   (W.M.E.B.)

9. Suppose you are a wholesale merchant. You find your customers tend to deal less with you and more with manufacturers directly. How might you stem this tendency?   (W.J.E.C.)

10. In recent years changes have taken place in the retailing of goods particularly in the grocery trade. Discuss these changes with regard to (*a*) mass distribution, (*b*) transport, (*c*) packaging, (*d*) goods conveyed to consumers' houses, (*e*) shopping after normal hours.   (A.L.S.E.B.)

11. What is meant by 'wholesaling'?
    Explain with reference to wholesaling the meaning of the terms 'voluntary group' and 'cash and carry warehouse'.   (L.C.C. & I.)

12. Suppose that you are a small grocer. What advantages would you expect to receive if you became a member of a voluntary chain of small grocers organised by a firm of wholesalers? What responsibilities would you thereby incur?
    (W.J.E.C.)

13. Show why cash-and-carry and discount stores have developed in recent years and how they are able to trade profitably.   (S.R.E.B.)

14. Explain the reasons for the growth of supermarkets in recent years. How do you account for the survival of the small shop?   (L.C.C. & I.)

15. Indicate the main functions common to both large-scale and small-scale retailers. How do you account for the fact that in large cities there are still some small retailers on the main shopping streets?   (W.J.E.C.)

16. What are the functions of a retailer? Illustrate your answer by reference to different forms of retail organisation.   (L.C.C. & I.)

Chapter 26

Mail order trading · Mobile shops · Vending machines

Many businesses, including some of the big department stores, rely on advertisements and the services provided by the Post Office to carry on mail order trading.

The **Post Office** will take parcels up to ten kilograms in weight so long as they are not more than a certain size. Goods most suitable for mail order business are those that are of small bulk but fairly expensive, such as clothes and clothing materials. The Post Office charges according to the weight and not according to the value. The postage on an article worth 25p may be 20p, the carriage increasing the cost by $\frac{20}{25} \times 100 = 80$ per cent. The postage on an article worth £20, but of the same weight, would also be 20p, but in this case the cost has been increased by $\frac{20}{2000} \times 100 = 1$ per cent only.

For an extra fee valuable packets can be registered so that the receiver must sign a certificate admitting that he has received the packet and the sender can claim compensation up to £150 if the packet is lost or damaged. To be able to claim more than £150 the sender can insure the packet up to a maximum of £500. For an unregistered packet a certificate of posting can be obtained for one penny showing that it was delivered to the Post Office. Parcels cannot be registered and can be insured only up to £100. Firms can arrange for parcels sent on approval to be returned postage forward, but they must pay extra for this service. Where parcels are sent in sufficient quantities, the Post Office will, if notified in time, collect them free of charge and may allow a discount on the postage.

Except for local deliveries, which are 5p cheaper, the Post Office takes no account of distance. The charge for sending a parcel 10 miles is the same as for sending it 100 miles or more. The longer the distance between buyer and seller, the more there is to be gained by using the Post Office.

Facilities for payment are also provided by the Post Office. The National Giro, as explained on page 47, can be particularly useful for mail order trading. Money and postal orders and stamps are available to those without current accounts. If a firm wants payment on delivery of the goods, it can use the cash on delivery-service (C.O.D.). The postman will collect up to £20 when he delivers the parcel and remit it to the seller. When the amount due is more than £20, the addressee must pay at the Post Office before receiving the parcel. The maximum that can be collected in this way is £50. A charge is made for the service.

Customers who prefer to use other banks can pay by cheque or by bank giro credits. By attaching National Giro or other giro forms to its invoices and requesting payment by these means, a mail order firm is relieved of the work of opening a large number of letters, sorting cheques, postal and money orders, and paying them into the bank.

A fast first-class post, a slower but cheaper second-class post, prepaid reply cards, express delivery, railex, recorded delivery, franking machines, telephones, postal services to foreign countries and air mail, are other services provided by the Post Office. Particulars of postal services can be found in the *Post Office Guide*.

The Post Office is a fairly quick and reliable way of sending parcels and it takes them to the most out-of-the-way places. In this country no place is far from a town to which people can go to see the goods before they buy them. Mail order business can get over this difficulty by sending goods on approval, the goods having to be returned within so many days if they are not suitable. This, however, means extra expense. In America, where so many small places are situated so far away from towns, mail order business is far more important than it is here.

Direct sales from makers to consumers are sometimes made through the Post Office. When this is the only method used by a maker, all middlemen are eliminated and no capital is required to open retail shops. Handling and packing costs are reduced because the goods are packed and dispatched once instead of being sent first to a wholesaler, then to retailers and finally to the consumers. There is also a saving in stocks, because all stocks can be kept in one place instead of being scattered among many traders. Some mail order houses do not keep any stocks, but instruct their suppliers to send goods direct to customers.

The **disadvantages** of mail order trading are the heavy costs of advertising to find and keep in touch with customers, the expense of printing and distributing catalogues, many of which may bring no orders or orders of small value, the heavy costs of parcelling, postage and carriage, and the cost of keeping accounts and dealing with payment by instalments. For the heavier and bulkier goods, like portable sheds and lawn mowers, orders are received through the Post Office, but the goods are dispatched by road or rail.

Women's and men's wear form over 50 per cent of **mail order sales**. Floor coverings, household textiles, furniture, bedding, sports goods and toys provide another 20 per cent. Although sales are increasing at 15 per cent per annum as compared with 4 per cent for shop sales, they still form only 3 per cent of the total. This rapid growth is partly due to worsening traffic conditions in towns and to women in employment having less time to visit the shops. Mail order firms say that they offer 'shopping with comfort, convenience and credit'.

Mail order firms fall into **three groups**. The great bulk of the trade is done by six big firms which have promoted sales by advertising a wide selection of reliable goods and by appointing local agents through whom they obtain most of the orders. The agents, many of them housewives working in their spare time, canvass for customers and collect the instalments due. Instead of sending expensive catalogues to all customers, a few are sent to the agent who lends them to customers. Expenses are saved by sending to the agent one parcel containing goods for several customers instead of posting separate parcels to individual customers.

Selling through local agents has enabled mail order houses to grant credit on 98 per cent of their sales. The standardisation and branding of more goods has helped to increase sales because when customers order branded goods they know the goods will be the same as those in the shops.

A second group of smaller firms dealing in a narrow range of goods, such as garden plants, do not employ agents but post small catalogues or brochures in answer to inquiries received after advertising. They may also use direct advertising by sending brochures to people they believe to be interested in their goods.

A third group of small firms do not even use catalogues, but rely entirely on advertising to bring orders.

Another retail outlet that has increased in importance recently is the **mobile shop**. The biggest owners of mobile shops are the cooperative societies which have one-third of the total sales made by mobile shops. Travelling shops are suitable for goods in regular demand and the great majority sell groceries, greengrocery and meat, the rest selling mainly oil and hardware. They are not suitable for heavy goods like washing machines, nor for fashionable goods for which a wide choice is desired.

Mobile shops are useful to people living in country districts, one-quarter of their sales being made in Scotland, but they are also increasing in towns where they serve customers in the suburbs. They save the housewife the time and trouble of going shopping and carrying goods home, and the roundsman can take orders for goods to be delivered on his next call. A mobile shop may offer less choice than a fixed shop because the amount of stock a vehicle can carry is limited.

By using a mobile shop a business can extend the area it serves and find more customers. Instead of waiting for customers to come to the shop, the shop is taken to the customers. The roundsman is in constant touch with the customers and learns their likes and dislikes. He is bringing goods to their notice and trying to sell all the time instead of waiting for them to ask as in a counter shop. There is no need for a special delivery service, and, if credit is given, the roundsman calls regularly to collect the debts while selling more goods at the same time.

Some traders possess only a mobile shop. It is easier and cheaper to acquire than a fixed shop and it may be cheaper to run, rent and rates being saved. There is no need to advertise as the travelling shop advertises itself.

Vending machines are also increasing in number. They are used to sell cigarettes, chocolates, drinks, fruit, refreshments, tickets, etc., and are found outside shops, in canteens and in busy places like railway stations. They are self-service outlets, open day and night, making goods available when other outlets are closed. They help to increase a retailer's sales and save time in handling goods and receiving payment. Some customers would rather use the machine than wait to be served in the shop. They can also be used for advertising.

Vending machines are expensive to install, but as they help to pay for themselves they are suitable for hire purchase buying or for renting. They are not suitable for all goods and can operate only with certain coins. Each machine, containing only a small quantity of goods, requires frequent restocking and the choice offered is limited. Their sales are less than 1 per cent of the total.

Some of the businesses described in this and the four preceding chapters are composite businesses. A composite business combines two or more functions. Some of them undertake retailing, wholesaling and manufacturing. Compound businesses are those that sell many kinds of goods, such as a general shop or a department store.

Questions

1. What is mail order business? Describe its methods of (*a*) contacting customers, (*b*) delivering goods and accepting payment. Give reasons for the recent growth of this form of retailing. (A.E.B.)

2. Mail order trading is the fastest growing retail outlet. Compare this method with that from a normal shop. (W.M.E.B.)

3. In what ways does the Post Office assist mail order trading?

4. What do mobile shops sell? What are their advantages and disadvantages to (*a*) the owners, (*b*) the customers? Why is their number increasing?

5. Which of these are compound and which composite businesses? A supermarket, a chain business owning factories, a big retail cooperative society, a department store, the CWS.

6. The retail trade has, in recent years, provided new methods of selling goods. Explain what contribution, whether good or bad, each of the following has made to retailing: (*a*) mobile shops, (*b*) automatic vending (slot machines), (*c*) discount shops, (*d*) stamp trading. (A.L.S.E.B.)

7. Briefly indicate the functions of retailers. How far is it true to say that large-scale retailers are similar to wholesalers? (W.J.E.C.)

8. Describe how the mail order system of retailing is operated showing how it helps the buyer and the seller. (S.R.E.B.)

9. 'Mail-order stores grew up in an age of cheap letter and parcel post services, and they will be wiped out by the sharp increases in GPO charges for these services that have taken place recently.'

    Do you think that this statement is true? How can mail-order businesses help themselves to overcome these big increases in postal charges other than by putting up their own prices? (R.S.A.)

10. What is 'mail order' trading? Explain the reasons for its popularity.
    (L.C.C. & I.)

Chapter 27

The rate of turnover

As the storing of goods is part of the wholesaler's work the period during which he has to store them is important. Storage costs money and the shorter the time the goods are kept the smaller the expenses to be deducted from the gross profit. The same is true of the retailer. The faster goods are sold, the greater the **advantages** as explained below.

Certain kinds of goods must be sold quickly if they are to be sold at all. Fish, meat and dairy produce will not last for long. Unless they can be sold within a few days, they will **waste** and the trader will have received nothing for them. Goods that last a long time, like furniture, cannot be sold as quickly as the cheaper goods that are consumed quickly and must be bought frequently, such as bread, but the faster all kinds of goods are sold the better for the trader.

A trader who takes £1000 out of his deposit account to buy goods which are sold immediately for £1050 has made £50 gross profit and he can put his £1000 back in the bank where it will earn interest for him. If, however, he had been unable to sell the goods until one year had passed, he would have made no profit. Had he allowed the £1000 to remain in the bank, it would have earned him £50 interest during the year. By locking up his money in goods, he has lost this £50 interest and this loss cancels the £50 made on the goods. When goods must be kept a long time before being ready for sale, as is the case with timber, wines and spirits, the loss of **interest on capital** locked up in them becomes very important.

Besides losing interest the trader would have had to store the goods for one year. Even if he used his own premises for **storage**, he would lose the rent he could have earned by letting the space to someone else. The longer the goods remain in stock the greater is the risk of their becoming soiled or **damaged** and having to be sold at a reduced price. The greater, too, is the risk of a loss through a fall in prices.

Goods that are slow in selling are more likely to go out of **fashion**, or out of date. If summer dresses are not sold by the end of the season, they will not sell during the winter, and have to be stored until the following summer, by which time fashions may have changed completely and no one would buy them. To avoid storage expenses and the risk of a change in fashions, shops hold **sales** at the end of the season to dispose of as much as possible at reduced prices. The loss due to reduced prices at the sales may be less than the costs of storage and the loss of interest that would be incurred by keeping the goods for several months longer.

When stock is sold quickly the trader has to replace it frequently. One trader may buy £600 worth of stock which is sold by the end of six months, when he buys another lot. Another trader may buy £300 worth of stock every three months, selling each lot in the period in which it was bought. The second trader, buying new stock twice as often as the first, has a much better chance of stocking the most recent and **up-to-date goods**. This is most important in connection with goods in which fashions change quickly, and new types of goods which are being constantly improved. It is one reason why annual radio and motor shows are held. The makers are now preparing new models, but these will not reach the shops until they have been exhibited at the next show. The retailers are thus given a year in which to sell their stocks before new models are released by the makers. Before the shows were commenced, retailers complained that new models appeared so frequently that their stocks were out of date almost as soon as they bought them.

Both traders sell the same amount of goods in a year, but the first trader lays out £600 to start with, while the second spends only £300. The second trader receives his money back quickly and can use it to buy again. He needs **less capital** than the one who buys enough stock to last six months and he loses less interest and requires less storage space.

The speed at which goods are sold is known as the **rate of turnover** or stock-turn. It is measured by the number of times a year that the average stock can be sold. A newsagent has a supply of papers every morning and he sells them the same day. His stock is turned over once a day.

To find the rate of turnover the stock in hand is averaged and divided into the sales at cost price. Given the following particulars the rate of turnover would be found as shown:

Stock 1 Jan. £1200. 1 June £800. 31 Dec. £1000.
Sales for the year, £18 000.
Gross profit, $33\frac{1}{3}$ per cent of sales.

$$\text{Average stock} = \frac{£1200 + £800 + £1000}{3}$$
$$= £1000.$$

Sales at selling price $\quad= £18\ 000$
Gross profit $= \frac{1}{3}$ sales $\quad= \quad\ 6\ 000$

Sales at cost $= £12\ 000$

$$\text{Rate of turnover} = \frac{\text{Sales at cost}}{\text{Average stock}}$$
$$= \frac{12\ 000}{1000}$$
$$= 12 \text{ times.}$$

This means that £1000 worth of stock can be sold twelve times in a year. The business s in the same position as if it bought £1000 worth of stock on

1 January, sold it all on 31 January, bought another £1000 worth on 1 February, sold it all on 28 February, and so on for the rest of the year. The average time any article remains in the shop before being sold is one month. Of course, some goods are sold in one day, while others may take months to sell, but the average is one month.

When stock remains the same and the rate of turnover is increased more can be sold in a given time. If the above rate could be increased from twelve to twenty-four the year's sales at *cost price* would be twice as much. In order to speed up sales prices may have to be lowered, so that the gross profit on each article is less. Were the gross profit lowered from $33\frac{1}{3}$ to 25 per cent of selling price the turnover and profit would be:

Sales at C.P. = £1000 × 24 = £24 000
G.P. = $\frac{1}{4}$ S.P. = $\frac{1}{3}$ C.P.   =   8 000
_____
Sales at S.P.   = £32 000
_____

The profit on each article is less, but it is realised more quickly and made more times in the year, giving a greater total profit. The net profit, as was shown in Chapter 14, would increase at a faster rate than the gross profit. A policy of 'small profits, quick returns' **(S.P.Q.R.)** may pay better than one of big profits on each article, but slow returns.

	Trade	Rate of turnover
1	Butchers	78
2	Dairymen	67
3	Greengrocers	53
4	Bread and flour confectioners	42
5	Fish and poultry	34
6	Groceries and provisions	15
7	Confectioners, tobacconists, newsagents	12
8	Electricity and gas showrooms	8
9	Books and stationery	6
10	Furniture	6
11	Chemists	6
12	Radio and electrical goods	6
13	Clothing and footwear	6
14	Cycles and perambulators	5
15	Hardware, china, wallpaper and paint	5
16	Jewellery, leather and sports goods	3
	Average for all goods	9

An increase in the rate of turnover which does not result in greater sales brings about a reduction in the average stock carried. In the above example sales at cost were £12 000. If this figure were the result of turning over stock twenty-four times the average stock must be

$$\frac{£12\ 000}{24} = £500,$$

as compared with £1000 when the rate was twelve times.

The formula

$$\text{Rate of turnover} = \frac{\text{Sales at cost}}{\text{Average stock}}$$

can be rearranged to give

Sales at cost = Average stock × Rate of turnover.

$$\text{Average stock} = \frac{\text{Sales at cost}}{\text{Rate of turnover}}.$$

Approximate rates of turnover are shown on page 122.

Questions

1. What is meant by the rate of turnover? What are the advantages of a fast rate of turnover?

2. A trader's average stock is £6000 and his sales for the year are £30 000. He makes a gross profit of 20 per cent on sales. Find his rate of turnover. What is the average time it takes to sell an article?

    Find the rate of turnover using stock and sales at selling price. Does it make any difference?

3.

Trading account

	£		£
Opening stock	1 500	Sales	12 000
Purchases	9 000	Closing stock	2 500
Gross profit	4 000		
	14 500		14 500

(a) Find the rate of turnover.
(b) What percentage of selling price is gross profit?
(c) Another trader, with the same sales and stocks, makes this percentage on cost price. What is his gross profit and his rate of turnover?

4. Mr Black and Mr White are two retailers. The following relate to their trading over the past twelve months:

	Average stock at cost	Mark-up	Rate of turnover
Mr Black	£2500	10 per cent	12
Mr White	£8000	25 per cent	2

Work out the gross profits of each retailer. Suggest methods by which greater gross profits could be achieved by each retailer. (A.E.B.)

5. In many countries shops are trying to operate a weekly stocktaking. What do you think might be the result of this practice? (M.R.E.B.)

6. The following relate to the trading of a business in two successive years:

	Year 1	Year 2
	£	£
Sales	44 000	50 400
Cost price of sales	33 600	37 800
Expenses	5 600	6 400
Average stock during the year	4 000	4 200

    (*a*) Calculate for each year (i) the gross profit and the net profit and express each as a percentage of turnover; (ii) the rate of stock-turn.
    (*b*) When you have completed the calculation of (*a*), comment on all the data you then have before you.   (W.J.E.C.)

7. Account for the fact that some shops have seasonal 'sales' and others do not. Give examples of shops which do not hold 'sales'.   (S.R.E.B.)

8. A retailer is offered £500 worth of goods with a trade discount of 25 per cent and a cash discount of 2½ per cent if paid within fourteen days. The rate of turnover for this type of goods is twelve. The balance on his account at the bank is £100.
    How much will the goods cost if paid for (*a*) within fourteen days and (*b*) at the end of the month? Giving reasons for your answer explain whether the rate of turnover is sufficient to finance the transaction or whether the bank should be asked for an overdraft and for what period.   (A.E.B.)

9. Explain what you understand by the phrase 'small profits quick returns'. A trader has an annual turnover of £32 000. If his rate of turnover is five and he writes up cost price by 30 per cent to obtain selling price, calculate the average value of stock. If you were contemplating purchasing this business what other information would you ask for?   (J.M.B.)

10. The rate of gross profit varies from about 16 per cent on groceries and tobacco to over 40 per cent on radio and electrical goods. Show if there is any connection between gross profit and (*a*) rate of turnover, (*b*) risk of loss through waste and changes in fashion, (*c*) capital locked up in stock, (*d*) space occupied by stock, (*e*) preparation and display of goods, (*f*) sales staff required.

11. Explain why trades 1 to 7 in the table on page 122 have a higher rate of turnover than trades 8 to 16.

12. (*a*) What is turnover?
    (*b*) What is rate of turnover? Give **two** methods by which it may be increased.
    (*c*) Give examples of business which would normally expect (i) a high rate of turnover and (ii) a low rate.
    (*d*) Calculate the rate of turnover from the following:

Opening stock £1000	Closing stock £500
Sales £5000	Per cent profit on selling price = 25 per cent.

                                                           (S.R.E.B.)

Chapter 28

Capital and the agents of production · Fixed, current and working capital

In order to carry on a business or to undertake any form of modern production, four things are necessary. First, there must be land, by which is meant not only soil but all that Nature provides. Next, somebody must work. In some parts of the world land and labour may be all that is required to satisfy the wants of the natives who gather wild fruit and hunt and fish. To increase the supply of fruit, the natives would have to save some fruit to use as seed instead of eating it all. The fruit saved for the purpose of producing more is capital. The natives could also save food to eat while they made tools and traps, by means of which they could again increase their wealth. Such tools and traps would be capital also. Without capital, production as we know it today would be impossible. As tools and equipment wear out, someone must save so that they can be replaced by new forms of capital. If all the potatoes in the world were consumed this year, none could be grown next year because no one had saved any to be used as seed.

Land may be plentiful in some parts, but there may be no labour and capital there. To commence production in such places, someone must arrange for the necessary labour and capital to be brought there and decide what is to be produced. This work is done by the organiser or entrepreneur, who also bears the risk that the venture may fail.

Land, labour, capital and enterprise are the factors or agents of production. They work together to produce wealth which must then be shared among them. The share taken by the landowner is rent, labour takes wages, capital takes interest and enterprise takes profit. Suppose A owns a plot of land, B is willing to work, C can provide seed potatoes and tools, and D arranges for B to plant the potatoes on A's land.

When the crop has been lifted, how much should go to A, B, C, D, for their parts in producing it? There is only a limited amount to share and the greater the amount taken by one agent the less there is left for the others. If the crop is sold for £20 and A, B and C had come into the scheme on condition that they were to receive £6 each, then D would receive only £2. In practice, this is what does happen: rent, wages and interest are fixed in advance, and the organiser runs the risk that there will be nothing left for him when he has paid out what is due to the others. If B goes on strike and succeeds in obtaining more wages, D will have to be satisfied with less. The only way in which all can obtain more is to produce more. Had D, the organiser, arranged for C, the capitalist, to provide £1's worth of fertiliser, the crop would have been greater and might have sold for £25 instead of £20.

This problem of sharing the **country's wealth**, or the national income, among the population, is known as the problem of distribution of wealth. Some believe that landowners should receive nothing and that the Government should own all land as in Russia. Others believe that too much is paid in interest and that practically all the wealth produced should belong only to those who have worked. 'Distribution' in this connection means sharing and not the movement of goods as in 'Channels of distribution'.

One person may represent all four factors of production. A shopkeeper may own the business premises, work in the shop, provide all the capital required, and organise and manage everything himself. The profit that he makes is then really made up of rent for the land he owns, interest on his capital, wages for the work he does, and what is left is profit for his enterprise.

Capital is, then, wealth saved in order to produce more wealth. Suppose a man has saved £4000 in money and he is going to start a business and make his £4000 earn more wealth for him. He must first rent or buy some premises. If he buys he will exchange some of his money, say £3000, for a building, and then he spends a further £200 in equipping it with counters,

Circulating Capital

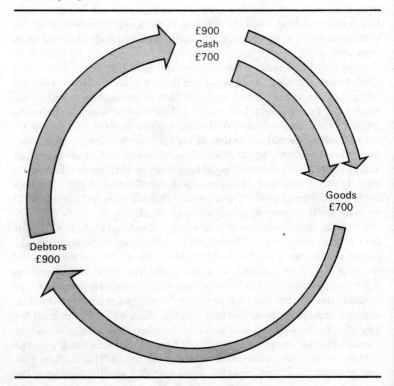

£900
Cash
£700

Goods
£700

Debtors
£900

etc., and making it suitable for a shop. He must have the building and equipment and he does not want to sell them but intends to keep and use them as long as they will last. They are his **fixed capital**.

£800 is now left in the form of cash and the business must be worked with this. It is by using this £800 capital that profit is made. This part of the capital is continually changing its form. £700 of the £800 cash may be spent on goods which are finally sold for £900. At first the £900 may be in the form of debts due to the trader, but, finally, these debts will be turned into cash which will be £200 more than the £700 capital which had been circulating. This £200 is the gross profit. The capital has been increased by £200 less expenses for wages, etc. Some of the £100 cash which had been left in the till was required to pay these expenses. It is the **circulating capital** that grows. Therefore, the bigger this part of the capital and the faster it circulates the better. The previous chapter showed how important it is to obtain a rapid stock-turn.

Fixed and circulating capital are also known as fixed and circulating (or current or floating) assets, an **asset** being cash or anything that can be turned into cash. Cash itself and assets that can easily be turned into cash are referred to as liquid assets.

The current assets of one business may become the fixed assets of another. Ships are floating assets to the builders who make them for sale, but to the ship-owners who buy them for use they are fixed assets. Some businesses need more fixed assets than others. The retailer needs more attractive premises and equipment than the wholesaler. Manufacturing concerns require much expensive machinery and a greater proportion of their capital is fixed than is the case with a trading firm.

When goods are bought on credit the assets of the business increase, but there is no increase in the capital owned because an equivalent amount of money will at some time be taken out of the business to pay for these goods. A debt due from the business is a **liability** and to find the capital owned it must be taken away from the total assets.

The **Balance Sheet** is a summary of the assets and liabilities of a business. The balances in the fixed assets accounts show the value of each asset after an allowance has been deducted to cover depreciation. It is unlikely that a depreciation figure would appear on a Land and Buildings account, since such assets usually appreciate in value, but motor vehicles, machinery and equipment become worn and obsolete in the course of time, and a realistic figure representing their true current value must be shown. Fixed and current assets are listed separately in the balance sheet; Liabilities are grouped under Capital, Long-term Liabilities and Current Liabilities.

It has been traditional to set out the balance sheet in the form of two sides, the left side being headed Liabilities and the right side Assets. Nowadays, however, balance sheets are usually set out in vertical form, as in the example shown overleaf.

Notice that this summary gives all the important facts about the business. We can see how much capital was in the business at the start of the year and how much net profit was made during the year. It is clear that the

Balance sheet (sole trader)

Balance sheet as at 30 June 19 . .

	£	£
Capital at start	4 629	
add profits	10 011	14 640
Long-term liabilities:		
Bank loan		6 000
Current liabilities:		
Sundry creditors		1 745
		£22 385
Fixed assets:		
Premises	11 325	
Plant and machinery	2 399	
Furniture and fittings	3 000	16 724
Current assets:		
Stock	2 600	
Debtors	2 030	
Cash at bank and in hand	1 031	5 661
		£22 385

business owes a debt to the bank and that some creditors' accounts are still unpaid. We can see how much the firm's premises and equipment are worth and what present stocks are held; we can also tell that there is £2030 to come from debtors, and an amount of £1031 is held in cash.

If we studied a balance sheet like this one for each year since the business began, we should have a very clear picture of the progress of the business since its formation.

It must be remembered that a balance sheet shows the position on a certain day only. A balance sheet made on the next day would be different because some of the goods would have been sold, some of the debts paid, etc., causing assets and liabilities and therefore the capital to be different.

The **capital owned** need not be the same as the **capital used** in the business. When he borrows £100, the trader debits cash account and credits loan account. Assets and liabilities are thus increased by the same amount and there is no change in the capital owned (assets minus liabilities), but the trader has £100 more to use. Similarly, when he buys goods without paying for them at once, he is really using capital borrowed from someone else. In the same way some of the capital he owns is being used by his debtors when he sells goods on credit.

The proprietor, having invested his savings in the business, can think of himself as a creditor to whom the business 'owes' the amount of the capital. As the business cannot exist without capital, the 'debt' must remain unpaid as long as he continues in business. He regards the capital as one of the **fixed liabilities** of the business.

The amount of the capital owned is the value of the business. If all the assets in the foregoing balance sheet were turned into cash, the owner would have £22 385, out of which he would have to pay £1745 to creditors, leaving him with £20 640, of which £6000 is owed to the bank. If the business were sold, the proprietor would expect to receive at least £20 640 for it, to get back his personal stake of £14 640 and to repay the bank loan.

The balance sheet shows whether a business is solvent or insolvent. If *all* the assets are greater than the creditors, the business can pay its debts in full, for, if need be, the assets can be sold and the cash received for them will be enough to pay the creditors. Such a business is **solvent**. If the assets are less than the liabilities, the business is insolvent and cannot pay its debts in full. This does not mean that it is bankrupt for matters may improve and the position become solvent again. But if a business continues to remain insolvent for any length of time, it will end in bankruptcy, when the assets are realised and shared out among the creditors in accordance with the Bankruptcy Acts.

So we can say that the **Trading Account** of a business shows the **gross profit** figure; the **Profit and Loss Account** shows the **net profit**. The **Balance Sheet** sets out the **liabilities** and **assets** of the business, which should balance exactly. The current stock figure, which has already been worked out for the Trading Account, is shown on the Balance Sheet as an asset; the net profit shown in the Profit and Loss Account appears on the Balance Sheet as an addition to the capital.

The greater the amount of capital invested in a business, the greater the profits expected from it. Some businesses make millions of pounds profit in a year but in order to be able to say whether or not this is a good result the profits must be compared with the capital in the same way as they are compared with sales. By expressing **profits as a percentage of capital** the results of one year can be compared with those of other years and the results of one business with those of others.

A business with a capital of £5000 and a net profit of £150 is earning $\frac{150}{5000} \times \frac{100}{1} = 3$ per cent on its capital. £100 invested in the business earns £3 in a year for the owner. This is a poor return. The owner could have lent £100 to the Government and earned £3 a year interest without any risk or worry. A business may fail and the capital be lost, but money lent to the Government is quite safe and the interest is paid regularly. Capital invested in a business is therefore expected to earn more than the rate of interest paid by the Government for loans, for otherwise nothing is gained by using one's capital in a business.

The owner of a business does not wait until the profit and loss account has been completed before he takes anything out of the business. During the year he draws out money for his private expenses, hoping that the profit will be at least equal to the sums he has drawn out. When the profit for the year is known, the total of these **drawings** must be deducted from it in order to find out how much profit is still due to him. If, for example, the net profit is £600 and the drawings are £400, £200 profit is still due to the owner. Instead of taking this £200 out of the business and spending it, the owner may decide to save it and leave it in the business so that it can earn more wealth for him. It is then added to the capital just as interest earned by money deposited in a bank is added on to the principal. Had the net profit been £300 the owner would have taken £100 too much and this amount would have to be deducted from his capital.

Unless some of the profit is saved, the business-owner may find it difficult to replace assets when they are no longer usable. A van bought for £1000 will not be worth £1000 after being used for a few years. The loss in value is called **depreciation**. Each year the value of the assets as shown in the balance sheet should be decreased by the amount of the depreciation, and the same amount counted as a loss to be deducted from gross profit. Eventually, it will be necessary to obtain a new van and the profit that has been saved can be used to purchase it.

As well as having to replace assets that become worn out, a successful business may wish to expand by acquiring additional assets. It may want to extend its premises, buy more machinery, or build new factories. To do this it must obtain more capital. If the owners have no more to invest, **to obtain more capital** they may:

1. Persuade people who have savings to lend them for a period.
2. Persuade them to become part-owners and invest their savings permanently in the business.
3. Instead of taking out all the profit made, they can leave some of it in the business and use it as capital. Profits employed in this way are 'ploughed back' in order to increase production and earn more profits in the future, in the same way as a farmer sometimes does not harvest a crop, but ploughs it in for fertilising the soil for the purpose of growing bigger crops in the future.

    Today many big businesses plough back much of their profits. The Government may encourage the ploughing back of profits by granting tax relief on such profits.
4. When capital is not available to buy assets the use of premises and equipment may be obtained by renting and by using hire purchase for buying as well as for selling.

Questions

1. How is capital formed? What is its purpose? How is the amount of capital found?

2. What is production? Name the agents of production and say what they earn for the parts they play.

3. A retail grocer starts with £5000 in the bank. When he is ready to open his shop, he has only £1000 in the bank. What has happened to the other £4000? Has the amount of his capital altered?

4. Of what does the capital of a newsagent consist? How do the various items differ from those making up the capital of a car factory?

5. Explain the difference between (*a*) fixed and current capital or assets, (*b*) fixed and current liabilities.

6. What is the difference between capital owned, capital used and working capital? How is the amount of each found? Why is working capital important?

7.

Balance sheet of A. Mills at 31 December 19 . .

Liabilities	£	Assets	£
Capital	2700	Furniture	500
Creditors	300	Stock	2000
		Cash	500
	3000		3000

Find the amount of:

(*a*) capital owned and capital used;
(*b*) fixed capital and current capital;
(*c*) fixed liabilities and current liabilities;
(*d*) working capital.

8.

Balance sheet of L. Love as at 31 March 19 . .

Liabilities	£	Assets	£
Capital	10 000	Premises	7 500
Trade creditors	5 700	Furniture and fittings	2 500
Loan repayable in ten years	5 000	Stock	5 600
		Trade debtors	4 600
		Cash	500
	20 700		20 700

(*a*) What is the amount of:

   (i) the capital employed in the business;
  (ii) the fixed assets;
 (iii) the current assets;
 (iv) the long-term liabilities;
  (v) the short-term liabilities;
 (vi) the working capital?

(*b*) For the year ended 31 March 19 . ., L. Love's turnover was £56 000, which gave him a gross profit of 25 per cent on his selling prices. His expenses were £11 000 and his average stock on hand (at cost price) throughout the year was £5250. Find his (i) net profit, (ii) rate of stock-turn. (w.j.e.c.)

9. Are the businesses in questions 7 and 8 solvent? Give reasons for your answers.

10. If the loan in question 8 had to be repaid on the day following the date of the balance sheet, would Love have enough working capital then? What could he do to increase the working capital?

11. Describe, with illustrations, the difference between fixed and circulating capital in the case of a retail shop. Explain whether the amounts of fixed and circulating capital normally vary with turnover.

    In the business of A. Jones the selling expenses represent 12.5 per cent of turnover, the rate of turnover is five and the write-up on cost price to give selling price is 20 per cent. If the net profit is £5000 find (*a*) the total value of sales and (*b*) the average value of stock.   (J.M.B.)

12. What is profit? When a trader says that his business made a net gain of £1000, what, besides profit, may be included in this figure? Why is it important to know?

13. A large company calculates its net profit as 20 per cent of its turnover and 5 per cent of its capital owned. Another similar company calculates its net profit as 5 per cent of its turnover and 20 per cent of its capital owned. Write a short account on the difference between the two companies' trading results.   (R.S.A.)

14. Your father, who has operated two filling stations for some years, wishes to expand his interests. What steps lie open to him? In the past he has sold several grades of three leading brands of petrol.   (M.R.E.B.)

15. Distinguish between capital, turnover and profit. A retailer turns over his stock four times a year. His selling price is obtained by increasing cost price by 40 per cent. Selling expenses amount to 15 per cent of turnover. If the turnover for the year was £20 000 find (*a*) the amount of the net profit, and (*b*) the average value of stock carried at cost price.   (J.M.B.)

16. Show how the amount of working capital required is influenced by increases in:

    (*a*) the stock carried;
    (*b*) the rate of turnover;
    (*c*) the wages and expenses;
    (*d*) the credit received;
    (*e*) the credit allowed.

17. Discuss the relationship between the rate of turnover and gross profit in the case of:

    (*a*) a retail grocery store;
    (*b*) a shop selling radio and television sets.

    What differences might be expected in the amount of working capital required?
    (A.E.B.)

18. Explain how business firms may obtain capital for expansion on a short-term and long-term basis. You should name at least two sources in each case.

    Show how the methods used by firms to obtain additional capital differ according to their size.   (L.C.C. & I.)

19. (i) What is a firm's capital?
    (ii) Why might a firm wish to increase its capital?
    (iii) Indicate how a public limited company may increase its capital.
    (U.C.L.E.S.)

20. What do you understand by the capital structure of a public limited company? Show how the company decides on its capital structure, referring in your answer to *two* different types of business capital used to finance outgoings.
    (L.C.C. & I.)

Chapter 29

Profitability · Break-even point · Costs · Budgetary control

A commercial business is judged by its profitability and a prospective buyer of a business compares the annual accounts of several years to see if there is any noticeable trend towards an increase or decrease in the net profit.

The final accounts of a **manufacturing business** show the total value of products sold during the year (the 'turnover') and to find the **gross profit** the expenses involved in making these goods must be subtracted from this total sales figure. These expenses include the cost of the raw materials used and the wages of the people employed in the manufacturing. To find the raw material cost, the value of the materials still held in stock must be taken from the total of stock held at the beginning of the year and stock bought during the year.

The figure of gross profit depends directly on the amount spent on materials and labour: if sales double, it is likely that the amount spent on materials and labour will also double (although the factor of productivity may come in here, and improved methods and materials may produce an increased volume of sales without a corresponding increase in costs).

To determine the true profit position, however, that is the **net profit**, many other costs must be taken into consideration. These 'overhead' expenses include such things as salaries of the administrative and clerical staff, rent, rates, lighting, heating, advertising, transport, postage, telephone, bad debts, insurance, etc.

Costs are usually classified as **fixed** or **variable** but it is sometimes difficult to determine whether an individual expense is fixed or not. Fixed costs are those which **do not vary with output** yet all costs, even those that appear to be fixed, are liable to vary over a period of time. However, if we accept this definition we can classify all indirect overheads as fixed costs, since whether business is booming or poor they must be met. On the other hand, the cost of raw materials and factory labour, and possibly also power, will be less when production falls and can be classified as **variable** costs. It may be argued also that such items as transport and postage are likely to be less if sales decline since fewer deliveries will be made and fewer invoices and statements sent out, so these costs might be termed variable too.

The procedures and calculations involved in the preparation of final accounts are illustrated in the diagram overleaf.

The break-even point: If we assume, in looking at the figure, that the sales of £50 000 represented 50 000 items sold for £1 each, we can see that it cost £20 000 in direct manufacturing costs (cost of goods sold) to make this

Preparation of final accounts

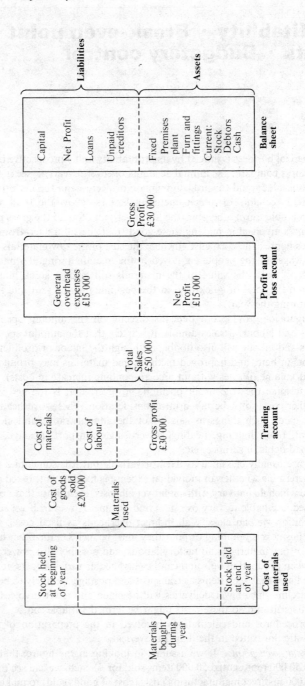

number of items. If we divide 50 000 into £20 000, we find that the cost of manufacturing one item was $£\frac{2}{5}$ = 40p. The remaining 60p of the selling price constitutes a 'contribution margin' towards the general overhead expenses and the net profit. To cover expenses, sufficient items at £1 each would have to be sold to absorb the figure of £15 000 spent on general overheads, bearing in mind that it costs 40p to make each item. To find this 'break-even' figure, we can divide the 'contribution margin' of 60p into the figure for general overheads, giving us the calculation

$$\frac{£15\ 000}{£0.60} = 25\ 000 \text{ items.}$$

Let us check the calculation:

25 000 items sell at £1 each	£25 000
25 000 items cost 40p each to make	£10 000
Fixed overhead expenses	£15 000
	£25 000

In this case, therefore, if fewer than 25 000 items are sold a loss will be made; if more than 25 000 are sold a profit will be made. The **break-even point** is 25 000 items selling at £1 each.

The Break-even point

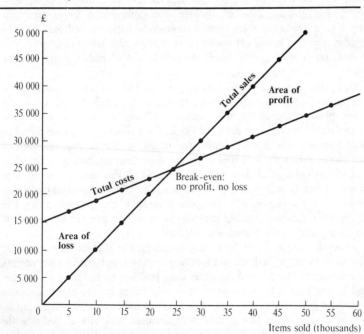

The formula for finding the break-even point may be stated as follows:

Calculate the 'contribution margin' for each unit made (i.e. its selling price less the cost of manufacture) and divide this into the fixed overheads.

A graph may be drawn to illustrate the break-even point, and the calculations given above are shown on page 135 in graph form. Total sales and total costs are plotted, to give two lines. The point of intersection marks the break-even point.

The **manufacturing cost** of a product contains three basic elements: direct material cost, direct labour cost and factory overhead. This third element includes the wages of maintenance men, engineers and works management staff, plus factory heating, lighting and cleaning – in fact, all the manufacturing expenses not included in direct labour and direct material costs. The cost accountants have the task of determining the percentage of the total factory overhead that should be charged to each product. They start from the basis of the operations concerned in the making of the product, e.g. if there is more machine time involved than direct labour hours, the overhead percentage includes a suitable proportion of the cost of power and of the maintenance, repair and depreciation of the machines used. To this must be added a percentage for the supervision involved in producing the article.

To the Manufacturing (or Factory) Cost must be added other percentages to cover the cost of maintaining all the other departments of the company, the fixed overheads, the depreciation of furniture, equipment and fittings, and any other charges that are applicable to the organisation as a whole. These costs are termed **commercial expenses** and may be subdivided into two broad categories: Distribution and Administration.

A diagram of the costs involved in each unit of manufacture may be drawn as shown on page 137.

Budgeting is a widely used system in modern business management. The essence of budgeting, whether in business, in private life, or in the wider sphere of Government, is planning. A Budget Committee is set up to formulate the budgets for each activity of the business that is considered to need a budget. The Budget Committee, usually under the chairmanship of one of the directors, is made up of the departmental managers or other executives in charge of these activities, e.g. Sales, Production, Purchasing, Research and Development, Maintenance. The Chief Accountant is also a member of the committee. Suggested budgets are submitted by the executives concerned, studied and discussed by the committee, revised if necessary, and finally agreed and adopted.

From the budgets that have been prepared, the Budget Department is able to work out a Cash Budget for the year, showing the probable receipts and payments of cash and the likely cash position both during and at the end of the year. This forecast is obviously based on the other forecasts contained in the individual budgets and is not therefore an infallible guide, but in practice it is found that if department and capital budgets are prepared with care the deductions worked out from them are valuable.

Analysis of cost

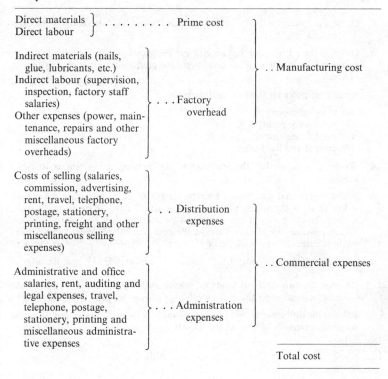

Direct materials ⎱ . . . . Prime cost		
Direct labour ⎰		
Indirect materials (nails, glue, lubricants, etc.)		
Indirect labour (supervision, inspection, factory staff salaries)	. . . Factory overhead	. . Manufacturing cost
Other expenses (power, maintenance, repairs and other miscellaneous factory overheads)		
Costs of selling (salaries, commission, advertising, rent, travel, telephone, postage, stationery, printing, freight and other miscellaneous selling expenses)	. . Distribution expenses	. . Commercial expenses
Administrative and office salaries, rent, auditing and legal expenses, travel, telephone, postage, stationery, printing and miscellaneous administrative expenses	. . . Administration expenses	
		Total cost

Other financial statements prepared from the budgets include: a forecast of profit and loss and a forecast balance sheet for the budget period.

The Chief Accountant, Head of the Budget Department or other appointed person acts as Budget Coordinator and prepares a **master budget** which brings all the budget plans together into one all-embracing programme of operations for the whole business.

The comparison of actual results with forecasts can pin-point areas of the business where investigation is called for: policies may need some revision or systems may need improvement. Control is possible throughout the financial year: wasteful or mistaken procedures are not hidden for twelve months until exposed in the final accounts.

Budgetary control obviously does not provide an instant cure for all management problems and it calls for enthusiastic team work, not only between the departments but also between executives and top management. For the system to work, all who participate in it must believe in it and must cooperate fully.

Questions

1. Outline a system of budgetary control and show how the budgets are sub-divided and inter-related.

2. Describe the advantages that an efficient budgetary system can give the management of a business. What conditions are prerequisite for such a system to succeed?

3. Write brief notes on three of the following:

   (*a*) working capital;
   (*b*) break-even point;
   (*c*) capital investment;
   (*d*) current and fixed assets. (R.S.A.)

4. Would you agree that the sole motive for running a business is to make profit? (L.C.C. & I.)

5. It is essential that a company knows its costs of operation, since it needs to reflect them in the selling price of its products. Taking **shoes** as an example, explain the categories of cost that must be considered in formulating a price. Where possible, use the language of the cost accountant. What other factors might influence the price of a pair of shoes? (L.C.C. & I.)

6. (*a*) Define budgetary control, and explain its importance to a manufacturer of machine tools.

   (*b*) Mention two different kinds of subsidiary budgets, and show briefly the meaning and importance of each budget chosen by you. (L.C.C. & I.)

7. Explain the difference between fixed and variable costs of production. Illustrate by giving examples of both kinds of costs. (L.C.C. & I.)

Chapter 30

Ownership · Sole traders and partners

The trader in business on his own is known as a **sole trader**. He is free to please himself as to the way he manages his business. He has all the profits that result from his work and efficiency, which is an incentive for him to work hard. He need not consult anyone and if he thinks a change is necessary he can carry it out at once. Usually his business is not big and he can therefore supervise most of the work and see that it is properly done. If he employs a few assistants, he knows them personally, and has the opportunity of making the best use of them. He also knows his customers and he may grant credit to those he thinks he can trust.

When a sole trader's business continues to increase, he may find that a **partner** to share the business with him would give many advantages. In the first place, the partner would bring more capital into the business and so enable it to be extended. If losses were suffered in some years, the partner would share them with him. Management of the business could now be shared and each partner could become a specialist in his own department. There would be somebody as interested as himself in seeing the business succeed, to discuss matters with him and to make suggestions, and to attend to affairs when he has to be away.

Sole traders and partners have the disadvantage of being subject to **unlimited liability**. If the business fails, and the assets are insufficient to pay the creditors, the traders are liable to lose everything they possess, and not merely what they invested in the business. A trader may have to give up his house, for instance. In a partnership every one of the partners, except those known as 'limited partners', is liable for all the debts of the firm. If some partners possess nothing when the business fails, those who do possess something will have to pay the debts in full if they can.

Partnership is the carrying on of business in common by two or more people for the purpose of making a profit. When partners decide to work together, they should draw up an agreement or deed, stating the conditions and terms of the partnership. If there is no agreement the **Partnership Act**, 1890, provides that:

1. Profit and losses shall be shared equally.
2. All partners have the right to invest equal amounts of capital in the business.
3. No partner can claim interest on his capital.
4. No partner can claim a salary or wage for working in the business.

5. Any difference of opinion among the partners must be settled by a majority vote, but all partners must agree to a change in the nature of the business, such as a change from selling boots and shoes to selling drapery.
6. The books of account must be kept at the place of business, and all partners have the right to inspect them.

These provisions apply only if there is no agreement. The partners can share profits and losses in any proportion agreed by them, and they can pay interest on capital and salaries if they wish. All these points should be settled in the written agreement which should also state the name of the firm, how long the partnership is to last and how much drawings each partner is allowed.

The maximum number of partners allowed is usually twenty, but there is no limit for firms of stockbrokers, solicitors, accountants and certain agents. There are different **kinds of partners**. Those taking part in the business are known as active or general partners. Sleeping or dormant partners are those who have the right to take part, but do not interfere. Both types have unlimited liability.

Limited partners were allowed by an Act of 1907. These can invest capital in the business and have their liability limited to what they have invested. In the event of the failure of the firm, they stand to lose only the capital they put into the business. In return for this advantage, they lose the right to take any part in managing the business. If they do take part, their liability is unlimited for debts incurred during the time they acted. A limited partnership must have at least one partner with unlimited liability.

When a partner leaves a firm and severs his connection with it, he should give notice of the fact, or he may find, perhaps, years afterwards, that he has to pay certain debts of the firm because some creditors may be able to prove that they would not have dealt with the firm had they known that this particular member of it had left. Anyone who causes others to think he is a partner, when in fact he is not, becomes a nominal partner, or a partner by estoppel.

The retirement of a partner or the admission of a new partner, or the sale of a business, raises the question of **goodwill**. To take over a business that is well established and has its regular customers is much easier than beginning an entirely new business which, until it is built up, will earn only small profits. The seller of an old business will want to be paid, therefore, not only for the net assets, but also for having saved the buyer the trouble of having to build up connections, i.e. for the goodwill. The amount to be paid for it is usually taken as being equal to the profits for one or more years. It cannot be accurately valued because there is no guarantee that the customers will continue to deal at the same place when the new owner takes charge. Goodwill may be included in the balance sheet as an asset.

Sole traders and partners own businesses that do not require a great deal of capital. These forms of ownership are also **suitable for** the non-trading businesses of professional men, such as lawyers, who sell services to people relying on their skill and character. The number of persons they can attend to is limited and, as they do not buy what they sell, they do not, in the event of failure, owe vast sums to creditors. The great majority of these firms have only one owner. Farmers are usually sole traders or partners.

Questions

1. What are the disadvantages of being (*a*) a sole trader, (*b*) a partner?

2. When a sole trader goes into partnership what does he gain and what does he lose?

3. Why should partners take interest on capital and salaries and count them as losses in the profit and loss account?

4. What is partnership? Describe the different kinds of partners a firm may have.

5. What are the main provisions of the Partnership Act?

6. Explain the difference between unlimited and limited liability.

7. What information should be given in a partnership agreement?

8. What is goodwill? When must it be valued?

9. In what kinds of businesses are sole traders and partners usually found? Give reasons for your answer.

10. Many family businesses operate as either sole ownerships or as partnerships. Describe the advantages and disadvantages of each business system.

    (W.M.E.B.)

11. (*a*) What advantages would be gained by a sole trader in converting his business into a partnership?

    (*b*) What are the disadvantages? (W.J.E.C.)

Chapter 31

Ownership · Limited liability companies

Big business undertakings need much more capital than can be provided by sole traders and partners. Many people would be willing to invest small sums if they were certain that they would not lose any more than they invested, and the total of these small sums would provide enough capital to set up the biggest business. The **limited liability company** enables investors to use their money in a business without bearing the risk of unlimited liability.

When the promoters have decided to form a company, they have next to obtain the necessary capital. This is usually done through an **issuing house** whose business it is to bring the opportunity of investment to the notice of the public and to induce people to become part owners of the business by providing a share of the capital. A company desiring to raise £10 000 capital could divide it into 10 000 shares of £1 each, and anybody contributing one or more pounds would become a shareholder in the company and would receive a share certificate (usually referred to as a 'share') showing how much capital he had invested.

The document advertising the shares is known as the **Prospectus**. It is usually printed in newspapers, as well as being posted to people who are likely to be interested. In order to persuade people to part with their money, extravagant or false claims about future profits may be made in the Prospectus, so to check such claims the Companies Acts required a copy of the Prospectus to be sent to the Registrar of Companies.

The Prospectus must give certain information so that investors can judge the business for themselves. In the case of an existing business advertising for more capital, for instance, the Prospectus must give the profits and losses for the last five years. Even if the capital can be raised without sending out a Prospectus, a Statement in Lieu of Prospectus must be sent to the Registrar.

Another document that must be sent to the Registrar is the **Memorandum of Association**. This must contain at least five clauses as follows:

1. The name of the company is the Radio Manufacturing Company Limited.
2. The registered office of the company will be situated in England.
3. The objects for which the company is established are:
   (a) To manufacture radio sets; (b) to trade, etc.
4. The liability of Members is Limited.

5. The capital of the Company is £500 000 divided into 500 000 Ordinary Shares of £1 each.

If the new company chooses a name already being used by another company, there will be a danger of the two companies being confused and the Registrar in that case would ask the new company to adopt some other name. The name must always have 'Limited' as the last word, so that people will know that its liability is limited. The company cannot alter its name without the permission of the Department of Trade.

All that need be said about the registered office is that it is either in England and Wales, or in Scotland. If it is situated in Scotland, the company will be controlled by different regulations. Once registered it cannot be changed.

The third clause gives the objects of the company or the purposes for which it was formed. There must be nothing that is illegal in these. A company is now allowed to alter its objects. The Radio Manufacturing Company can, for instance, add the making of television sets to its objects. As the capital was obtained from the shareholders to be used for the objects first stated, if a sufficient number of shareholders think the alteration is unjust to them, they can appeal to the court, which, if it thinks it right to do so, can cancel the alteration.

The fourth clause states in words that the liability of each member is limited. If the company does not succeed and cannot pay its debts, the creditors can claim nothing from the shareholders once these have paid to the company all the capital they agreed to provide. The liability of the directors can, if the company so decides, be made unlimited.

The capital stated in the Memorandum is the maximum the directors can raise unless the shareholders decide to increase it.

The five clauses mentioned above must be included in the Memorandum. Clauses dealing with other points can be included, but if they are they can be altered by the company itself.

The Registrar requires, besides the Prospectus and the Memorandum, a copy of the rules which are drawn up for running the company. These rules are known as the **Articles of Association** and can be altered just as the company likes, but the Registrar must be notified of any changes made. At the end of the Companies Act, there is given an example of a set of Articles, known as Table A. It gives such regulations as the following:

The Chairman, if any, of the Board of Directors shall preside as chairman at every general meeting of the company.

On a show of hands every person present in person shall have one vote. On a poll every member shall have one vote for each share of which he is the holder.

The remuneration of the Directors shall from time to time be determined by the company in general meeting.

Persons dealing with the company are supposed to know the Memorandum, but they need not know the Articles because these are liable to change frequently. Details of the Memorandum and Articles can be obtained on application to the Registrar.

When the directors have complied with the provisions of the Act, the Registrar gives them a certificate of incorporation and a trading certificate which allow them to begin the business for which the company was formed.

Sole traders and partners usually do the organising or managing themselves. The owners of a limited company may number thousands, and as they live in different parts of the country and even in different countries they cannot all be interfering in running the business. The **organisation** of a limited company enables the owners to leave the management to a **Board of Directors** elected by the shareholders. The directors are elected for their ability and reputation and may have very little invested in the business, being paid salaries and fees for their services. They are elected for a term of years at the end of which they can usually be re-elected.

Some directors merely attend directors' meetings to decide policy, such as deciding to build new factories and how much dividend, if any, should be paid. They cannot do exactly as they like because their powers may be limited by the Articles of Association.

The day-to-day running of the business is left to a managing director or a general manager. He appoints the heads of the various departments, such as purchasing, selling, accounting, transport, etc. These heads appoint people to work under them and report regularly to the managing director who then reports to his fellow directors. At the annual general meeting the chairman of the board of directors reports to the shareholders who can vote on any questions put to them.

Because shareholders let directors handle their money and manage the business there must be safeguards for investors. The **Companies Acts provide these safeguards**, some of which have already been mentioned in connection with the Prospectus, Memorandum and Articles. A limited company must call a meeting of its members at least once a year. It must keep proper books of account and an auditor must report on them. At the annual meeting a profit and loss account and a balance sheet must be submitted to the members. These accounts must show certain information, e.g. how much has been paid to the directors. Copies of the accounts must be sent to all shareholders and to the Registrar. At the meetings the members can criticise the directors and vote on any proposals put forward. These meetings are attended mainly by big shareholders who have the real power because votes are usually granted according to the number of shares owned. Any member who owns over half the shares can outvote the others and have his own way in most things.

The protection afforded by the Companies Acts, the granting of limited liability and the right of shareholders to sell their shares at any time attract, not only wealthy investors, but also a large number of **small savers**. The appointment of directors to manage the company's affairs enables people who know nothing about industry and commerce to invest in them and to share in the profits. Without these advantages it would be impossible to raise the immense capital required by the big companies.

A partnership comes to an end with the death of the partners, but the law regards a limited company as existing, even although all its original members are dead. **Public limited companies** are therefore suitable for businesses like insurance in which the agreements may last fifty years or more, as well as for big businesses.

So far this chapter has dealt with public limited companies. The Act also allows the formation of **private limited companies**. A private company can be set up with only two members, whereas a public company must have at least seven members. There is no limit to the number of shareholders in a public company, but a private company cannot have more than fifty not counting present and past employees. A private company is not allowed to advertise its shares and cannot sell them in the same way as a public company.

Private companies do not require a trading certificate and need only one director instead of two. They must now publish their accounts like public companies. As the members cannot exceed fifty, they are not suitable for undertakings requiring large amounts of capital but are suitable for small 'family' businesses. They are forty times as numerous as public companies. A private company can turn itself into a public company by removing from its Articles the clause which restricts the right to transfer shares, after which the shares can be dealt in on the Stock Exchange.

We have now mentioned three **types of business ownership** – the sole trader, partnerships, public and private companies. To these must be added cooperative societies (which have limited liability under the Industrial and Provident Societies Act of 1862), local authorities who own such businesses as waterworks, passenger transport, market halls, baths, etc., the Government and the corporations and boards which have been created by Acts of Parliament. Municipal and state undertakings have unlimited liability. Cooperative retail societies were dealt with in Chapter 24. The others will be discussed in Chapter 40.

Questions

1. What advantages and disadvantages do limited companies have as compared with (*a*) sole traders, (*b*) partnerships?

2. How does a public limited company obtain its capital? What documents must be sent to the Registrar of Companies? Why are the documents important?

3. What protection do the Companies Acts give to investors?

4. What is a board of directors in a public limited company? What does it do? To whom is it responsible? How does it direct the company?   (A.E.B.)

5. What are the advantages and disadvantages of public limited companies to investors?

6. A private company is planning to become a public company. Why should it make the change? Explain the difference between public companies and public enterprise. (R.S.A.)

7. What are the fundamental differences between a partnership and a private company? Why is it that many professional concerns are partnerships rather than companies? (R.S.A.)

8. One form of ownership in industry is the limited liability company. Describe the following features of such a company: (*a*) the prospectus, (*b*) company directors, (*c*) shareholders, (*d*) dividends. (A.L.S.E.B.)

9. Using the following headings distinguish between the public company and a partnership: (*a*) the provision of capital, (*b*) control of day-to-day running of the business, (*c*) disposal of profits. (A.L.S.E.B.)

10. What is meant by the organisation of a business? Describe the organisation of (*a*) a department store, (*b*) a chain business.

11. Explain (*a*) Issuing House, (*b*) Memorandum and (*c*) Articles of Association.

12. Tabulate the differences between a private limited company and a public limited company. (W.J.E.C.)

13. Explain *the difference* between a retail cooperative society and a public limited company in respect of (*a*) ownership, (*b*) control and (*c*) disposal of profits. (A.E.B.)

14. (*a*) 'A limited company is a legal entity, or legal unit, separate from its members.'
    Give **brief** answers to the following:

    (i) Who are the members of a limited company?
    (ii) What, in this context, is meant by *limited*?
    (iii) Who controls a limited company?

    (*b*) A limited company has a paid-up capital of 200 000 ordinary shares of 50p each; its net profit for the year is £20 000. It resolves that three-quarters of this sum shall be distributed as dividends.

    (i) How much will the owner of 1000 ordinary shares receive? (*Ignore taxation.*)
    (ii) What happens to the other quarter of the net profit? (W.J.E.C.)

Chapter 32

Stocks and Shares

The Prospectus, which is printed in the newspapers, has attached to it a form which can be filled in and posted to the company. On this **application** form the investor states how many shares he wants. The Prospectus states how much he must pay on application. It may be the full price or part of the price.

Allotment takes place when the applicant is informed that he can obtain a certain number of shares, and once this has been done he is the owner of the shares. If all the price was not paid on application, the balance is usually payable on allotment. When only a part of the price is due on allotment, the directors will make one or more 'calls' for the rest when they need the money. Once the full price has been paid, no further claims can be made on the shareholder because his liability is limited to the capital he agrees to invest.

The promoters of a company run the risk that not enough capital will be subscribed, in which event they must return the money received and cannot start the business. The least amount, or the minimum subscription required, must be stated in the Prospectus. This risk can be met by **underwriting** the shares. In return for a commission, insurers undertake to buy the shares unless they can be sold to the public. Sometimes the issuing house, which is usually a merchant bank, buys all the shares itself, and after advertising an **'offer of sale'** sells them to the investing public.

If 100 shares are issued but 300 are applied for the issue is oversubscribed. The issuing house must then decide how to allot, e.g. it might give each applicant one-third of the number he asked for. Speculators who believe that the price will soon rise, and that they will be able to sell the shares quickly at a profit, may ask for many more shares than they could pay for if the full price were demanded on allotment, particularly when they think that the shares will be greatly oversubscribed. Instead of stating a price for the shares an issuing house may fix a minimum price, say £1.50, and ask investors to **tender** for the shares and pay in full on application or allotment. If

A offers £1.80 for 40 shares
B offers £1.70 for 60 shares
C offers £1.60 for 70 shares

A and B together will take all the shares which, unless the Prospectus states otherwise, will be allotted to them at the 'striking price' of £1.70, even although A offered more. C will get none. Tendering and payment in full on allotment reduce speculation and may raise more capital for the company.

A. Shareholder is given a certificate, like the one illustrated below. This certificate shows that, out of the total capital of £500 000, A. Shareholder has provided £1000. He owns one-five-hundredth of the business and, as in this case all the shares are of the same kind and have equal rights, he is entitled to one five-hundredth of the profits.

All shares, however, are not of the same kind. To obtain large sums of capital, an appeal must be made to different types of investors. Some are prepared to take big risks; others are not. Wealthy investors may be willing to do without profits for a while provided they believe they will receive big profits later. Many small investors prefer a moderate profit which they can rely on each year rather than a big profit one year and nothing in the next year. They want a regular income, and to appeal to them a company can issue preference shares.

Preference shares are given preference in claiming profits. They have the first claim on profits, a limit being placed to the amount they receive by making it equal to a certain percentage of the capital they provide. A company that has allotted 10 000 5 per cent preference shares of £1 each will have to pay $£\frac{5}{100} \times 10\ 000 = £500$ to the owners of these shares before any other class can receive anything. If the total profit is £500, it will all go to the preference shareholders leaving nothing for the others.

When a company ceases to exist (when it is said to be wound up or to go into liquidation), the capital, if there is any left after all the assets have been sold for cash and creditors paid, is returned to the shareholders. The

---

Share Certificate

No. 1   No. of Shares. 1000

The Radio Manufacturing Company Limited

Incorporated under the Companies Act, 1948

Capital – £500 000

This is to certify that ...... A. Shareholder .... 26, High Street, Birmingham .... is the registered holder of ... 1000 .. Ordinary Shares of one pound each, fully paid in the above-named Company numbered from . 1 .. to . 1000 . inclusive subject to the Memorandum and Articles of Association of the Company.

Given under the common seal of the company

This .. 1st ... Day of .. April .. 19 ..

(Seal)   T. Martin }
                          A. Brewster } Directors

K. Robinson, Secretary.

No transfer of the above-mentioned shares can be registered until this certificate has been deposited at the company's office.

---

preference shareholders may have the right to demand repayment of their capital first.

As preference shareholders run less risk, they do not have the same voting rights as others.

A company cannot pay dividends unless it has made sufficient profits. Preference shares that do not receive a dividend in one year may claim two in the next year, if there is enough profit. Shares that are entitled to arrears of dividends out of future profits are known as **cumulative preference shares**. Preference shares are assumed to be cumulative unless otherwise stated.

Some preference shares, as well as receiving a fixed percentage on capital, also take a share in the profit that may be left. These are **participating preference shares**.

With one exception, a company is not allowed to return capital to shareholders. If the shareholders could claim back their money at any time, it would be impossible for the company to continue in business. The only part of the capital that can be repaid is that provided by **redeemable preference shares**, and this is repaid when the company decides to do so and not when the shareholders may want it.

Redeemable preference shares are the only shares that can bought back by the company issuing them (but a company can buy shares issued by other companies). The Companies Acts lay down conditions for the issue of this type of share.

The terms of issue state when the shares are redeemable, such as at any time during the next fifty years. There are two ways in which they can be redeemed. The company, instead of sharing out all the profit, can save some of it until it has accumulated enough to buy back the shares. Or it can bring out a new lot of redeemable preference shares and with the money received for these buy and cancel the first lot. The first method reduces the number of shareholders, leaving more profit for the remainder. The second method may be used when capital is plentiful and rates of interest low. The new shares may offer a lower rate than the first issue, which again would leave more profit to be shared among the other shareholders.

The kinds of preference shares already mentioned may be combined in one type. Some companies, for example, issue cumulative participating redeemable preference shares. There may also be 'A' and 'B' preference shares, 'A' having the first claim and 'B' the second.

After the claims of the preference shares have been met the rest of the profits belong to the **ordinary shares** (or equities). They may make big profits or they may make none. They are more risky than preference shares and have more voting rights. Recently a few companies have issued ordinary shares which do not carry voting rights.

Deferred shares are more risky still as they are not entitled to any dividends until all other types have received a certain amount first. They are sometimes known as 'founders' shares', being given in part payment to those who began and built up a business that is being bought by a limited company. They are also known as 'managers' shares'. Their value may be as low as 5p, but, as each share may carry a vote, they are the means of giving control to the managers who by owning twenty 5p shares have twenty votes, while the owner of one £1 share has only one vote.

When a company is in need of more capital, it may decide to borrow it instead of issuing more shares. If the capital is required for a short period, it may be able to borrow from the banks, but capital borrowed for long periods will be raised by issuing **debentures**. The debenture is a document stating that money has been borrowed and setting forth the terms and conditions for repayment. The debenture-holders are entitled to a fixed rate of interest on their money which is due whether the company makes a profit or a loss. As debentures are not shares, they do not carry votes, and the lenders have no voice in controlling the business. If money can be borrowed at low rates of interest, the company may prefer to issue debentures instead of shares, because then there will be more profit left for the shareholders and, when the loans have been repaid, the profit to be shared will be greater still.

Debenture-holders may be given security for their loans. They may, for example, if the company fails to pay the interest or repay the capital according to the terms of issue, have power to take over and sell the business in order to recover their money. Debentures with such security are 'mortgage debentures', while those without security are termed 'naked debentures'.

The loans may be repayable after a stated number of years or by drawings. When they are repayable by drawings the company repays a certain number each year, the particular debentures to be repaid in that year being decided by drawing lots.

Shares are numbered and every shareholder has the number he owns on his share certificate and in the company's register of shareholders. After all the shares have been fully paid for, it does not matter who owns any particular share as neither the company nor its creditors will be able to claim any more from the shareholders. The company can then dispense with the numbers and save itself a lot of clerical work. It can, too, if it likes, turn fully paid shares into **stock**, also unnumbered. When shares are converted into stock they are all combined into one. Instead of saying that its capital is made up of 500 000 separate shares of £1 each, the company now says its capital is composed of stock worth £500 000, without dividing it into any parts. A shareholder owning 50 £1 shares would have his certificate cancelled and receive instead a certificate stating that he owned £50 worth of stock. For convenience stock is usually bought and sold in £100 lots. Fractions of shares cannot be bought, but any fraction of a stock can. Investors may find stock more convenient than shares because they can buy, say, £1000 exactly of stock but £1000 exactly could not be invested in shares which are worth £1.20 each as this would mean buying $833\frac{1}{3}$ shares. To buy a whole number of shares, an awkward sum for calculating yields, either £999.60 or £1000.80, would have to be invested. The same applies to debentures, which, when fully paid, can be turned into debenture stock.

All that was said about capital in Chapter 28 applies to limited companies as well as to sole traders and partnerships. In the case of limited companies, however, **capital may also mean** any of the following:

Nominal, registered, or authorised capital. This is the amount named in the Memorandum and registered with the Registrar. It is the maximum amount the company has authority to raise unless the shareholders vote in favour of an increase. All this capital may not be needed at once and only a part of it may be asked for at first.

The issued capital is the amount the public has been asked to provide. If all the nominal capital has been asked for, the issued capital will be equal to the nominal capital.

The subscribed capital is the amount investors have agreed to provide. It is the total value of the shares allotted. Unless all the shares issued have been taken, the subscribed capital will be less than the issued capital.

Called-up capital is the amount the directors have asked shareholders to pay on application, allotment and in calls. If no more can be claimed from the shareholders the called-up capital will be the same as the subscribed capital.

Paid-up capital is the amount actually received in cash from the shareholders. When all the shares have been paid for in full, paid-up capital will be the same as called-up capital.

Capital is highly **geared** when a considerable part of it, about one-third or more, consists of debentures and preference shares. The more highly geared it is, the greater the amount that must be paid out to owners of debentures and preference shares before other shareholders receive anything.

Questions

1. How would you obtain shares in a new company?

2. When are shares undersubscribed? How can a company make sure that it will receive the minimum subscription?

3. Describe how allotment by tender works. What are the advantages of this method to the company and to investors?

4. Describe the different kinds of preference shares. Why are different kinds of shares issued?

5. What are the advantages of redeemable preference shares to the company and to investors?

6. Distinguish between preference shares and deferred shares.

7. In what ways does stock differ from shares?

8. Discuss the different forms of capital raised by a large public limited company. Assuming that such a company has a successful year, how would it dispose of the profits that were available? (A.E.B.)

9. How does an ordinary share differ from a debenture? What would be your rights as an ordinary shareholder compared with those of a debenture-holder? (A.E.B.)

10. Classify shares and debentures according to the risks and rights of the holders.

11. A company's capital, fully paid, is made up of:

   8 000 000 ordinary shares of £1 each.
   1 000 000 5 per cent preference shares of £1 each.
   10 000 7 per cent debentures of £100 each.

   Its profit is £2 000 000 and it places £280 000 to reserve. How much per cent will the ordinary shareholders receive? Is the gearing high or low?

12. Explain (*a*) authorised, (*b*) subscribed and (*c*) paid-up capital.

Chapter 33

The Stock Exchange · Brokers · Jobbers

Although a company is not allowed to repay the share capital (except for redeemable preference shares), the investor can turn his shares into cash by selling them to anyone who is prepared to take them. The company must be informed of the change in ownership so that it can make the necessary alteration of names, etc., in its books and issue a new certificate to the new owner for a slight charge.

The certificate on page 148 says that the shares are ordinary shares of £1 each. This value stated or 'named' on the shares is their **nominal or par value**. It may be £1, £10, 25p, or any other amount. If A. Shareholder sells his shares, the price he obtains for them is their **market value** at that time. The market value may be at par when it equals the nominal value, or it may be above par or below par.

If a company starts with a capital of £1000 and by the end of the year has made £500 profit, it has increased the capital to £1500 and each of the 1000 £1 shares now represents a value of £$\frac{1500}{1000}$ = £1.50.

The holder of a share, therefore, would expect to receive £1.50 if someone wanted to buy it from him. If the company declares a dividend of 50 per cent and pays out all the profit at the rate of 50p per share, the shares will still be worth more than £1, because it is likely that a good profit will be made next year again. The amount of next year's profit is uncertain, and so the price that will be given for the shares will vary according to people's estimates of what the profits will be.

A profit equal to 50 per cent of capital is very good, and there may be very few businesses that are so successful. It may pay to give more than £1.50 for the shares. Suppose an investor gives £2 each for them. He is then entitled to receive the next dividend which may again be 50 per cent. He will receive 50 per cent of £1, the nominal value of the share, and not 50 per cent of the £2 he paid for it because that £2 went to the shareholder and not to the company. The profit on his outlay, known as the **yield**, is (£0.50 ÷ 2) × 100 = 25 per cent. Even if he gave £5 for a £1 share, his investment would yield 10 per cent and, if he could not earn 10 per cent elsewhere, it would pay him to buy at £5 per share.

When a company makes losses, there will be many shareholders anxious to sell its shares but very few people willing to buy. Their market value will be less than their nominal value or below par. They may become worth nothing.

Profits and losses are not the only causes of **changes in the market value** of stocks and shares. The degree of risk involved must also be taken into account. There is no guarantee that a company that pays 50 per cent this year will pay it next year, but it is more certain in some businesses than in others.

The greater the risk the less will the investor be willing to give for the shares. The possibility of strikes, wars, new taxes, etc., all have effects on the market value of shares.

Blue Chip Stocks is the name used to describe the shares of companies that are considered to be sound and unlikely to be adversely affected in the long term by temporary trade depressions.

Gilt-edged Securities are British and other Government stocks noted for their regularity and reliability in the payment of interest and redemption at the stated time. Money loaned to Local Government authorities in Britain also comes under this head.

The owner of shares can find a buyer for them himself, or he can request his banker to arrange the sale, or he can employ a stockbroker. When buying shares, it is always advisable to obtain them through a bank or a broker because one can easily be deceived into buying worthless shares from dishonest dealers. To try to prevent this selling of worthless shares it was made compulsory in 1939 for all stockbrokers who were not members of some body like the Stock Exchange to obtain a licence to carry on their businesses.

Most stocks and shares can be bought and sold on the **London Stock Exchange**, although other big cities and towns have Exchanges, too. The Exchange is a place where buyers and sellers of shares meet. Those doing business there must be qualified and be accepted as members of the Exchange; for which privilege they must pay and they must abide by the rules of the Council which is elected by the 3500 members for the purpose of governing the Exchange.

The Exchange is a market place for stocks and shares, Government and municipal bonds, debentures, and other securities approved by the Council. The Exchange cannot guarantee that the securities dealt in will always pay good dividends, but it does see to it that the companies which have issued the shares comply with the law and publish the information considered necessary to judge the value of the shares before it allows them to be quoted or dealt in on the Exchange. By selecting the men and women to be admitted as members and by refusing permission to deal in shares not complying with its rules, the Exchange is safeguarding the interest of investors. It is an **organised market** where business is done only by members and according to rules formulated by the Council of the Exchange.

Members have unlimited liability and a broker who sells to a buyer who fails to pay him is nevertheless expected to pay his client. Brokers who cannot pay their clients are 'hammered' and cease to be members, the Exchange paying compensation to their clients. The same applies to the delivery of shares bought for clients.

On British Stock Exchanges there are two kinds of members, brokers and jobbers. The **stockbroker** is an agent acting on behalf of the person who employs him. He buys and sells shares for somebody else and not for himself. He is paid by means of a commission, known as 'brokerage', which is usually a percentage of the value of the shares bought or sold. The **jobber** is a principal, buying and selling for himself. He trades in shares, buying at one price in order to sell at a higher price. His gross profit is the difference between his buying price and his selling price, and is known as the 'turn'.

A broker who has **to buy or sell shares** goes to a jobber who deals in that kind of share and asks for a price, not disclosing whether he wants to buy or sell. The jobber gives him two prices, the lower being the price at which he is prepared to buy the shares, and the higher the price at which he will sell them. As he does not know whether he will have to buy or sell the shares, he makes the difference between the two prices as small as he can. If the broker is not satisfied with these prices he can try another jobber. The first jobber, if approached again, may quote different prices from those he gave in the first instance.

The actual share certificates are not produced on the Exchange. The names, such as Western Airways Ordinary Shares, tell brokers and jobbers exactly what they are. When a price is accepted, broker and jobber note the 'bargain' in their books, and on the next day their clerks meet in the Settling Room to check and agree the notes.

Shares bought on the Stock Exchange need not be paid for at the time of purchase. The year is divided into twenty-four 'Accounts', usually of a fortnight each and ending on a Friday. The following Monday, when a new Account begins, is **Continuation Day**. On this day arrangements can be made to postpone settlement of transactions made in the Account just ended. Some will wish to postpone payment and others to postpone delivery. Usually the buyer who is not ready to settle must pay a charge known as 'contango' to the seller who is postponing delivery. Sometimes the charge is borne by the seller when it is known as 'backwardation'. Settlement for dealings in Government and some other securities cannot be postponed.

Tuesday is **Making-up Day** when the brokers make up their books. Wednesday is Ticket or **Name Day** when the last buying broker makes out tickets bearing the names of his clients and the shares bought, and passes them on to the jobbers from whom he bought the shares. The jobbers again pass on the tickets and finally they reach the broker who first sold the shares during the fortnight covered by the Account. This broker then gets in touch with the last buying broker in order to claim the money and to arrange for the transfer of the shares.

Meanwhile the selling broker sends his client a **transfer form**. The client signs the form to show that he is parting with the shares named on it and returns it, together with the share certificate, to his broker who passes the documents to the buying broker. The form and the certificate are then sent to the company concerned which alters the share register, cancels the old certificate and sends a new one bearing the purchaser's name to the buying broker who will forward it to his client. Investors who bought and sold during the Account do not need a certificate and can be ignored for the purposes of transfer.

Contract notes are sent to clients, showing how many shares were bought or sold, the amount of the brokerage and the expenses, and the amount due to or from the client.

Tuesday, eleven days after the close of the Account and the clerical work has been completed, is **Pay Day**, when accounts which are not to be carried forward are settled.

Shares of a private company cannot be sold on the Exchange. They must be sold privately and the directors may have to approve the sale, especially if it is a family business and the family wants to retain control.

Questions

1. What are the uses of the Stock Exchange to investors? What protection does it give them?

2. What causes the market value of shares to rise and fall?

3. A company has paid a dividend of 100 per cent and its 25p shares are now being bought on the Exchange at £6 each. How much per cent does the investor who buys at this price earn on his outlay?

4. If you have lent £100 at 5 per cent per annum, would it pay you to get it back and use it to buy 25 £1 shares at £4 each in a company that is paying 15 per cent dividend?

5. The broker is an agent and the jobber a principal. Describe the work of the broker and of the jobber.

6. It is the broker's duty to obtain the lowest possible price for a buyer of shares and the highest possible price for a seller of shares, even although they are the same kind of shares sold and bought on the same day. Show how the Stock Exchange enables him to do this.

7. What is an organised market? Show how the Stock Exchange is an organised market. For what is it a market? Name some other organised markets.

8. What takes place on (*a*) Continuation Day, (*b*) Making-up Day, (*c*) Ticket Day and (*d*) Pay Day?

9. You are a shareholder in a public limited company. You wish to sell a part of your holding. How can this be done? Would your answer be different if your holding was in a private company?   (A.E.B.)

10. What is a Stock Exchange Account? Describe how brokers and jobbers settle for shares bought and sold during the Account.

11. A successful private limited liability company wishes to extend its business. To do this it must increase its financial resources. Discuss three of the methods by which this may be done.   (A.E.B.)

12. Write notes on (*a*) 'gilt-edged', (*b*) par value, (*c*) brokerage, (*d*) 'turn', (*e*) 'bargain', (*f*) 'hammered', (*g*) contract note, (*h*) contango.

13. Write an account of the reasons why people and firms use the services offered by the London Stock Exchange. Describe the activities of those who do the work of the Stock Exchange. Explain the importance of what goes on in the Exchange to the commercial and industrial life of the country.   (W.M.E.B.)

Chapter 34

The Stock Exchange · Speculators · Unit trusts · Institutional investors

The Stock Exchange rule allowing postponement of payment and delivery is taken advantage of mainly by speculators who deal in shares, not for the sake of the dividends they will earn, but for the profits they can make through buying and selling shares. These speculators are of three main kinds. **Bulls** buy shares believing that the price will rise and that they can sell them quickly at a profit. Suppose a Bull instructs his broker to buy 1000 shares at £1 each. When the settlement arrives, the price is still £1 each, and as he does not want to pay for the shares he will pay contango for postponing payment. In a few days the company whose shares have been bought by the Bull declares a very good dividend and the price rises to £1.30. The Bull now sells the shares for £1300. He has not used any money, and now the broker owes him £1300 less £1000 and the brokerage and expenses.

Bears are speculators who sell shares hoping that the price will fall so that they can buy them back at a lower price. They may sell shares they do not possess, but hope to be able to obtain at a lower price before the settlement. If a Bear sells 1000 shares at £1 each but the price does not fall, he will arrange to postpone delivery and pay backwardation. If, later, the price falls to £0.70, he will order his broker to buy 1000 at that price and deliver them to the purchaser. He now receives £1000 less £700 and the brokerage and expenses from his broker.

Stags are speculators who buy new issues because they believe that the price fixed by the issuing house is too low and that once the Stock Exchange starts to deal in the shares they can sell them quickly at a profit, perhaps before they have paid in full for them. Tendering for shares to be paid for in full on application or allotment, as described on page 147, now gives them less chance to speculate.

Of course, prices do not always change in the way speculators think that they will, and then they may lose heavily and may have big sums to pay their brokers. Certain goods are also bought and sold on Exchanges, e.g. wheat on the London Corn Exchange, and speculation takes place in goods as well as in stocks and shares. One claim made in support of speculation is that it evens out prices because speculators buy goods when they are very plentiful and prevent the prices from falling very low, and they sell them in times of scarcity thus keeping the price down.

The London Stock Exchange is **the only one with jobbers**. Elsewhere brokers deal with brokers, but on some British exchanges a few brokers may act sometimes as jobbers. The advantage of dealing with jobbers is that they are always prepared to buy or sell. A broker buys or sells only when his clients instruct him to do so, but a jobber, being in business on his own account, is prepared to deal at any time. In other Exchanges brokers may be unable to find buyers and sellers for certain shares, but the London jobber is always ready to buy or sell, at the prices he quotes, the shares in which he deals.

Because jobbers have shares to sell when there is a demand for them, and are ready to buy when the demand lessens, they help to prevent great fluctuations in price. A jobber tries to keep his book balanced. When buyers of a particular share are plentiful he sells easily, but he must also buy in order to have a supply of shares available, just as a shopkeeper must replace his stock. If his supply becomes low, he raises the price to discourage buyers and encourage sellers. Similarly, he reduces prices when his supply is overbalancing his sales. Jobbers deal with one another as well as with brokers and competition among them tends to keep prices down.

Share **prices are quoted** in the newspapers, e.g.:

Radio Manufacturing 97p − 4p

This means that the owner of shares in the Radio Manufacturing Company can expect to obtain rather less than 97p per share and the buyer would have to give rather more than 97p per share. Minus 4p means that the price has fallen 4p during the day. Had the price gone up by 4p the quotation would have been 97p + 4p.

When preparing to pay dividends, companies will not register transfers of shares because they do not want to have to alter the lists of shareholders entitled to the dividend. At such times share prices may include the next dividend. The price will then be stated as 97p cum div. (or cum in.), meaning that the buyer of the share buys it with the dividend or interest about to be paid. If the seller wishes to retain the next dividend for himself, the price will be quoted as ex div. or ex in. (without the dividend or interest).

A company may not share out all the profit it has made, but may retain some of it to be distributed in years when it has made little or no profit, or it may retain it because it needs more capital. Sometimes a company turns this retained profit into share capital by issuing **bonus shares** to its members, who pay for them out of this retained profit which is then kept permanently in the business.

After a bonus issue the share capital has been increased, but the net assets owned by the business are the same. Each share then represents a smaller part of the assets and profits. As a result the market value of the shares falls. This may be an advantage to the shareholder because the shares being cheaper may be easier to sell. Instead of owning 15 shares representing assets worth £60, and selling at £4 each, he owns 20 shares representing the same assets and selling at £3 each.

The Exchange itself does not issue shares to the public. It merely enables shares that have already been bought from public limited companies to change hands easily. It is a market for secondhand shares which is of great **importance to the country**. Many would not invest in new shares unless, in case of need, they could be turned easily into cash. This is why a Prospectus states that the Exchange has been asked for a 'quotation' for the new shares. By providing the means for turning shares quickly into cash, together with the safeguards already mentioned, the Exchange makes it much easier for companies to obtain buyers for new shares. The lists of prices published in the daily papers keep investors informed of changes in the values of their shares and they can compare these prices with the prices obtained for them by their brokers.

There is more risk in investing in a new business than in an established successful business. Those willing to take the risk, if they have no money available, can sell their shares in the old companies to the more cautious investors and use the proceeds to provide capital for the new companies. In this way the Exchange helps to make new ventures possible.

When a private company becomes a public company, but is not asking for more capital, the Council may give its shares an 'introduction' to the Exchange, i.e. it allows its shares to be bought and sold on the Exchange. If the company requires more capital, but only a small amount, it may be allowed a 'placing', in which case it can sell the new shares to a firm of brokers which then sells them to, or places them with, its clients. For small issues this is much cheaper than an appeal to all investors.

The free market of the Exchange is also important to businesses which are not asking for capital. A business wishing to build up a fund for the replacement of an asset or for some other purpose can invest the sums it sets aside each year for the purpose in shares which can be sold when the cash is required. Banks and insurance companies handle big sums which may be claimed from them at short notice. Some of this money can be made to earn by investing it in shares which can be sold quickly when there is a sudden demand for cash. The Government finds it easier to borrow vast sums at favourable rates of interest because the lenders know they can, whenever they like, turn the bonds into cash by selling them on the Exchange. The large numbers of securities dealt in allow funds to be invested in different securities thus spreading and minimising the risk of loss.

Small investors who cannot buy shares in several companies in order to spread the risk of loss can invest in **unit trusts**. The organisers of a trust employ experts to buy and sell shares, the shares bought being deposited with a bank which acts as a trustee. If a trust buys shares in 20 different companies for a total of £100, it may divide the investment into 500 parts or units, each unit being worth 20p. An investor who buys 100 units is then spreading an investment of only £20 over 20 different businesses. He can buy as many units as he likes, either directly from the trust or through brokers or banks.

The owner can sell units and fractions of units to anyone. Units cannot be dealt in on the Stock Exchange, but a trust acts as a jobber to buy back its own units and to sell them again. The lower price at which it buys back is the 'bid' price and the higher price at which it sells is the 'offered' price. These prices depend on the dividends earned by the shares owned by the trust. Dividends received are, after deducting expenses, shared out to unit holders at so much per unit. For the protection of investors trusts must be managed in accordance with the law relating to them.

Buyers of stocks and shares are not necessarily private individuals investing their own money. Big investments are made by the **institutional investors**. These are organisations such as insurance companies, banks, investment trusts, unit trusts and the pension funds of big companies, that have a great deal of other people's money to invest, for example: insurance premiums, bank deposits and pension fund contributions. These organisations are concerned primarily with the safety of the money invested, and the banks in particular invest mainly in Government or Local Government stock. Investment and unit trusts, however, are looking for profitability also; they spread their investments over a wide range of stocks.

Questions

1. How does a Bull gain by a rising market and a Bear by a falling market? Do speculators serve any useful purpose?

2. What are the advantages to the London Stock Exchange of having jobbers? Describe the work of the jobber. Why may one jobber quote higher prices than other jobbers for the same kind of shares?

3. What is a quotation? Why does a Prospectus state the Exchange has been asked to give a quotation for the shares?

4. The main functions of the Stock Exchange are:

   (a) to provide a market for stocks and shares and Government bonds by enabling buyers and sellers to get easily in touch with one another;
   (b) to even out the prices of shares;
   (c) to indicate by the share prices quoted for which kind of businesses it will pay to ask the public for more capital;
   (d) to make the raising of new capital easier and cheaper.

   Show how the Stock Exchange fulfils these functions.

5. Describe the work of the London Stock Exchange and discuss its importance to industry and the Government. (A.E.B.)

6. Explain the part played by the London Stock Exchange in enabling trade and industry to raise funds for capital development. (J.M.B.)

7. Explain what is meant by the term 'unit trust'. How does this form of investment differ from one made through a Stock Exchange? (M.R.E.B.)

8. Explain cum div., ex div., bonus shares, issuing house, brokers, stags, jobbers.

9. What would be the results of there being no Stock Exchange? (M.R.E.B.)

10. 'Buyers of stocks and shares are not necessarily private individuals investing their own money.'

    If this statement is true, what other investors buy shares, and what kinds of investment do they look for?

11. What are the functions of the Stock Exchange? Describe the nature of speculation on the Stock Exchange   (A.E.B.)

Chapter 35

Business expansion · Productivity · Amalgamation · Growth industries

Most manufacturing businesses study ways of increasing their sales and we know that there are many forms of advertising and different types of sales outlet available. Some of these, like mail order, vending machines, mobile shops and supermarkets, have expanded swiftly in the last two decades, to meet the increasing consumer demand for manufactured goods of all kinds.

Increased sales, however, may not necessarily result in increased profits. The cost of manufacturing the extra products must be carefully considered. In a previous chapter (pp. 133–6) we saw the importance of knowing the 'break-even' point: the number of manufactured items that must be sold to cover all out-goings. A manufacturer with a plant of a certain size, employing a certain number of operators, knows therefore the size of the daily or weekly ouput that he must maintain to show a certain net profit figure. If it is proposed to increase production in order to sell more goods, several factors must be considered.

1. It may be possible to **increase productivity**. If more goods can be produced by the same number of workers and machines through improved methods and organisation, this is a sure way to increase the profits. On the other hand, any increase may have to be counter-balanced by expenditure on new machinery and equipment if a rise in productivity is to be achieved. In this case, sales may expand at once but net profit may increase only in the long term.

2. **Economies of scale** may be possible; that is, once the new methods and equipment have become established, large increases in production may be possible with no extra outlay beyond the prime cost of additional raw materials. In other words, the larger the scale of operations the lower the cost per unit of manufacture. However, further expense may have to be borne if the increased production cannot be handled in the existing warehouse – it may be necessary to build a bigger one.

3. A greater increased output may be derived from the same labour force, if economies of scale are realised, but pressures on office staff are bound to be severe. If existing production control and accounting methods are inadequate to deal with the expanded business, a reorganisation in this area also may become necessary.

It is clear that the following progression may take place:

$$\left. \begin{array}{l} \text{Modern machines,} \\ \text{equipment,} \\ \text{methods} \end{array} \right\} \longrightarrow \left\{ \begin{array}{l} \text{Increased} \\ \text{productivity} \end{array} \right\} \longrightarrow \left\{ \begin{array}{l} \text{Expanded production} \\ \text{with economies} \\ \text{of scale} \end{array} \right\} \longrightarrow \left\{ \begin{array}{l} \text{Higher} \\ \text{net} \\ \text{profits} \end{array} \right.$$

A manufacturer may, nevertheless, have reservations about increasing his production and profits by this means. For example:

He may not wish to expand his company in order to raise further capital for new plant and buildings;

He may feel that the rise in demand is temporary and does not justify a long-term expansion;

Any further building may be impossible on his present site; a major expansion may necessitate moving to another area.

We have already seen that an established company needing capital for expansion or reorganisation may obtain it by several methods. Capital may be 'ploughed back' into the business, the company may make a further share issue, or it may seek a loan either from a bank or in the form of debentures.

Expansion may also take place by a company taking over another established business. The fact that stocks and shares can be bought and sold has made this possible. If one company obtains over half the shares or over half the voting power in another it gains control over it in most matters. The controlling company is then known as a **holding company** and the other as a **subsidiary company**. Sometimes a special company is formed in order to buy up shares in a large number of companies so that they can be run together from one centre. Combines and trusts are set up in this way.

Holding and subsidiary companies are created for several reasons. In the first place competition may be so keen that a leading company decides to curtail it by buying or controlling its competitors. It may then decide to specialise by using certain factories for certain kinds of work only and so gain in efficiency. It may also be able to order in bulk for all its factories. Or it may decide to close down some factories and concentrate production in a few of the best equipped. By centralising the work it may be able to save in advertising costs, office work and in research work.

When this process takes place between businesses of the same kind it is known as **horizontal amalgamation**, e.g. two groups of retail grocery shops, or two motor-car factories.

The term also describes the integration of firms that each make a variety of products requiring similar processes or raw materials; the merger allows knowledge, techniques and plant to be shared, to mutual advantage. Examples of this type of amalgamation (sometimes called **lateral**) are Reckitt & Colman Ltd, whose range of products includes many well-known household items, and Imperial Chemical Industries Ltd, which produces many man-made fibres, dyes and a host of other chemical products. Both these organisations were built up as a result of amalgamation between companies manufacturing products that required similar materials and comparable production and sales techniques.

Control of other businesses may be desired in order to secure supplies. A steelworks may obtain an interest in iron mines in order to be certain that it will get the raw materials it needs, or a jam factory will buy up orchards so that it can be sure of obtaining sufficient fruit of the right kind for its factories. Amalgamation of this kind between businesses at different levels of production is known as **vertical amalgamation**.

Vertical amalgamation also takes place in the opposite direction. An ironmining company may obtain control of a steelworks in order to make certain that it will be able to sell its output, or the makers of clothes may buy up retail shops for the same reason. These are examples of forward vertical amalgamation, while the former were examples of backward amalgamation.

Diagonal amalgamation occurs when a business takes control of firms that make products used by the business in its production process. For example, a small firm making boxes or some other type of packing might be taken over by a large company seeking to ensure an uninterrupted supply of packing materials at a lower cost. Often the capacity of the integrated firm is developed so that it becomes a valuable subsidiary, supplying the parent company's needs and also producing for other customers.

When a firm integrates a certain 'diagonal' activity, it may not do so by absorbing an existing firm; it may develop the activity within its own organisation.

A clothing manufacturer, for example, might decide to print his own silk labels for sewing into his garments: these usually carry the maker's name and the washing instructions. If he finds that the machinery is not fully occupied in printing his labels, he may offer this service to other clothing manufacturers and supply them with silk tags, and this becomes a profitable sideline. Similarly, a firm that buys plastic bags for its products may decide to set up a department to make its own; this firm too might supply other firms with their plastic bag requirements, and thus develop an additional source of profit.

Disintegration may also take place. A company that has branched out into making a component or accessory product previously bought from a supplier, in the expectation of saving money, achieving a more reliable quality level, or ensuring future supplies, may discover that the enterprise is, after all, uneconomic. He may find that the new plant loses money because his own demands do not fully employ it and he cannot attract enough outside business to make it pay; or he may encounter labour difficulties that he had not anticipated. In this case, the new enterprise is 'hived off' from the parent organisation.

There is an old adage, 'If you want something done properly, do it yourself', and the directors of a company must decide how much they will do for themselves and to what extent they will rely on outside suppliers. Such decisions involve parts and accessories that are vital to the manufacture of the finished product, packing materials and transport.

Instead of buying shares on the Stock Exchange, a company may make an offer, known as a **takeover-bid**, to the shareholders of another company to buy their shares at a stated price. To obtain control of a company it is not necessary to buy all the shares but only a majority of the shares carrying votes.

Amalgamation of business

Vertical Amalgamation

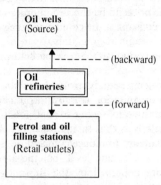

Horizontal Amalgamation

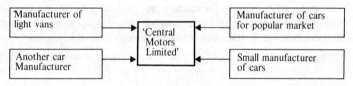

Lateral Amalgamation

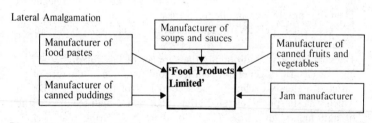

Diagonal Amalgamation

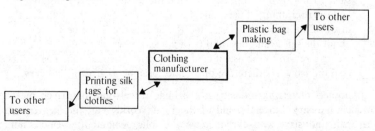

There are **other ways of gaining control**. When the same directors serve on the boards of several companies, they can consider them together and may decide to sacrifice one or more for the benefit of the others. Such control is referred to as control by means of interlocking directorates.

Voluntary agreements between companies are also made. Such agreements may deal with the prices to be charged in order to prevent undercutting by some, or to the division of the country into regions, each company being allowed to sell in certain regions only, or to fix the output of each business during a certain period, so that the market is not flooded by a big output from all factories.

Sometimes a special organisation is created to sell the product of a group of companies. Such an organisation is known as a 'cartel'. It can save in advertising costs and arrange its selling so that goods are provided from the factories nearest the buyer, thus saving transport charges.

The objects in each case are to reduce competition, save costs and keep prices from falling below a certain level, but the agreements cannot be enforced unless they are approved by the Restrictive Practices Court. Amalgamations that may lead to a monopoly can be forbidden by the Government after the question has been considered by the Monopolies Commission.

Growth can be seen in an **industry** as a whole and not just in a single enterprise, but not all industries can be regarded as 'growth' industries. Two industries in Britain have interesting records in this respect:

1. **The gas industry**, having been superseded by electricity for lighting purposes before the First World War, concentrated on domestic cooking and heating supplies and the supply of gas to industry. For several decades up to 1960, the growth rate of the gas industry was negligible. Then the rapidly-growing demand for central heating boosted sales to unprecedented high levels. The discovery of natural gas has further stimulated this growth.

2. **The coal industry**, traditionally the supplier of fuel for domestic heating, for electricity generating stations and for the manufacture of gas, suffered a steady decline in the second half of the twentieth century which was sharply accelerated after 1960. As we shall see in our study of nationalised industries (Ch. 40), there was during that period a steady run-down of capacity through the closing of less profitable pits and the re-training of personnel for other work. Since the dramatic rise in world oil prices, however, and the doubts that have been expressed about the safety and desirability of nuclear power stations, we are now seeing a return to the use of coal for electricity production. The British coal industry has therefore once more become a 'growth' industry.

Another interesting industry is the huge petrol- and oil-driven motor vehicle industry. Since the end of the First World War, this has been a 'growth' industry, with ever-increasing public demand for vehicles and petroleum fuels. In recent years, however, the development of electrically-powered vehicles has become the subject of research in several countries amidst growing concern for the noise and air pollution which motor vehicles cause. The 'growth' days of the vehicle industry as we have known it may be numbered.

Two modern industries which have proved to be remarkable growth industries are the manufacture of aluminium, and the various types of plastic. Three new large aluminium smelters came into production in Britain between 1970 and 1974, and new uses are constantly being found for this strong, lightweight material. The plastics industry, in its various forms, has proved to be one of the fastest-growing industries of our time, and rapid expansion is going on. Both these industries account for a very satisfactory 'slice' of Britain's exports.

The most recent example of a growth industry in Britain is the development of the newly-discovered oilwells, both off-shore and inland. Because of the steep increase in world oil prices in 1974, the need to accelerate production is of paramount necessity, and this industry must prove one of the fastest-growing of modern times.

Questions

1. Explain and give some examples of: (i) backward and forward vertical integration, (ii) horizontal and lateral integration, (iii) diagonal integration – does it always involve the amalgamation of firms?

2. Commercial enterprise has become increasingly concentrated in the hands of large organisations. Outline the advantages from the point of view of increased efficiency and economies that might be expected. What disadvantages might be involved?

3. Explain: (i) holding company, (ii) monopoly and the Monopolies Commission, (iii) R.P.M. Is it legal today?

4. What is meant by productivity? How might this concept be applied to a large department store? What steps might be taken in such a business to improve productivity and thus increase profits?

5. Write briefly on 'growth' industries. Give some examples.

6. Mention six different types of activity that have been developed in the form of international businesses.

7. Describe some of the restrictive practices that could result from agreements made between manufacturers, mentioning how these might affect other commercial enterprises and the consumer. What arrangements exist under British law to keep track of such agreements?

8. Increasingly business enterprise is concentrated in the hands of large firms. From a production point of view, what are the possible advantages? What are the likely disadvantages to such a firm?   (R.S.A.)

9. The past decade has seen a great rise in the number of mergers and takeover-bids in industry. These can be put into three broad categories: (i) horizontal mergers (linking of organisations doing the same type of work), (ii) vertical mergers (linking of organisations engaged in the different stages of production or distribution of a product) and (iii) 'conglomerate' mergers (linking of organ-

isations whose activities are entirely different). For each category, suggest the major reason(s) for such mergers to take place. Wherever possible, give actual examples. (L.C.C. & I.)

10. Name what you consider to be a 'growth' industry, and put forward your reasons why it merits such a description. (L.C.C. & I.)

11. Growth may be a means by which a firm achieves a higher rate of profit. Outline how this higher rate of profit may occur, distinguishing between growth from within and growth by merger. (R.S.A.)

12. What are (*a*) holding companies, (*b*) subsidiary companies?
In what other ways can one company obtain control of another?

13. Why do companies amalgamate and combine (*a*) horizontally, (*b*) vertically? Give examples.

Chapter 36

Middlemen · Agents · Markets · Futures

Anyone who comes between the producer of the goods and the final buyer can be termed a **middleman** or an intermediary. The wholesaler and the retailer are middle men and so are the brokers and jobbers discussed in the previous chapter. Before the goods reach the consumer they may have been bought and sold several times.

The middlemen are frequently blamed for the big difference that may exist between the factory or farm price and the retail price. Each middleman who deals with the goods has to make a profit and sell them at a higher price than he paid for them.

It is true that in some cases there may be too many middlemen and this is one reason why there has been a tendency to cut them out by direct dealing between the maker and the retailer or by the maker opening his own retail shops. A maker sells goods for £100 to wholesaler A, who, after storing and packing them, sells them for £120 to wholesaler B, who immediately sells them to C for £130. In return for his profit, A has given service but B has not. C, by cutting out B, could just as well have bought the goods from A for £120.

Besides middlemen, who are traders on their own account, there are others who are engaged to help in buying and selling. Some of these may not even see the goods but they must be paid, and their earnings must be added to the cost of distribution. Some of them will be described later.

To **justify their existence** middlemen must provide some necessary service and provide it at less cost than it could have been provided by the original owner or the final buyer. They claim that they do this for the following reasons.

In the first place they are **specialists** in the kind of work they do. The manufacturer's job is the making of goods and the more time and attention he gives to manufacturing the more skilful he should become. To undertake wholesaling as well would divide his time and energies and both jobs would suffer. If the manufacturer gives all his time to his factories and the wholesaler to his warehouse both would become more efficient, just as one who does nothing but shorthand should be better at it than one who does typewriting and bookkeeping as well. Middlemen should be experts, not Jacks-of-all-trades and masters of none. Division of labour means more efficient labour.

The middleman, then, knows all that there is to know about his job. The stockbroker can advise which shares are not worth buying, and he knows where, how and when to buy or sell to the best advantage, what documents must be used, how to transfer shares from one person to another, and all the details about stamps and fees, about which the principal may know nothing and with which he does not want to be bothered. The stockbroker can do the work much more quickly and without making mistakes.

Middlemen can often do their work for less than it would cost the maker to do it, and instead of increasing the costs of distribution they may actually reduce them. They can do this because they are experts who know the best and cheapest way of doing the work, and because they obtain business from many people. By collecting goods or work from a large number they secure a **big turnover** and can, like the wholesaler, spread their overhead charges so much that they can afford to operate for a small charge or commission. The stockbroker has so many clients and during the course of the year he buys and sells such a vast number of shares that a commission as low as three-eighths per cent is enough to give him a considerable income. It would cost much more than the brokerage for someone to equip and staff an office to handle just the shares in which he himself deals.

The stockbroker can make savings in ways which are not possible to his principals. Instead of investing £500 in War Loan for me and £1000 for you in two separate transactions, he can combine the orders and obtain both lots in one transaction thus saving time and expense. Brokers who deal in goods can do the same and **buy in bulk**.

For these reasons most businesses, particularly the smaller ones, prefer to use the middlemen rather than try to do the work themselves. Even some of the biggest businesses found that it did not pay them to do without the wholesaler.

The work of wholesale and retail middlemen has been dealt with in previous chapters. Below are described some middlemen who are not traders on their own account. They are mainly **agents** acting on behalf of someone else, known as the 'principal'. An agent may be employed by sellers to find buyers for their goods or services, or by buyers to find sellers of the goods and services they require. Agents bring buyers and sellers into touch with one another. It is their business to know where buyers and sellers can be found and where the best prices can be obtained.

Brokers are agents who never have possession of the goods. They merely sell or arrange to sell on behalf of their principals, in the same way as the stockbroker buys or sells shares that he has not seen. They are employed in many kinds of trades: coal, grain, wool, tea, fruit and many others. Some of them do more than strictly falls within a broker's work. The **wool brokers** are examples of these. Unlike wheat and cotton, wool varies so much in quality that it cannot be accurately graded and sold by grade or by description. A buyer wants to see the wool and to sample it first. Importers instruct the brokers to sort and classify the wool in the warehouses, to prepare catalogues, send them to likely buyers, arrange for the wool to be auctioned in Spitalfields and give the bidders an opportunity to sample the wool in the warehouse first. In a similar way brokers arrange tea auctions at Mincing Lane, and fruit auctions at the London Fruit Exchange and elsewhere, and Billingsgate is famous for its fish auctions.

On the Metal Exchange dealings take place in copper, tin, zinc, silver and lead, without the intervention of brokers. The principals meet and deal directly with one another, five minutes being allowed for trading in each metal in turn. This method is referred to as ring trading.

London with its vast import and entrepôt trade is the main centre for these organised markets where raw materials are bought and sold according to rules drawn up by the Exchange concerned. Foreign, as well as British, businesses make use of these markets to buy or sell raw materials. In addition to those already mentioned London has important organised commodity markets for maize, barley and other cereals, cocoa, sugar, oils and fats, rubber, furs, gold and silver bullion, and diamonds. Trading in these commodities of extractive industries also takes place otherwise than through the Exchanges.

The output of extractive industries can vary a great deal. At times supplies may be plentiful and difficult to sell and at other times they may be scarce and difficult to buy. This uncertainty can be overcome by means of **forward contracts**. A farmer, for example, can agree with a miller that, when he harvests his crop in three months' time, he will deliver it to the miller at an agreed price. In this way the farmer makes certain of selling his crop and the miller is sure that he will receive supplies in three months.

Forward contracts are suitable for goods that can be graded, the prices of all grades rising or falling together. Such goods can be bought without being seen, buyers and sellers knowing exactly what the grades mean. If the wrong grade is delivered, the rules of the Exchange state what must be done to adjust matters.

Because output varies prices can also vary considerably. They will be very high in times of scarcity and very low in times of abundance. If during the three months prices had risen it would have paid the farmer to wait before selling. If prices had fallen, it would have paid the miller to wait before buying. By entering into forward contracts, they run the risk that prices may change to the advantage of one party and to the disadvantage of the other party to the agreement.

This risk of loss through changing prices can be avoided and insured against by dealing in **futures and hedging**. For this purpose the Exchange selects a standard grade and all futures contracts are agreements to deliver a certain quantity of this grade at a future date. Suppose that a cocoa manufacturer buys spot, that is, for immediate delivery, some raw cocoa and reckons that he can sell the finished goods at the end of three months at a profit of £100. The price of the raw cocoa he bought then falls by £100 and the price of the finished goods also falls by £100 (although in practice it is not likely to fall by the same amount) so that the maker has no profit when he sells the finished goods.

To safeguard his profit the maker hedges. When he buys spot, he also sells forward binding himself to deliver to an importer the same quantity of cocoa in three months' time and, we shall assume, at the same price as he has just paid. When the time comes for him to deliver he can buy the cocoa for £100 less than the price for which he sold it in the futures contract. He thus gains £100 on the future to balance the £100 profit lost on the finished goods.

As a rule there is no need for the maker to deliver because he can buy back the future. The importer probably does not want the standard grade and, if he took it, he would have to sell it for £100 less than he gave for it. As he does not want this grade, and the maker merely wants his profit, he prefers to give up the future and pay the difference of £100 to the maker and be free to buy spot the correct grade when he wants it.

Just before buying the future, the importer agreed to supply a merchant with the same quantity in three months. He fixed his selling price at £100 more than it would cost him to buy at that time. Like the merchant, he did not want to store cocoa for months and decided to buy later. In doing so he ran the risk that prices might rise and his profit disappear. To protect himself, he bought the future. In fact, prices fell and he now buys for £100 less than he bargained for and, as his selling price remains the same, he gains £200. But, as explained above, he pays £100 to the maker which leaves him with the £100 profit he expected to make. Had prices risen by £100, he would make no profit on the cocoa, but would receive £100 from the maker to make up for it. In this way both the maker and the importer safeguard the profits they plan to make.

In practice the £100 is not paid in one sum. If prices alter £20 by a date fixed by the Exchange, that £20 is paid on that date, and so on at other dates during the three months. Transactions do not balance exactly as in the example, but any losses on futures plus brokerage and expenses are regarded as the cost of insuring against much greater losses caused by changing prices. The **purpose of a futures market** is to enable makers and traders in the goods to ensure their business profits and not to make profits just by buying and selling futures; although Bull and Bear speculators who never handle goods try to do so.

Futures markets are also known as **terminal markets** because commodities are bought for delivery after a certain time or term. Dealings in futures take place in cocoa, coffee, sugar, certain cereals, oil seeds, rubber, wool, cotton and some metals. Some futures markets, such as those for wheat and cotton, have declined greatly in importance because the supply and prices of these commodities are now controlled by governments and by international agreements so that there is much less uncertainty about the future supplies and prices of these products.

Factors or mercantile agents are given possession of the goods and they can deal with them as if they were the owners, selling and buying in their own names. They can even borrow money using the goods as security. Brokers, when acting as brokers, cannot deal as principals but must make it known that they are acting for someone else. Factors are employed to buy and sell coal, boots and shoes, fruit, etc. They are frequently referred to as 'commission salesmen'.

Auctioneers are agents employed by sellers for selling their goods at auctions. They have possession of the goods.

Agents are important in foreign trade as well as in the home trade. A del credere agent is one who receives goods on consignment undertaking to sell them only to buyers who will be in a position to pay. In return for guaranteeing payment to the exporter, he is entitled to an extra commission on the sales, known as a del credere commission.

The consignor sends a pro forma invoice to the agent informing him of the quantity and value of the goods supplied to him. The consignee later forwards an account sales to his principal showing which goods have been sold and the prices at which they were sold. From the receipts the agent deducts his commission and any expenses he incurred in connection with the goods, and remits the balance due as shown by the account sales.

Agents are also employed to collect orders abroad, to advertise, to distribute goods, to buy and to sell, to pack goods, to arrange transport and shipping, while the banks act as agents for sending abroad documents, and for collecting money from foreigners, as will be explained in Chapter 52.

Middlemen, then, are often essential to the smooth working of a market. A **market** is not a place or a building, but is made up of the buyers and sellers who deal and compete with one another. Markets can be classified according to the type of transaction that takes place, such as the wholesale market through which goods pass from the makers and importers to the retailers, or according to the type of goods bought and sold, such as the wool market, the coal market, etc.

When buyers and sellers are really competing in a market, there can be only one price in that market. Buyers will buy from the seller who will take the lowest price and other sellers cannot charge more if they wish to dispose of their goods. If there are two prices for the same kind and quality of goods, then there are two separate markets for those goods. Two or more markets may exist for the same sort of goods because the dealers in one market do not know what is happening elsewhere; or it is too much trouble and expense to travel to or get in touch with buyers and sellers at a distance; or the product may be perishable and cannot be transported long distances without losing quality.

Some markets are purely local, serving the people living in the immediate neighbourhood only, like the poultry market in a country town or the market for a small town's weekly newspaper. Others are national and cover the whole country like the markets for clothing and for the chief newspapers. Worldwide or international markets exist for goods which are in universal demand like rubber and wool.

In order that buyers and sellers all over the world may compete, the goods must be such as can be sold by description or by grade without being seen first, and be capable of being transported over long distances without deteriorating. The dealers, too, must have immediate knowledge of what is happening in other parts of the world. Today a change in price or in conditions at one centre is immediately known at other centres through radio and cable messages, so that, after allowing for transport and other expenses, the price of the goods in these worldwide markets tends to be the same everywhere.

Questions

1. Define a middleman. Give at least four reasons to explain why middlemen may lessen the costs of distribution. Give examples to illustrate your answer.

2. What are (*a*) brokers, (*b*) factors, (*c*) del credere agents? Describe the services they give to commerce.

3. Which goods are bought and sold by means of brokers? Describe the work done by brokers in connection with any one of them.

4. Mention some of the commodity markets in London and describe the work of any one of them. (R.S.A.)

5. It is sometimes said that there are too many middlemen in the distributive trades. Enumerate some types of middlemen, state the special services they render and discuss alternative means of securing these services. (J.M.B.)

6. Explain the importance of a wholesale produce market (e.g. Nine Elms, Smithfield) and its importance to (*a*) the producer, and (*b*) the retailer. (R.S.A.)

7. Describe the importance of markets in the modern world. Give an example of each of the following:

   (*a*) an international market;
   (*b*) a local market;
   (*c*) a market for capital;
   (*d*) a futures market. (J.M.B.)

8. Describe how wool from an Australian farm reaches a Yorkshire mill.

9. What are futures? What kind of goods are sold in futures markets? Show how a manufacturer can hedge against a fall in prices.

10. Why may the retail price of meat be much higher than the price the farmer gets for the animals? Say what happens after the farmer has sold the animals.

11. Why is London an important centre for organised commodity markets? Explain, in relation to organised commodity markets, the meaning of the following terms: (*a*) forward contracts, (*b*) futures, (*c*) hedging. (A.E.B.)

12. Select one commodity market and explain (*a*) its purpose, (*b*) who deals there, (*c*) the method of selling. (L.C.C. & I.)

Chapter 37

Transport · Rail · Road

Transport **aids trade in many ways**. By moving goods from places where they are plentiful to places where they are scarce, transport adds to their value. The wheat of the Canadian prairies would be of no use to us unless it could be carried to this country. The more easily goods can be brought over the distance that separates producer and consumer, and the smaller the cost of carriage, the better for trade. When there were no railways, no good roads, no canals and only small sailing ships, trade was on a small scale. Only expensive goods, such as silks and gold, could afford to pay the heavy costs of carriage for long distances.

The great advances made in transport during the last two hundred years were accompanied by a big increase in trade. Bigger and faster ships, fitted with refrigerators, enabled a trade in meat to develop between this country and New Zealand, for instance. Quicker transport enables supplies to be obtained at short notice so that less capital need be locked up in idle stocks. It has helped to develop direct trading between maker and retailer. It makes possible mass production and big business, drawing supplies from, and selling goods to, all parts of the globe. Big factories could not exist without transport to carry the large number of workers they need to and from their homes. Big city stores could not have developed unless customers could travel easily from the suburbs and goods be delivered to their homes. Big cities could not survive unless food could be brought from a distance.

Transport, like warehousing, prevents waste. Much of the fish landed at the ports would be wasted if it could not be taken quickly to inland towns. Transport has given us a much greater variety of foods and goods since we are no longer obliged to live on what is produced locally. Foods which at one time could be obtained only during a part of the year, can now be obtained all through the year and obtained more cheaply by being imported from foreign countries. Transport has raised the standard of living.

By moving fuel, raw materials, and even power, as, for example, through electric cables, transport has led to the establishment of industries and trade in areas where they would have been impossible before. Districts and countries can specialise and concentrate on making things which they can do better and cheaper than others and then exchanging with one another. The cheaper and quicker transport becomes the longer the distance over which goods can profitably be carried and the more it pays to specialise, to trade and to exchange. Countries with poor transport have a lower standard of living.

Commerce requires, not only the moving of goods and people, but also the carrying of messages and information. Means of communication, like telephones, cables and radio, send information about prices, supplies, and changing conditions in different parts of the world. Messages to ships and aircraft save time and prevent accidents and loss. Makers and consumers at opposite ends of the globe can get in touch with one another easily and quickly. Air travel enables representatives to reach potential foreign customers at once and to obtain orders that would otherwise be lost. A business can make the whole world its market.

When **railways** were built after 1830 they had a monopoly of land transport. For this reason they were not allowed to charge what they liked. Goods were divided into classes according to value. The more valuable the goods the more they cost to move by rail. Railways charged more for carrying one tonne of machinery for one kilometre than for carrying one tonne of coal for one kilometre, although the cost to the railways might have been the same in both cases. The rates had to be published and be the same for all users of the railways. They could not be increased without the consent of a Rates Tribunal, which is now known as the Transport Tribunal.

After 1918 road transport by motor vehicles developed rapidly and the railways no longer had a monopoly and began to lose traffic. In 1921 more than one hundred companies were compelled to combine into four big companies in order to secure the advantages of amalgamation described on pages 163–4. In 1947 railways were nationalised and formed into one system, but they continued to lose.

To enable the railways to compete on better terms with the roads, the old system of charging was abandoned in 1957. Railways now base their **charges** on the cost of carrying the goods and are free to quote any rates they like. Their overheads are very heavy. The expenses of getting the trains ready, signalling, repairing the track, etc., are the same for small as for big loads. It is therefore much cheaper per tonne per kilometre to move wagon loads and train loads for long distances than small lots for short distances because the overheads are spread over weight and distance.

With certain exceptions railways offer a choice between owner's risk rates and carrier's risk rates. C.R. rates are higher than O.R. rates, but they enable the consignor to claim for loss or damage.

Railways collect and deliver goods and a charge is made for this service, and also for the use of railway equipment such as cranes. The consignor can, if he likes, pay station-to-station rates and take the goods to the station himself and arrange for them to be collected at the destination station. Or he can arrange for the railway to do the cartage at one end only.

When the consignee is to collect the goods, the railway staff inform him when they have arrived by sending him an advice note. Unless he takes the goods away within a certain time, the railway will be losing income because the wagons will be kept idle, and to compensate them for this loss he will have to pay demurrage, or if the goods have to be stored at the stations he will be charged rent.

When goods are sent by goods train a **consignment note**, supplied by the railways, must be filled in. On it must be given particulars as to the weight and description of the goods, to whom they are sent, who pays the carriage and at which rates, owner's or railway's risk. The carman takes the note and signs the counterfoil which is retained by the consignor as a receipt for the goods. When delivering goods, the carman will obtain the signature of the person receiving them as evidence that the goods have been delivered. If the goods arrive damaged, the one signing for them in the delivery book should add a note to that effect after his signature.

Parcels weighing up to about fifty kilograms can be sent by **passenger train**. The rates are higher than for transport by freight train, but the parcels get to their destination more quickly which is important for mail and goods urgently required, for perishable products like fruit, and for newspapers that go out of date in a few hours.

Road transport has many advantages over railway transport. Motor vehicles can go anywhere where a road exists. They can go into the warehouse or factory for loading the goods and take them straight to the unloading point. Goods sent by rail must be taken to the station and there be unloaded, sorted and loaded on to the railway wagons, while at the end of the railway journey they must be unloaded and loaded again. Wagons and goods may be delayed in marshalling yards while they are taken off one train and added to another. This handling can be avoided by taking the goods all the way by road.

Roads are faster than railways for short journeys. Railways have the advantage in carrying big quantities of heavy, bulky goods for long distances. A crew of three at most can take 1500 tonnes in one train, but it would require 150 ten-tonne lorries and 150 men to move the same quantity in the same time by road. Road transport is handicapped by the lack of motorways and by traffic congestion in towns.

Some road carriers collect small parcels and sort them according to their destinations before handing them over in big lots to the railways which then allow them cheaper rates. Some run regular services between certain towns. Many specialise in furniture removal, or in bulk transport in full lorry loads of coal, liquids, etc. There is no standard consignment note in road transport.

A firm can buy lorries and vans and carry its own goods which then remain under its control during transport with less risk of theft and damage. It can send the goods as soon as they are ready, but if they were collected by the railways or by road carriers they might have to wait until trains or lorries were available and be delayed. The driver can deliver at several points on the route, collect the amount due, give receipts and bring back empty cases. The vehicles can advertise the owner's business.

These advantages must be weighed against the extra capital required and the charges of independent carriers. Unless the vehicles can be fully employed, it may be cheaper to use the railways or other carriers. These can spread expenses to a greater extent because they may have more work per vehicle and may carry goods from several consignors in the same vehicle and obtain return loads to share the cost of the outward and homeward journeys.

The railways are making **efforts to regain traffic from the roads**. They have won the right to charge in the same way as road carriers, i.e. on cost of service. This is more difficult for the railways to determine because they have so many fixed overheads incurred for the whole system. It is difficult to say, for example, how much of the wages paid to signalmen should be charged to a particular parcel. Their wages must be paid whether the trains are full or empty.

Handling and sorting have been reduced by stacking goods on large trays called **pallets**, and by packing them in big boxes called **containers** which can be lifted on to and off railway wagons and ships without being unpacked. As the consignors load the goods and seal the door-to-door containers which are not opened again until they reach the consignees, goods need not be so stoutly packed and the loss through damage and theft is reduced and insurance rates are lower.

Wooden wagons are being replaced by bigger steel wagons fitted with continuous brakes so that express goods trains can be run between important centres. Steam engines have given way to diesels, and electrification of main lines is proceeding. Many small collecting and delivering depots are to be replaced by one big modern depot at a 'railhead' which will collect and deliver over a radius of forty kilometres, thus reducing handling and transference of small lots from train to train. Marshalling yards are being modernised and better signalling introduced.

Some of the lines that do not pay are being closed and efforts concentrated on the main routes, more traffic being carried in trainloads between big towns. A firm that can send regular trainloads may do so in its own special wagons. Such 'block' or **'company' trains** carry, for example, oil from Southampton to Birmingham. For goods that cannot be moved in trainloads fast, long-distance **'liner' trains** carrying containers run regularly between big centres, such as Glasgow and London. There is no need to marshal these trains and the wagons are permanently coupled. The long, low, flat wagons make it easy for special cranes to load and unload containers.

The **National Freight Corporation** set up in 1969 is responsible for integrating British Road Services (the nationalised section of road transport) and its associated firms with rail services. It decides whether goods brought to its depots by road should be sent forward by road or be transferred to the railways. It deals with railway 'retail traffic' in wagon loads. It collects and delivers parcels and sundries (consignments of less than one tonne) and controls most of the freightliner traffic. Wholesale traffic, in bigger lots and in trainloads, is the concern of the Railways Board.

Iron, steel, coal and coke provide most of the **railway freight** which totals more than 200 million tonnes a year carried for an average distance of 112 kilometres. Road vehicles move about 1500 million tonnes a year for an average haul of 45 kilometres, over half the weight being carried by the consignors' own vehicles. Tonne-kilometres, obtained by multiplying the weight by the distance, show that roads are now doing three times as much work as the railways.

Over 50 per cent of **railway receipts** come from freight traffic, over 10 per cent from parcels and mails, and over 30 per cent from passengers.

While railways have won greater freedom, road haulage has become subject to more regulation. Vehicles are taxed to pay for the roads which are provided for them, the railways having to build their own tracks, and there are regulations about safety, insurance, etc. The country is divided into regions under licensing authorities; these authorities consider applications for **licences** from road hauliers. Vehicles weighing not more than $1\frac{1}{2}$ tonnes unladen do not require a licence, but all others must have an operator's licence. Railways and the National Freight Corporation have the right to oppose the granting of a licence to a newcomer on the grounds that there is not enough work for another carrier in the area they serve and that they already provide satisfactory services at reasonable prices, but the decision whether or not to grant a licence rests with the licensing authority. Passenger transport is also licensed.

Questions

1. Why can transport be described as productive? Why is it a branch of commerce?

2. What benefits have resulted from better methods of transport?

3. Describe the contribution of the railways to Britain's commercial life. (A.E.B.)

4. Why have the railways lost traffic to the roads? In what ways are they meeting competition from the roads?

5. How would you account for the very large quantity of goods now being carried in Britain by road transport? Do you consider this advantageous to commerce and industry? (R.S.A.)

6. If the estimated cost of transporting a particular commodity by road is 3p per kilometre and it would cost $2\frac{1}{2}$p per kilometre if the railways were used how far would this influence your choice of transport? (A.E.B.)

7. Give examples of three types of goods which are sent by (*a*) passenger train, (*b*) goods train. Why in such cases are these methods preferred to transport by road? (W.J.E.C.)

8. What are the advantages and disadvantages of the liner train system? Candidates may wish to use the following headings in their answers: (*a*) why introduced, (*b*) liner train routes and timings, (*c*) speed of delivery, (*d*) effect on cost, (*e*) possible advantages. (A.E.B.)

9. How do containers and pallets reduce the cost of transport by road and rail?

10. Why do so many traders obtain their own vehicles instead of using the services provided by firms of road carriers and by railways?

11. Write notes on consignment notes, demurrage, road vehicle licensing, block or company trains, C.R. and O.R. rates, the National Freight Corporation.

12. A manufacturer with nation-wide sales has the choice of either operating his own fleet of road vehicles or hiring the services of a road transport firm.

    Describe the advantages and drawbacks to the manufacturer of each choice. (L.C.C. & I.)

13. In the 1960s and 1970s a study of the index of tonne miles for inland goods transported shows that road transport has been gaining freight, the railways losing it. What advantages does road transport possess that might account for this?

    What transport policies have been adopted to reverse this trend? (A.L.S.E.B.)

14. What factors should be considered in choosing to dispatch goods by either road or rail transport? (L.C.C. & I.)

Chapter 38

Transport · Canal · Sea · Air · Common carriers

Water transport is cheaper than land transport. A horse can pull in a barge a load many times heavier than the load it can pull in a cart. Although Britain was the first to develop canals, transport by canal is not so important in this country as it is on the Continent. Belgian and French canals which are wider, deeper and longer, carry five and six times as much as British canals. In some countries the governments have helped the canals by adjusting the railway rates so that the canals can obtain a good share of the traffic.

British waterways are divided into broad waterways and narrow canals. The broad waterways, mainly canalised rivers, can take boats with up to 400 tonnes and the Manchester Ship Canal and the Caledonian Canal can take seagoing vessels. Most of the narrow canals constructed before the days of railways which captured some of their traffic, take barges carrying only about 25 tonnes. These barges travel in pairs, a motor barge towing a 'dumb' barge. The canals are so narrow that barges cannot travel at more than 10 kilometres per hour in case the wash destroys the banks. A pair of barges can carry more than a lorry, but a lorry can make several journeys in the time a barge takes to make one.

Canals cannot go everywhere like roads. They must be level and any change in level means building locks which cause delay to barges passing through. In Britain the canals and locks vary a good deal in size, so that only a very small barge can travel right across the country. In winter there is the possibility of the water freezing and bringing traffic to a standstill for days at a time.

Canals, in following a level course, may take a longer route than roads or railways. Businesses not situated on the canal banks may in any case employ road or rail transport for a part of the journey. For short journeys the expense of transferring goods from one vehicle to the other at either end of the journey may mean that the goods are carried all the way by road or rail. Where barges can travel right up to a ship for loading and unloading over the side, port charges and handling expenses may be saved.

Canal traffic is mainly in goods which are heavy and for which speed is not important. Canals are also suitable for goods which cannot stand a lot of jolting, such as pottery. Coal accounts for about half the weight they carry. Oil, grain, flour, metals, timber, sand, cement, pottery and chemicals are their other main cargoes. Inland waterways carry about 8 million tonnes a year for an average distance of 20 kilometres. Tonne-kilometres show that the railways do 150 times as much work as the waterways.

Canal-owners carry only a small proportion of the goods, most of which are transported by independent carriers. These carriers pay tolls for the use of the canals and their **charges** for carrying must be low enough to compete with road and rail transport. Until 1963 the tolls were controlled by law and were not the same for all canals, each canal company having obtained its own Act of Parliament when it was formed. Generally, the tolls were based on the value of the goods carried, the goods being placed in one of eight classes, the most valuable attracting the highest tolls. They tapered up to 48 kilometres so that the longer the journey the cheaper per kilometre were the average tolls. Canal-owners are now free to charge as they like for the use of the canals and alterations in the toll system are being considered. They may also charge for collecting and delivering, for the use of equipment, for loading and unloading, for storing goods in their warehouses, and for supplying water to factories and farms. They also operate four ports.

Narrow canals now carry very little and are being used more and more for pleasure, anglers and boat-owners paying for a licence to use them. To enlarge and improve them would be a very costly undertaking especially in built-up areas.

After being advised of the load, the carrier obtains a declaration and permit from the Waterways Board. On one part of this form the carrier declares particulars of the load and journey. The other part, which states the tolls due, is also a permit allowing the boat named to travel on the canal, and is completed by the canal officials. Two copies are kept by the officials and one is given to the boatman who can use it as a delivery note.

In 1947 railways and the docks which they owned, British Road Services, and most canals were nationalised. At present the Railways Board is responsible for the railways, the Docks Board for the former railway docks, and the Waterways Board for the nationalised canals and their four docks.

Sea transport is most important for the British Isles that import and export so much. Ships can go almost anywhere across the sea, but require expensive installations at both ends of the voyage. **Tramps** are vessels that go wherever they can obtain cargo, while **liners** sail on a fixed 'line' or route calling at certain ports only and sailing at fixed times whether the ship is full or not. Liners are usually bigger and faster than tramps and often carry passengers as well as general cargo. Tramps take cargoes of coal, ores, wheat, timber, rice, etc., in bulk. **Tankers** are ships which are specially built for carrying liquids. Many are owned by the oil companies which also charter tankers, sometimes for a period of several years.

When goods are delivered to a ship the shipper is given a signed **bill of lading** admitting that the goods have been received and setting forth the terms upon which they are to be carried. The bill must be sent to the importer who must produce it when claiming the goods at the destination port.

Shipowners have formed associations in order to protect and further their common interests. It is much easier for liner companies working on the same routes to do so, than it is for the more numerous tramp-owners whose ships sail the seven seas. Liner-owners organise **conferences** for fixing the rates to be charged. As they give shippers a regular service, their ships sailing irrespective of the amount of cargo received, it is essential that the shippers use the service whenever they have goods to be carried, and not take advantage of a lower rate that may be offered now and then by a shipowner who does not provide a regular service. To encourage them to use the same line, a rebate is allowed to those who have been loyal to one line during the period.

Rail and road transport can adjust the number and size of the vehicles to suit the load. A liner cannot alter its capacity and its expenses are incurred for the ship as a whole whether it is full or empty. The cargo it can take is limited both as to weight and volume. If the charge were so much per tonne, and the holds were filled with light bulky goods, earnings would be less than if some heavy goods were carried as well. On the other hand, a cargo of heavy goods, taking up little room but weighing as much as the ship can safely carry, would leave empty space earning nothing.

Liners charge, therefore, on a weight or volume basis, selecting the method that gives the higher freight (or charge). If one cubic metre is taken as equal to one tonne, a case measuring one cubic metre, but weighing less than a tonne, will be charged on volume and rated as if it were a tonne. If it weighed two tonnes it would be charged on weight. The rates are port to port rates, e.g. wooden doors from a United Kingdom port to Cape Town, £13.80 per tonne. Certain expensive goods like jewellery and furs are charged on value, if this gives more freight than weight or volume, while others, like insulin, are always charged on value. When a package contains different kinds of articles, the rate applicable to the article that gives the highest freight is applied to the whole package. A bill for the amount of the freight, called the 'freight note', is sent to the shipper.

Liners charge what the traffic will bear, i.e. they charge as much as they can without losing traffic. The rates are determined by the Conference which may alter them at any time. Unlike railway rates, they have never been controlled by a tribunal because the ships of all owners, and of all countries, can go to any port and compete against one another, and, if necessary, they will reduce rates in order to get cargoes.

Liner companies advertise their services and usually make their own arrangements for obtaining **cargo**, having offices and agents in important centres. Their ships always take on cargo at the same ports. The cargo is general cargo, made up of a large number of consignments received from different exporters. Tramps take cargo in bulk at any port where it may be available. The liner is certain of some cargo for the outward and homeward journeys, but a tramp may have to travel in ballast from one port to another in order to pick up another load. Tramp-owners must get in touch with shippers of bulk cargoes all over the world. They do so by employing specialist middlemen.

The owner of a tramp seeking work for his ship informs a shipping broker, who is a member of a Shipping Exchange. The **Baltic Exchange**, London, is the world's greatest freight market. On the floor of the Exchange the broker meets other brokers who have been instructed to secure ships for moving cargoes in bulk, and he is almost certain to find one who has suitable cargo to offer and who is prepared to pay a rate acceptable to the shipowner. He then arranges a 'fixture' for the tramp. Tramp freight rates are a result of bargaining between the brokers and vary much more than liner rates.

As the cargo is usually enough to fill the vessel the whole ship together with its crew is hired. The agreement is set forth in the **Charter Party**, drawn up according to the rules of the Exchange. A Voyage Charter hires the ship for a particular voyage, while a Time Charter hires it for a certain period. When the cargo is loaded, a bill of lading is used, even though the ship has been chartered.

Containers are of great importance to shipping. A ship wants a quick turn-round. While in port it earns nothing, but incurs expenses totalling hundreds of pounds per day. Unless the cargo is unloaded within an agreed number of days, known as 'lay days', its owner must pay demurrage. It takes much less time and labour for cranes to load and unload containers full of packages than it does to handle and record those packages one by one. To stow containers, standardised in shape and size, in ships specially built for them is much quicker and cheaper than to stow their contents separately. Ships spend less time in port and make more voyages and earn more in a year. As containers can be transferred without being unpacked from or to road and rail vehicles at either end of the voyage, they make through door-to-door transport quicker and cheaper.

For short journeys across the Channel, handling costs are reduced by trailers rolling-on at one end of the journey and rolling-off at the other to continue the journey by road. Hovercraft and hydrofoils are at present used mainly for passengers.

For a country with a long coastline and no part being far from the sea, **coastal shipping** is important. It can compete with road and rail traffic and it can ask the Minister of Transport to stop railways taking away its traffic by charging unfair rates below the cost of carriage.

British coasters sail mainly from ports on Tyneside, the Bristol Channel and Merseyside. More than half their cargoes are destined for London. They carry over 50 million tonnes a year, 80 per cent of which is made up by oil, coal and coke, the rest consisting mainly of minerals, cement and cereals. If we take into account that the average haul is 320 kilometres against the railways' 112, coastal vessels do about two-thirds as much work as the railways.

Coasters are losing traffic to roads and railways. Lorries and trains can pick up loads wherever they become available and deliver at many more points than coasters, which are confined to the ports. Most cargoes must in any case be carried overland for a part of the journey.

The perils of the sea make insurance a very important matter for ship and cargo-owners as we shall see in the next chapter.

Air transport has so far been used mainly for passengers. Goods are carried in the same liners as passengers, as well as in all cargo planes. The great **advantages** of air transport are speed, particularly where distances are long, and the ability to carry in any direction, over land and sea, without breaking bulk at the coast. Goods sent by air need not be so stoutly packed as goods sent by sea, and because of the shorter travelling time there is less risk of theft and damage. For these reasons insurance rates are lower, and the expenses of handling, storing and port dues are less than for sea transport. The lighter packing may save customs duties when these are levied on gross weight. The speed at which supplies can be obtained reduces the capital that need be locked up in reserve stocks and makes a bigger and faster turnover possible. The documents required are fewer and simpler than for sea transport.

The document setting forth the terms of carriage and giving particulars of the goods is the 'air consignment note' or 'waybill', three copies being required, one for the consignor, one for the carrier and one which the carrier must deliver with the goods to the consignee. It is not a document of title.

Some of the **disadvantages** are that costly airfields are required and bad weather may restrict flying. The airfields are usually situated on the outskirts of towns, and, as they are comparatively few in number, goods may have to be taken a long way by surface transport before and after the flight. For transport within a small country this is a disadvantage, but for export trade the airports may be nearer than the seaports, and on long flights time lost in travelling to and from the airfields can be made up.

Compared with land and water carriage, air transport is expensive, although in some cases it may be cheaper when allowance is made for savings in packing, stocks and insurance. A big plane can carry more than a lorry, but it cannot take anything like the weight and bulk that can be transported by a train or a ship. Air cargo is made up mainly of expensive goods of small weight and volume, such as machines and gold for which transport is a small part of the total cost. British air services, including their foreign services, do less than 2 per cent of the railway tonne-kilometres.

Charges for air transport, like those for ocean liners, are based on weight or volume, the cargo which an aircraft can carry being limited in both respects. The method yielding the higher freight is selected, 7000 cubic centimetres being reckoned as equal to 1 kilogram. Air liner rates, unlike ocean liner rates, are not affected by the value of the goods. Air lines, like shipping lines, agree on the rates to be charged on various routes. Over 100 air lines are members of the International Air Transport Association which determines the rates.

Rates are divided into three classes. General commodity rates are the same for all goods between the same two airports. Shippers of goods which are sent regularly and in sufficient quantities may be granted lower rates known as specific commodity rates. These rates are different for different goods and apply only between specified airports and usually only in one

Means of cargo transport

	Suitable for	Advantages	Disadvantages	Other details
Roads	All types of goods	Swift; direct; Specialised vehicles: tankers, tip lorries transporters, etc. Door-to-door	Comparatively small quantity per vehicle	Partial nationalisation: National Freight Corporation to integrate road and rail services; use of containers
Railways	All types of goods	Huge quantities moved in one train	Goods must be moved to and from station unless there is a private siding	1947 — Nationalisation. Easy inter-city service, company trains, car transporters, tankers, containers
Canals and Rivers	Heavy cargo Bulk liquid Pottery	Direct links; smooth journey; economical if geographically convenient	Slow; locks; canals may freeze in winter	Nationalised 1947; under control of British Waterways Board. Big ships can use Manchester Ship Canal and Caledonian Canal

	Suitable for	Advantages	Disadvantages	Other details
Air	Gold, diamonds, other precious goods, delicate machinery, live animals, perishable foods	Swift; less handling; cargo does not 'break bulk' at the coasts	Costly; bad weather may affect flying; amount of weight restricted	2 nationalised airlines —BOAC and BEA combined to form British Airways. Other (independent) air carriers
Sea	Liners	Follow scheduled routes ('lines'); liner companies fix rates at Conferences; obtain cargoes through own offices and agents throughout the world		
	Tramps	Call at any port to pick up cargo; charter parties; obtain cargoes through shipping brokers at shipping exchanges (e.g. Baltic Exchange in London)		
	Coastal shipping	Suitable for heavy cargo moving between ports. Economical if geographically convenient		

direction. On main routes most of the cargo is carried at specific rates. Class rates are the highest and apply to special cargo, like bullion and live animals needing special care.

There are several 'breakpoints' in some rates so that the bigger the consignment the lower the rate. Agents who collect goods from several consignors and forward them 'grouped' on one set of documents can obtain these lower rates and pass on some of the saving to the consignors. There are big reductions in the charges for goods shipped in one of the standard containers or pallets specified by the air lines.

Air lines will collect and deliver, store, insure and forward goods by suitable transport from the terminal airport, and in some cases provide a C.O.D. service. Extra charges are made for these services.

British Airways is the name of the organisation which resulted from the amalgamation of British European Airways (BEA) and British Overseas Air Corporation (BOAC) in 1971. Details of its constitution and responsibilities can be found in Chapter 40 (Nationalised industries).

There are also about forty independent air companies in Britain, operating on routes not served by British Airways. These companies arrange to carry cargo wherever it becomes available (as ocean tramps do), and to do special work such as spraying crops. Air services must be licensed by the **Civil Aviation Authority**.

The Baltic Exchange is the main air charter market, the rates being settled by the air brokers. Passenger fares on regular domestic routes are controlled by the CAA. The **British Airways Board** governs the nationalised lines.

Pipelines exist for moving liquids like oil. A network of pipelines from the refineries to the main population centres already exists and is being extended. It has been calculated that the annual tonnage of oil moved in this way is equal to about one-tenth of the work done by the railways.

In the last few years, with the development of the North Sea oilfields, extensive submarine pipelines have been laid, to bring the crude oil ashore to the refineries. Details of this important new development in Britain's industrial resources can be found in Chapter 40 (Nationalised industries).

A person who is ready to carry goods for anybody is a **common carrier** who, under the Carriers Act, has certain rights and obligations. He must accept the goods if he has room for them and they are the kind of goods he professes to carry. He must take them by the shortest or usual route and deliver them in a reasonable time. While the goods are in his possession he must take care of them and he is liable for any loss the owner suffers as a result of negligence on his part or on the part of his employees. He has a right to demand payment in advance, having a lien on the goods until his charges are paid, i.e. he can keep the goods until he has received what is due to him. When goods like jewellery and furs are sent and they are over £10 in value, the carrier must be told what the goods are. He then has the right to charge more than the usual rates, because in taking charge of the goods he is running a bigger risk. In all cases the goods must be suitably packed if the carrier is to be held responsible for the damage.

The majority of carriers are not common or public carriers, but private carriers. They reserve the right to choose the loads that pay best and to refuse the others.

Questions

1. Discuss the relative advantages of the different forms of transport available for the carriage of goods in Britain. (L.C.C. & I.)

2. How important are canals in Britain's transport system? Discuss their contribution in relation to other methods of transport which are available as alternatives. (A.E.B.)
   (Consider tonne-kilometres, goods carried, speed, routes, cost.)

3. Describe the services provided by 'coasters', 'tramps', 'cargo liners' and 'liners'. How do shippers arrange for the carriage of their exports and imports, and how are the freight charges determined? (R.S.A.)

4. (a) How is the hire of a tramp steamer arranged? What would be three of the main conditions of the contract of hire?
   (b) Why would a tramp steamer be used for the transport of timber from Quebec to Cardiff, whereas machinery exported from Liverpool to Montreal would probably be sent by cargo liner? (W.J.E.C.)

5. Describe three methods of transport used by business organisations, giving details of the types of goods carried by each method. (S.R.E.B.)

6. What are the advantages and disadvantages of air transport?

7. An increasing quantity of goods is being transported by air but the greak bulk of the foreign trade of the United Kingdom continues to be by sea. How do you account for these facts? (W.J.E.C.)

8. What are the current and future effects of the 'container revolution' in transport? (A.E.B.)

9. Describe how charges for transport by rail, road, sea, canal and air are determined.

10. Air transport carries only 13 per cent of the *value* of our imports and exports. The cargo of greatest value is easily machinery, including electrical machines. Then come non-metallic mineral manufactures, clothing and footwear, non-ferrous metals, scientific instruments, transport equipment and spare parts, chemicals and medicinal products. Why are these goods particularly suitable for air transport? (Deal first with common features, e.g. all are valuable.)

11. State with reasons which means of transport you would employ in the following cases. Consider points of departure and arrival, (e.g. Swansea and Plymouth are ports), size of load, are the goods perishable or not, the distance, the urgency, the speed, the cost.

   Timber, 40 tonnes, London to Birmingham
   Fruit, 300 kilograms, Evesham to Gloucester
   Coal, 1000 tonnes, Swansea to Plymouth
   China clay, 100 tonnes, Falmouth to the Potteries
   Steel girders, 10 tonnes, Newcastle to Carlisle
   Milk, 6000 litres, Somerset to London
   Petrol, 20 000 litres, Liverpool to Chester
   Films, 10, New York to London

12. Write briefly on: common carriers, the Baltic Exchange, the Channel Tunnel, coastal steamers.

13. Write on the importance of pipelines as a means of transport in Britain. Why have pipelines increased in importance and in extent recently? Mention the important centres of industrial and commercial activity that they connect.

14. In connection with the transport of goods by sea:

    (*a*) Distinguish between a charter party and a bill of lading.
    (*b*) Why is it that a charter party is only sometimes required whereas a bill of lading is always required?
    (*c*) Why is a bill of lading sometimes used in banking transactions?

    (U.C.L.E.S.)

15. In deciding which method of transportation of goods is to be used there are a number of factors to be considered. Explain briefly six of them.
    Which form of transportation would you choose for each of the following? State why you chose it.

    (*a*) A valuable small picture urgently needed for an exhibition in New York.
    (*b*) Heavy drilling machinery to be sent to Saudi Arabia.
    (*c*) Ten tonnes of coal to be delivered to the other end of your county.
    (*d*) A small packet to be sent to Inverness.   (S.R.E.B.)

Chapter 39

Insurance · Classes of insurance · Lloyd's

Another aid to trade is insurance, by means of which some of the **risks** incurred in business can be overcome. The risks run by a retailer include risk of loss through fire, burglary, broken plate-glass windows, injuries to his assistants in the course of their work and accidents involving his delivery van. The loss, even in a small business, might run into several thousands of pounds, and many would be unwilling to undertake a business venture unless they could protect themselves by means of insurance. 'Insurance' refers to events which may happen, like fire, and 'assurance' to events which must happen, such as death.

Insurance is based on the principle of the fortunate helping the unfortunate. It is known from past records that every year a certain number of houses are destroyed by fire, but which particular houses they will be is not known. All house-owners run the risk of loss through fire. If all of them pay a small sum each year into a fund, anyone who does lose his house can draw enough money from the fund to build another. Instead of the loss being borne by one man, it is shared between a large number. People are willing to lose a small sum in order to be certain that they will not lose a much bigger sum. The sum that is paid in order to be insured is called the **premium**, and the agreement whereby the insured promise to do this and the insurers promise to pay out so much if a certain event happens is called the **policy**.

The purpose of insurance is to compensate for loss and not the making of profit (although the companies that carry on the business may make a profit). If my house is destroyed by fire, I shall suffer a loss, but if your house is destroyed that will cause no loss to me, i.e. I have no **insurable interest** in your house and I have no right to insure it. If I did insure it, I may be tempted to set it on fire deliberately in order to obtain the insurance money and make a profit. Similarly, I might be tempted to kill a man whose death would cause me no loss, if I were allowed to insure him. Insurable interest must exist before one has the right to insure anything.

Statistics are essential for insurance. They provide the information that insurance companies must have in order to run their businesses successfully. If an insurance company is asked to insure people against accidents, it must be able to foretell the approximate numbers of such accidents in order to charge a premium that will be enough to meet the claims and expenses and leave something for profit. Official records show that between 600 and 700 people are killed on the roads each month. From these figures the companies can estimate what claims will be made on them and decide upon a suitable premium. For the same purpose the companies collect records of fires in different kinds of buildings and revise the premiums if necessary.

Statistics of births and deaths are essential for life assurance. From the records of a series of years, tables can be compiled showing the expectation of life for any age. For persons aged 30 now, the expectation of life is 40 years. Some of these people will die in a year, others in two years, and so on until they are all dead, but the average time they will live will be 40 years. If 10 of these people take out a whole life policy for £100 each, the company knows that it will have to pay out £1000 in the future. It also knows that the number of premiums it can expect to receive from the 10 assured is equal to 40 per person. If it charges a premium of £1.75 a year it will receive a total of £700. The premiums are invested and the compound interest earned must be added to the total of the premiums. £17.50 invested each year for 40 years would, at 5 per cent per annum, amount to over £2100, enough to pay the claims and leave something for expenses and profit. The actual calculation is complicated, being done by experts known as 'actuaries'.

Before issuing a policy an insurance company will require information about what is to be insured. This information is given on a **proposal form**. The questions asked must be answered truthfully. Insurance must always be conducted with the **utmost good faith**. All information that may assist the insurers to judge the risk correctly must be given. The older a person is the greater the risk that he will die soon, so that if he states on the proposal form that he is several years younger than he is in fact, he is deceiving the insurance company into charging him a lower premium and the company need not pay the claim. Suppose that cans of petrol were sometimes kept in a building and this fact was withheld from the insurance company. Later, the building was destroyed by a fire which broke out when no petrol cans were on the premises. If the insurance company discovers that information about the petrol cans had been withheld, it can refuse to make good the damage, although the fire was not in any way caused by the petrol. The presence of petrol increased the risk of fire, and had the company known this it might have charged a higher premium.

There are many branches of insurance, but we shall deal briefly with only a few of them.

Life assurance gives protection against loss caused by death. There are two main kinds of policies. One is a **whole life policy**, whereby the premiums must be paid as long as the assured person lives. The other is an **endowment policy**, which states that premiums must be paid until death, or in any case for not more than a certain number of years. Many people prefer an endowment policy because they know then how much they must pay in premiums at most and they can arrange for the policy to fall due at a time when they may need to spend money, e.g. to spend on the education of children or to buy a new machine when the present one is worn out. The endowment policy is a useful method of saving for a known future expense.

A person who takes out a whole life policy on his own life will never receive the money himself, but if he takes out an endowment policy he may live longer than the maximum period for which he has to pay premiums and so be alive to receive the money himself. The disadvantage of an endowment policy is that the premium per £100 assured is greater than for a whole life policy, because the insurance company is likely to receive fewer premiums when the policy is taken out for a certain number of years only, instead of for life.

Both whole life and endowment policies can be with or without profits. On a with profits policy for £1000, the company may pay out more than £1000 because the assured is entitled to a share of the profits made by the company. How much will be received depends on how much profit is made. A without profits policy will realise only £1000. The premiums for a with profits policy are, of course, higher than those for a without profits policy.

If the premium is not paid when due, the policy **lapses**, i.e. it becomes void, and the assured loses all rights in connection with it, and the sums he has already paid. This can be avoided by borrowing money to pay the premiums, the policy being given as security. The insurance companies are prepared to lend money at interest to enable the premiums to be paid or to alter the policy. They will also accept surrender of the policy when the assured gives it up and obtains back a proportion of the premiums he has paid.

Insurance gives **indemnity** to the insured, i.e. it makes up his loss, and no more than the loss. When a house insured for £40 000 suffers damage by fire to the extent of £4000, £4000 is the sum the company will pay. If the insured could claim more, he could make a profit by deliberately setting his house on fire. Assessors are employed to value the damage. When a policy contains an 'average clause', the property must be insured for its full value before the owner can claim for all the damage. If the house mentioned above, worth £40 000, had been insured for £20 000, only £2000 would have been paid for the damage because only half the real value had been insured. Had it been insured for one-quarter of its value then only one-quarter of the damage would have been paid. Some fire policies provide for the insuring of 'consequential losses', such as the profits which may be lost as the result of a fire.

In life assurance, however, the sum assured is paid in full, because it is very often impossible to measure the loss one person suffers through the death of another.

Third party motor insurance is compulsory for the owners of road motor vehicles. The third party is anyone who may suffer injury as a result of an accident caused by the vehicle. The other two parties are the owner of the vehicle and the insurance company who make the agreement. Many owners could not pay compensation which may amount to £20 000 or more. To make certain that the third party and passengers will receive compensation, the owner must insure them, so that the company pays instead of the owner. The owner can, if he likes, insure other risks, such as injury to himself or the loss of his car. A comprehensive policy covers all risks that a company will take and which are listed in the policy.

A **Fidelity guarantee** policy is used in cases where a person is appointed to a position of trust which gives him the opportunity to embezzle. It gives the employer the right to claim from the insurance company any sums stolen by the employee.

Marine insurance deals with risks connected with the sea. The chief place for taking out policies is **Lloyd's** of London, so called after the owner of a coffee-house who obtained information about ships for the marine insurers who used to meet in his coffee-house. Lloyd's is the name of an association of people who find it convenient to carry on their businesses in the same place, all of them sharing the expenses.

There are over 6000 members grouped into syndicates, each syndicate carrying on business on its own. Every member of a syndicate has unlimited liability for his share of any loss, and on becoming a member he must deposit security which in case of need can be used to meet claims against the syndicate. Like the Stock Exchange, Lloyd's is prepared to compensate those whose claims cannot be met by the syndicate which undertook the risk.

All members of a syndicate do not work on the Exchange. They choose one member to carry on the business for them and pay him for doing so. These men representing the syndicates are the **underwriters** who write their names under the policy. A shipowner who wishes **to insure at Lloyd's** must ask an insurance broker to do it for him. The broker writes details of the insurance required on a 'slip' and takes it to Lloyd's. To have all the underwriters in one place is advantageous to brokers as well as to underwriters. Competition among the underwriters keeps the rates low. The underwriters have their own places or 'boxes' in the Exchange, and the broker knows where he can find those who are likely to offer the best rates for the insurance he wants. If not satisfied with the first offer, he can, without wasting time in travelling, approach other underwriters.

The first underwriter to accept the risk or part of it is called the 'lead'. He signs the slip and states the sum which he is willing to risk. If this sum does not cover the insurance required the broker submits the slip to another underwriter who may be more ready to accept when he sees that a lead has been obtained. Several underwriters may be approached before the 'lines', or sums stated opposite each underwriter's name, total the amount required. In the event of a claim, each syndicate is liable to pay out these sums. Underwriters who think that they have undertaken too big a risk may reinsure some of it with other underwriters. Reinsurance prevents very heavy losses falling on any one syndicate.

After obtaining the necessary signatures the broker prepares a cover note giving particulars and the premiums to send to his client, who may accept or refuse. If he agrees, the broker makes out the policy and has it checked and signed at Lloyd's Signing Office. He then sends his client a debit note for the premiums and expenses due. The broker is not paid by the client, but is allowed a commission by the underwriters.

In order to judge the risks involved, the underwriters must know details of the ship they are asked to insure, its machinery, its age, etc. For this purpose they use Lloyd's **Register of Shipping**, prepared by an independent organisation composed of representatives of underwriters, shipowners and others interested in shipping. The ships are classified according to reports made by inspectors and a ship built according to their recommendations can be insured for a lower premium. Agents all over the world send information about ships and their sailings to Lloyd's.

Lloyd's underwriters accept all classes of insurance from any country, except whole life assurance. As the members of a syndicate may change, a Lloyd's policy does not cover more than three years so that newcomers are not made responsible for risks undertaken a long time ago by other underwriters.

Insurance companies which are not members of Lloyd's also insure marine risks. It is not necessary to employ brokers when dealing with these.

Employers must pay compensation to employees injured while carrying out their duties. Employers' **accident liability** insurance gives protection against this risk. Customers, too, may claim compensation. Ladies' hairdressers, for example, insure against causing injuries to their customers.

Sometimes people join together to arrange their own insurance scheme, the policyholders electing and appointing officers and staff to manage the business. This is known as **mutual insurance**. A group of business men may cooperate to run a mutual insurance scheme for risks that Lloyd's and the insurance companies will not accept.

Industrial insurance is a branch of life assurance in which premiums are collected by agents at intervals of two months or less. The policies were intended mainly for the provision of burial expenses and were for small amounts. Although there is now less need to make such provision, because National Insurance gives a grant towards burial expenses, industrial insurance has continued to grow, because it is a convenient means of saving for known future expenses.

Assurance and insurance

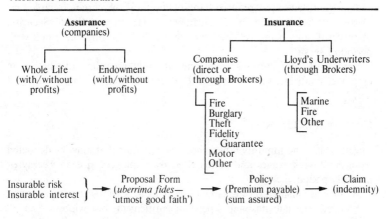

The **National Insurance Scheme** in Britain is financed by contributions made by both employers and employees. Contributions are related to the earnings of employees and are collected under the same procedure as is used for income tax (P.A.Y.E.). This arrangement came into force on 6 April 1975 (under the Social Security Acts of 1973–4) and it replaced the former system of sticking insurance stamps on employees' cards. The total contribution consists of two parts: the employee's contribution and the employer's contribution.

Employees' contributions are at one of two rates:

(*a*) Standard rate payable by most employees;
(*b*) Reduced rate payable by certain married women and by most widows entitled to National Insurance widow's benefit.

Employees who are not liable for contributions include:

(*a*) Men over 65 and women over 60 who have retired for National Insurance purposes;
(*b*) Men over 65 and women over 60 who have not retired and at age 65 (or 60) did not qualify for a retirement pension on their own contributions;
(*c*) All men over 70 and women over 65.

Employees may be contracted out of part of the new scheme if they are members of an occupational pension scheme providing equally good benefits. The State scheme has a 'ceiling' in employees' earnings (at present just over £4000 per annum), and those contracted out are protected by the State scheme up to that level and by the employer's scheme for that part of their salary which is above that level.

Contributions are calculated on gross pay, but certain emoluments such as benefits in kind, expenses, gratuities, redundancy payments and pensions are not included in the gross pay figure.

Those entitled to pay reduced liability and those who are non-liable may obtain certificates from the Department of Health and Social Security, these certificates being retained by the employer during the employee's period of service.

Employers' contributions are at one rate only, regardless of whether an employee contributes at the standard or reduced rate, or is non-liable.

Contribution tables

These weekly and monthly tables show the amounts that must be deducted from employees' wages and contributed by employers in each weekly or monthly period.

Women are insured on the same basis as men. A widow's pension works out to half the late husband's pension entitlement, but widows over 50 years of age and widowed mothers may inherit their late husband's total pension entitlement.

Self-employed persons are also included in the scheme: their contribution is at a special rate.

Non-employed persons are not compelled to contribute. If they decide to do so, they generally qualify for the same range of benefits as are available to working contributors.

Benefits

The retirement pension is payable at age 65 for men and 60 for women and works out to approximately half the annual pay being earned prior to retirement, the best twenty years of an employee's earnings being used to calculate the pension.

Other benefits include cash payments during periods of sickness and unemployment, and for women for a certain number of weeks before and after the birth of a child, widows' pensions, death grants and compensation for injury.

Questions

1. 'Insurance companies constitute an important section of commerce.' Discuss the work of such companies and state on what principles insurance is based.
   (R.S.A.)

2. Compare and contrast whole life and endowment assurance.

3. (*a*) Why is it possible for A to insure:

   (i) Against loss by fire, but not against loss which is the result of bad management?
   (ii) Against loss by fire to A's premises, but not against loss by fire to B's premises?

   (*b*) A effects a fire insurance on his stock for £4000. One half of the stock is completely destroyed; the replacement value is £3000. State with your reasons how much A might recover under his insurance policy.   (U.C.L.E.S.)

4. How does the insurance company fix the premium you have to pay? (M.R.E.B.)

5. Mr Blank would like to insure for £2000 his mini-van which cost £600. He uses it for private journeys as well as for business. Bearing in mind the terms 'indemnity' and 'utmost good faith' advise Mr Blank as to his insurance position.   (A.E.B.)

6. Write a paragraph on each of the following:

   (*a*) The importance of Lloyd's insurance exchange to Britain's commerce.
   (*b*) The work of actuaries.
   (*c*) Fidelity Guarantee.
   (*d*) The work of assessors.

7. A shopkeeper employs assistants to help in the shop and has a van for delivery work. Describe four risks against which the trader should insure his business. Write fully.   (S.R.E.B.)

8. (*a*) Find the premiums payable by a retailer who insures against the risk of fire to his premises valued at £5000 at 7p per cent and to his stock valued at £6500 at 20p per cent.
    (*b*) State three other insurable risks of a retailer.
    (*c*) Indicate his other risks which are uninsurable and explain why they are uninsurable. (W.J.E.C.)

9. What is Lloyd's? Who works there? What kind of policies can be obtained there?

10. Describe how a ship is insured at Lloyd's. Mention the documents involved.

11. What is covered by a full-time adult worker's National Insurance contributions? Is such a person likely to take out personal insurance in addition? Give reasons. (M.R.E.B.)

12. Explain third party, Register of Shipping, industrial insurance, mutual insurance.

13. (*a*) What is the purpose of insurance?
    (*b*) List the main types of insurance available.
    (*c*) Explain the importance of (i) life assurance, (ii) household insurance.
    (W.J.E.C.)

14. Mr Lewis wishes to insure against fire in his village shop, with a thatched roof, for £15 000.

    (*a*) Name the **three** principles of insurance involved in taking out cover on such property.
    (*b*) Explain how each principle works in this case.
    (*c*) Name **one** risk against which Mr Lewis cannot insure. State a reason.
    (M.R.E.B.)

15. Describe the *purpose* of each of the following documents used in insurance: (*a*) proposal form, (*b*) policy, (*c*) renewal notice.
    Explain how statistics are important to insurance companies. (A.E.B.)

16. Describe the means of (*a*) chartering a ship to transport a bulk consignment, (*b*) insuring the ship and cargo. (L.C.C. & I.)

Chapter 40

Nationalised industries · Docks

Railway transport is an example of a public utility undertaking. **Public utilities** provide essential services rather than goods. Their capital consists largely of fixed assets and their expenses are for the most part non-variable. The cost of running railway trains is only just over one-third of total working expenses, whereas the cost of running road vehicles is nearly two-thirds of the total. Other examples of public utilities are the Post Office, gas, electricity and waterworks. All these have been nationalised.

Even before nationalisation these public utilities had a monopoly, only one undertaking being allowed to supply a certain area. It would be very wasteful, for example, to allow several gas companies to lay different systems of mains along a street when one system was quite enough to do the work required. Because these undertakings were granted a monopoly, they were subject to control and regulations as to the prices they could charge. Many of them were owned and run by local authorities. As they already had a monopoly and were controlled, they were easily nationalised.

Businesses owned by the State or by local authorities are carried on by **public enterprise**. Those owned by individuals or companies whose main object is to make profit for themselves are run by private enterprise.

An advantage claimed for **nationalisation** is that it brings a whole industry under one control so that it can be planned and developed as a whole. Economies can then be made by avoiding unnecessary duplication. One gasworks and one office may now serve where two existed previously. Materials may be purchased at a lower price because they can now be bought in greater bulk. A big industry with a monopoly is in a better position to raise capital and to pay high salaries to attract the experts whose services it requires. It can afford to spend money on equipping laboratories for carrying on research, the results of which will benefit all the industry. These advantages apply to all big concerns as well as to the nationalised industries. The State can provide essential services, like transport, although they do not make profits.

Private enterprise opponents of nationalisation argue that it creates an undertaking that is too big to be well managed, and that monopoly may lead to inefficiency. The men in control, not being owners who have risked their capital in a business whose success or failure is vital to them, may show less initiative than private entrepreneurs. When several businesses compete, an improved efficiency in one enabling it to sell at reduced prices must be followed by improved efficiency in the others unless they are to be driven out of business. This spur to progress is lacking in the case of a nationalised industry, and as a result prices may be higher than they would be under private enterprise and there may be less choice for consumers.

To meet these criticisms the industries are managed regionally, the managements of the regions competing to achieve the best results. Advisory and Consumers' Councils are set up to voice the views and criticisms of the customers, and the industries are discussed in Parliament.

On the question of **entrepreneurship**, it is arguable nowadays whether the directors and managers of vast business companies do in fact take a financial risk such as the proprietors of small businesses have done in the past. Their enthusiasm probably arises from the satisfaction they derive from doing the job and meeting the numerous challenges that are offered; such men, it is felt, would bring the same qualities to a similar responsible managerial position in a nationalised industry.

The Acts that brought about nationalisation did not make the same arrangements for each industry, but the general pattern is the same. An industry was to be taken over and run by a **public corporation** whose members were appointed by the Minister of the appropriate department. The corporation must prepare annual reports and submit them to the responsible Minister who may be questioned on them by Members of Parliament. The Minister may issue general directions as to the policy to be followed by the corporation, but he does not interfere in the day-to-day working of the industry. The corporation has unlimited liability. It can borrow money from banks at a lower rate of interest than that charged to other borrowers, because the Government guarantees the loan. New capital, which must be repaid with interest over a period of years, can be obtained from the Government. The Acts also provided for the setting up of Advisory and Consumers' Councils.

The former owners were to give up their shares and receive instead Government stock bearing a fixed rate of interest. When a limited company has not made enough profit to declare a dividend, the shareholders receive nothing; but the holders of stock in a nationalised industry are entitled to receive the interest on it each year whether the industry has made a profit or a loss. As a result a nationalised industry can make an 'operating' profit but, after allowing for the interest on the stock, its accounts may show a net loss. In similar circumstances the accounts of a limited company would show a net profit.

The prices to be charged by a nationalised industry must be such as will prevent a loss 'taking one year with another'. It may make a loss in some years and parts of the industry may lose, but over a five-year period the industry as a whole is expected to earn at least 10 per cent on the capital employed. Some industries are expected to earn more than others. As a public corporation has no voting shareholders, it cannot distribute any profit it makes. Profits must be retained to be used as capital, or used for paying higher wages, or for reducing prices.

In the remainder of this chapter a short account is given of the organisation of the industries and services that have been nationalised in Britain up to the present time.

Fuel industries

Coal

National Coal Board – 1946. Chairman and between eight and eleven members appointed by the Secretary of State for Industry. Answerable to the Secretary of State and, through him, to Parliament.

The National Coal Board raises capital by borrowing from the Secretary of State for Industry up to a limit of 950 million pounds. Under the Nationalisation Act it is supposed to 'break even' on its current account 'taking one year with another' after meeting all charges and making proper provision for reserves.

Research: There are two research organisations: The Coal Research Establishment at Stoke Orchard in Gloucestershire, where basic general research is carried out; and the Mining Research and Development Establishment at Bretby in Derbyshire, where research into underground problems and the development of new machines and equipment are undertaken.

For many years Britain's coal mines represented one of her most important natural resources and after the Second World War productivity in the mines increased spectacularly. Unproductive pits were closed and the latest mechanised techniques, both in the production of coal at the coal face and in handling it below ground and at the surface, ensured high levels of production at the lowest possible cost. Unfortunately, the demand for coal steadily declined after the war and the industry was unable to 'break even' in competition with other sources of fuel.

Traditionally, large quantities of coal were used in the production of electricity, but the post-war years saw the development of other methods of generation, using oil, natural gas, hydro-electric and nuclear power. During those years many workers in the coalmines transferred to other industries and the Government sought to protect the coal industry by making the conversion to other fuels in the generation of electricity a gradual process.

The unexpected and steep rise in the price of oil in world markets in 1974, together with growing doubts about the use of nuclear power in electricity generation, brought about a reversal of this policy, and Britain's coal has once more become an extremely valuable resource.

Electricity

1881: First public supply of electricity – in Godalming, Surrey.

1919: The creation of the Electricity Commissioners – a supervisory body aimed at reorganising the industry on a national scale through voluntary agreement among the various municipal concerns and private interests.

1926: **The Central Electricity Board**. This was set up to construct and operate a national grid, inter-connecting individual power stations. For the first time, the two activities which make up the electricity supply industry – **generation** and **transmission** – were coordinated.

1947: **Electricity Act**. British Electricity Authority set up and fourteen regional boards. All municipal and private electricity undertakings in England and Wales were acquired.

1954, 1957: Two subsequent Acts amended the structure of the industry somewhat to take its present form, as follows:

In England and Wales, the **Central Electricity Generating Board** is responsible for the generation and transmission of electricity, which is distributed by twelve area electricity boards. Scotland and Northern Ireland have their own boards, which both generate and distribute.

The **Electricity Council** is the central coordinating body. It has the general over-all responsibility for electricity supply and is answerable to the Secretary of State for Trade and Industry. The Council consists of: Chairman; two deputy chairmen; the chairman and two members of the CEGB; the chairmen of the twelve area electricity boards; up to three other members.

The CEGB operates and maintains the power stations and the national grid, supplying electricity in bulk to the twelve area boards. Each board is responsible for selling and distributing electricity to the customers in its area.

Area Consultative Councils have been set up to look after the interests of consumers in each area: their chairmen are automatically members of their area boards.

The Secretary of State for Industry appoints the chairmen, deputy chairmen and members of the CEGB, the Electricity Council, the area boards and the consultative councils. The research programmes and the board's capital development plans are approved by the Minister.

Generation: The conventional coal-fired generating stations still account for a large proportion of the electric power generated for the public supply in Britain. Oil-fired stations and gas turbine units are also in use, and in the mountainous areas of Scotland and Wales hydro-electric stations have been developed. Nuclear power stations account for about 20 per cent of Britain's public supply and much research and experimentation are going on in connection with different types of nuclear reactor.

Electricity supply in Britain has increased spectacularly in recent years. The high rate of expansion is apparent from the fact that between the years 1965 and 1971 the output capacity of the generating stations rose by 50 per cent.

Gas

The first public supply of gas in Britain was installed in 1807, when Pall Mall in London was lit by gas. In 1812 the London and Westminster Gas Light and Coke Company was granted a royal charter to supply gas lighting to London. For many years gas was used solely for lighting, and was supplied by a number of gas companies and municipal authorities. Competition from the developing electricity industry caused gas lighting to be superseded, and by 1939 the gas industry was concentrating on supplying gas for heating and cooking.

1948: the **Gas Act** brought the gas industry under public control, and twelve area Gas Boards took the place of no less than 991 separate gas undertakings, of which 269 were run by local authorities.

The Gas Council was the central body, its members being appointed by the Secretary of State for Industry.

With the discovery of large fields of natural gas in the North Sea and in some land areas, the area boards which had the responsibility for the local manufacture of gas and its distribution to consumers became increasingly unsuitable as a distribution structure for piped natural gas, and were abolished in 1973, when the **British Gas Corporation** was set up, formed from the old Gas Council.

Gas consumption in Britain has shown a steady rise for many years, both in the domestic field and in industry. In homes, offices, shops and other premises, gas-fired central heating has become popular, and in many industrial installations natural gas is used wherever a fine, easily-controllable degree of temperature accuracy is required.

Research: There are four main research centres and a number of smaller ones. Much research has been done in connection with the transformation of the industry from the use of manufactured gas to that of indigenous, natural gas, including the problems of large-scale distribution and the construction of storage facilities.

The main source of gas in Britain now is natural gas. It accounts for about 95 per cent of total gas supplies.

Oil

The development of the oilfields discovered in the North Sea is one of the most important industrial activities in Britain today. Extensive submarine pipelines have been constructed to bring the oil ashore to storage tanks and refineries situated in Scotland, Teesside, Wales, the Midlands and the Thames Estuary. It is believed that by 1980 production of oil from these and the newly-discovered smaller land-based oilfields in Britain will be sufficient to make Britain totally independent of imported oil.

The first licences to prospect for natural gas and oil in the North Sea were granted in 1964–5, and in the last ten years development has proceeded rapidly. The Government has set up the British National Oil Corporation (BNOC) to keep control over the level of production and to watch over future exploration and development. The Corporation will also aim to extend its activities to the refining and distribution of oil, as the importation of foreign oil declines and is replaced by home-produced supplies, and the Government will take steps to acquire a majority stake in existing commercial oilfields.

Water supply

The production of water supplies first became a general public service in the middle of the nineteenth century, following the passing of the **Public Health Act** of 1848. Many different undertakings were set up to provide water for the growing urban populations, and for many years the water supply system was under the control of many different bodies.

1963: **Water Resources Acts**. The Water Resources Board was set up as a central authority to work with the river authorities in various parts of the country. The Board was an expert advisory body responsible to the Department of the Environment. At that time there were more than 1400 separate bodies in Britain in control of water supply, and eventually a major reorganisation was undertaken, culminating in the passing of the **Water Act** in 1973.

1974: The **National Water Council** replaced the Water Resources Board and ten regional water authorities were created. Responsibilities of the National Water Council include:

Treatment of water for public use;
Public supply of water;
Building up of supplies by storage schemes;
Dealing with sewerage;
Prevention and control of the discharge of pollution into rivers and estuaries;
Development of rivers and canals for public recreation.

Research: Various research establishments exist, providing information on the yield and behaviour of surface water resources, the construction of dams and barrages across estuaries, and the development of other reservoirs. The Water Pollution Research Laboratory at Stevenage investigates problems concerning the treatment of polluted water, the disposal of sewage and industrial waste and the prevention of pollution of water.

Transport

Inland transport

Railways: Over 100 privately owned railway companies were amalgamated under the **Railways Act** of 1921 to form four regional organisations, but competition from the fast-growing road transport still brought losses to the railways.

1947: **Transport Act**. This brought the railways under public ownership as a single entity – **British Railways** (afterwards shortened to **British Rail**); but the railways continued to run at a loss. The ways in which the railways have sought to recapture both cargo and passenger traffic during the intervening years, and the measures taken by the Government to make the railways financially sound, are described in Chapter 37, p. 176.

Roads: Road haulage in Britain was only partially nationalised by the setting up in 1953 of **British Road Services**, and this organisation was superseded by the **National Freight Corporation** established in 1968, to promote the integration of road and rail freight services with a view to making the maximum economic use of rail transport.

The **London Transport Executive**, appointed by the **Greater London Council** (the G.L.C.), and responsible to them, manages and operates the London Underground rail services and the London buses. Many other local authorities throughout the country operate bus services in their areas.

Rivers and canals: Inland water navigation is the responsibility of the British Waterways Board set up in 1947. A detailed account is set out in Chapter 38, p. 181.

British Rail, the National Freight Corporation and the British Waterways Board are all responsible to the Secretary of State for the Environment.

Air transport

Two public corporations were set up to handle air transport between Britain and Europe – British European Airways (BEA), and between Britain and other parts of the world – British Overseas Air Corporation (BOAC). Apart from these nationalised corporations, there are today about forty independent air transport companies.

1971: **Civil Aviation Act**. Two new bodies set up to take control of British civil aviation: the **Civil Aviation Authority** (CAA) and the **British Airways Board** (BAB). BOAC and BEA were combined to form **British Airways**.

The CAA handles such matters as the provision of air navigation services at airports, the issue of licences for air services and regulations covering the safe operation of aircraft (the responsibility of its Air Worthiness Division). It also ensures that every aircraft operator possesses an Air Operator's Certificate, and that each member of a flight crew holds the appropriate official licence. Air traffic control is also its responsibility, in conjunction with the Secretary of State for Defence.

The **British Airways Board** controls seven divisions of British Airways: British Airways Overseas, British Airways European, British Airways Regional, British Airways Associated Companies Ltd., British Airways Helicopters Ltd., British Airways Engine Overhaul Ltd., and International Aeradio Ltd. The responsibilities of the seven divisions are:

Overseas Division: long-range services around the world;

European Division: shorter-range services in Europe, North Africa and the middle east;

Regional Division: domestic flights within Britain, and to Channel Islands and parts of Europe;

British Airways Associated Companies Ltd: investments in hotels and other airlines;

British Airways Helicopters Ltd: provides helicopter services;

British Airways Engine Overhaul Ltd: engine overhaul for British Airways and other airlines;

International Aeradio Ltd: airport technical services and communications; manufactures specialised equipment for these purposes.

The Secretary of State for Trade appoints the Chairmen and the members of the CAA and the BAB.

Ports

The control of ports and their facilities is in the hands of four different types of organisation: nationalised undertakings, public trusts, local authorities and some private companies. Nationalised ports include Southampton, Hull, Cardiff and Swansea; the Port of London Authority and the Tees and Hartlepools Ports Authority are examples of public trusts administered by representatives of all those using the ports – shippers, shipping companies, local authorities and trade unions; local authorities own and operate about one-third of all Britain's ports, including the important port of Bristol; and ports owned by limited liability companies include Manchester, Liverpool and Felixstowe.

The Port of London Authority, formed in 1908, bought docks from different owners so that they could, under one owner, be developed as a whole in the best interests of shipping using the port and not for the making of profit. It must have at least fifteen and not more than sixteen members who serve for a specified period and represent associations of people concerned with the port. After consulting these associations the Minister of Transport appoints three members each for the shipowners and the shippers, two each for the National Ports Council and the trade unions, and one each for the wharf owners, the lighter and barge owners, the Greater London Council, the City of London, and the Corporation of Trinity House which is responsible for lighthouses and pilotage. The Director-General of the port is coopted as the sixteenth member. Like a public corporation the Authority can raise capital at a fixed rate of interest and, having no shareholders, it must use any profit to improve the port or to lower charges.

Those who support nationalisation envisage a scheme to bring all ports under the control of one central organisation, but at the time of writing this has not been accomplished.

The **National Ports Council** advises the Government on port developments and recommends improvements. The increasing use of big tankers and container ships has required the provision of more deep-water berths, facilities for handling containers and more mechanised equipment for the handling of general cargo. Capital investment in ports has more than doubled in the last ten years. Britain's three major ports are London, Liverpool and Southampton. Other important ports include Bristol, Port Talbot, Newport, Swansea, Milford Haven (now Britain's major oil port), Manchester (inland port linked to the sea by the Manchester Ship Canal), Newcastle, the port of Tees and Hartlepools, Hull and Grimsby. In Scotland, the Clyde is the principal port; and in Northern Ireland, Belfast.

Tanker terminals: These specially equipped terminals are owned and operated by the oil companies. Crude oil is discharged and piped direct to the refineries. The ports involved, such as Milford Haven in Wales, and Finnart in Scotland, can accommodate fully laden tankers of 250 000 tons, and will be able to cater for the half-million tonne tankers that are planned. Besides serving the Scottish refinery at Grangemouth, the Finnart terminal supplies oil by pipeline to refineries in Wales and Lancashire.

Dock labour: For many years dock workers were employed on a casual basis: they sold their labour when and where they could. In 1947, the **National Dock Labour Board** was established with a view to ensuring a minimum wage for each docker attending for work, and an effort was begun to end the casual employment of dock workers. In 1967, each registered dock worker was placed in permanent employment with an employer licensed by the port authority: the decasualisation process was complete.

The Post Office

Prior to 1969 the Post Office was a Government department but under the Post Office Act of that year it became a public authority under the control of a Chairman and Board appointed by and responsible to the Minister of Posts and Telecommunications. In 1974, however, this ministry was abolished. Postal and telegraph services became the responsibility of the Secretary of State for Industry, and the Home Secretary became responsible for radio and broadcasting.

Broadcasting

The Minister of Posts and Telecommunications was at the head of British broadcasting from 1969 to 1974, when that ministry was abolished and responsibility for broadcasting was handed over to the Home Office.

Two public bodies are licensed to provide television and radio broadcasting services: the British Broadcasting Corporation and the Independent Broadcasting Authority.

The BBC operates two national television services, four national radio services and nineteen local radio stations. It is financed out of sales of television and radio licences and profits from sales of such journals as *Radio Times* and *The Listener*.

The IBA controls the operation of one independent television service and a network of some sixty local radio stations. IBA is financed out of advertising revenue paid as rentals by the programme companies.

Organisation

BBC: Twelve Governors, each appointed for a period of not more than five years; responsible, through a number of advisory bodies, for the whole broadcasting operation – programme planning and production, and provision and maintenance of equipment. Director-General of the BBC is chairman of the Board of Management.

IBA: Chairman, Deputy-chairman and nine other members of governing body – appointed by the Home Secretary. It appoints the programme companies that provide the programmes and has power of control over programme output and advertising; it also maintains the necessary transmitting stations. Director-General is chief executive officer. Advised by committees of experts in various fields.

Iron and steel

British Steel Corporation was set up in 1967 under the Iron and Steel Act. Thirteen major steel companies were nationalised, bringing 90 per cent of

Nationalised industry in Britain

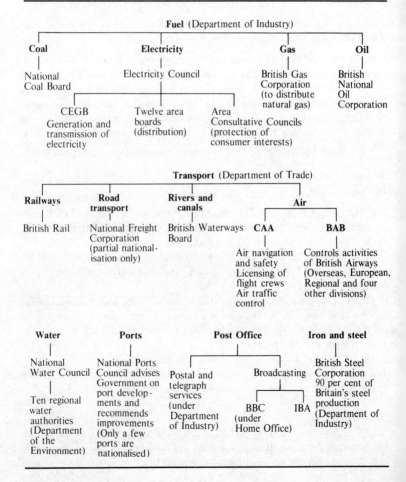

Britain's steel production under public control. BSC aims to promote the efficiency of the industry, improve productivity, expand exports and develop research.

Private sector
About 200 independent firms remain in production.

Since nationalisation, there has been greater emphasis on modernisation of plant and productivity improvement rather than increasing total output. Britain now has some of the most up-to-date steel-making plant in Europe.

Although the State has taken over some public utilities, like gas and electricity, formerly provided by many local authorities, **municipalities** still own waterworks, housing estates, market halls, airports, etc. The necessary capital may be raised by the issue of municipal stock and debentures bearing a fixed rate of interest and by loans from the Government. Profits can be used in ways decided by the local authority. They may be used to reduce the rates and, similarly, losses may have to be made good out of the rates.

Questions

1. What are public utilities? How do they differ from other businesses?

2. Describe some of the arguments used against the nationalisation of industry. What safeguards have been built in to the nationalised undertakings in Britain to meet these criticisms?

3. Although most of our goods and services are provided through private enterprise some are provided through the Government. Give examples and explain why this is so. (R.S.A.)

4. Outline the general organisation of any public corporation you have studied. From what sources does it obtain its capital? (A.E.B.)

5. Give examples of (*a*) a public limited company, (*b*) a public corporation. How do they differ in respect of (i) provision of capital, (ii) ownership, (iii) control, (iv) allocation of profit or surplus? (W.J.E.C.)

6. Describe the services provided by port and harbour authorities and explain why these services are commercially important. (R.S.A.)

7. Give reasons for and against nationalising the docks. Describe four ways in which ports are owned and controlled.

8. What businesses are owned by your local authority? Why does it own these rather than others? From what sources does it obtain its capital? What is its prices and profits policy?

9. Write notes on: 'turn-round', Passenger Authority, Transport Tribunal, National Ports Council.

10. Account for the consistent losses suffered by the Railways in Britain after nationalisation in 1947. Were the railways a profitable enterprise before that date – if so, when? Mention some of the ways in which they are now seeking to recapture some of their lost business.

11. Discuss the reasons for nationalising an industry, indicating how the purposes, responsibilities and attitudes of state corporations may coincide with, or differ from, those of private industry. Illustrate your argument with any nationalised industry of your own choice.

12. Explain the meaning of (*a*) private enterprise and (*b*) public enterprise. Describe briefly the forms of business units which comprise each system. (L.C.C. & I.)

13. Give an account of the work and aims of the National Freight Corporation.

14. Distinguish the different forms of long-term capital available to a public company.

    How do these forms of capital differ from those available to a public corporation? (A.E.B.)

Chapter 41

Government measures to protect workers and consumers · Consumer Credit Act

Protection of workers

In the last chapter we traced the development of industrial relations in Britain from the early nineteenth century to the present time and saw how important the role of Government has become in this field. Apart from legislation in connection with industrial relations, the following important measures for the protection of workers were also passed. They consolidated earlier laws dealing with safety and welfare.

1952: **Agriculture (Poisonous Substances) Act**.

1956: **Agriculture (Safety, Health and Welfare Provisions) Act**.

The requirements of these two acts, which specified the conditions that must be provided for the safety and welfare of agricultural workers, are enforced by the Agricultural Inspectorate of the Ministry of Agriculture, Fisheries and Food.

1954: **Mines and Quarries Act:** made similar stipulations for the safety and welfare of miners and workers in quarries. These are enforced by the Inspectorate of Mines and Quarries of the Department of Employment.

1961: **Factories Act** sets out safety requirements for factories and workshops, including compulsory fire precautions and the prompt reporting to the authorities of a fatal accident, and of any other accident resulting in more than three days' incapacity; the Act also made it compulsory to report anything in the nature of a dangerous incident concerning machinery or dangerous substances, so that an investigation could be conducted; and it laid down rules for the fencing of machinery, for the employment of women and young people and for the training and supervision of young persons working with dangerous machinery.

1963: **Offices, Shops and Railway Premises Act** supplemented the provisions of the Factories Act by widening the spectrum of employees protected by legislation. Very far-reaching in its provisions, its aim being 'to secure the health, safety and welfare of persons employed in shops and offices', the Act sets out compulsory fire precautions, standards of cleanliness, defines overcrowding, prescribes levels of temperature, standards of ventilation, lighting and sanitation; requires the provision of drinking water and first aid and deals with the safe condition of premises where people are employed.

Factory inspectors working under the authority of the Department of Employment are responsible for enforcing the provisions of these laws in respect of factories and factory offices; railway employment inspectors working under the Department of the Environment are responsible for inspecting railway premises.

1963: **Contracts of Employment Act** specified employers' and workers' rights and obligations in respect of terms of employment. It was superseded and amended by the far-reaching provisions of the Industrial Relations Act of 1971 and the subsequent legislation that replaced it.

Protection of consumers

Food

Laws relating to the purity of food date back to the middle of the nineteenth century, the principal Acts of Parliament being:

1860: **Adulteration of Food and Drink Act**. This Act prohibited the addition to food of any substance dangerous to health.

1975: **Public analysts** to be appointed by local authorities and regular sampling of food to be undertaken.

Several subsequent measures dealt with various aspects of the manufacture and supply of food, the most important being:

1938: **Food and Drugs Act**. Laid down standards of cleanliness for all persons engaged in food handling.

1955–6: **Food and Drugs Acts**. Manufacturers required to give information about substances used in manufacture and processing of food. Certain substances and processes considered to be injurious to health were prohibited. Food inspectors were empowered to visit shops, examine articles of food, and buy samples for submission to the public analysts.

Weights and measures

1871: **Weights and Measures Act** was the first legal basis for the imperial system. It was supplemented by later acts. Metric measurements had been recognised and legalised in 1864: they came into use in certain trades during the nineteenth century. In recent years, as we know, there has been a change-over in Britain from the imperial to the metric systems.

Local inspectorates undertook the regular verification and stamping of traders' weights in accordance with government regulations.

1963: **Weights and Measures Act**. Laid down the basic units of measurement and weight; specified the equipment to be used in trade and the public weighing and measuring equipment to be used by local authorities; and required that containers must state on the outside the weight or quantity contained in them. Responsibility for enforcing these provisions rests with the local authority Weights and Measures Inspectors.

Other measures

There have been other Acts of Parliament aimed at various aspects of consumer protection and some of these have already been referred to in

Chapter 18. They are referred to again here, together with further developments in the field of consumer protection.

1893: **Sale of Goods Act**. Goods must conform to the description or sample submitted by the buyer; they must be fit for sale and able to perform the job for which they were supplied.

1965: **Consumer Protection Act**. Weight, volume and a statement of the ingredients must be printed on all containers.

1968: **Trades Descriptions Act**. Descriptions of goods in advertising and on containers must not mislead or deceive buyers.

1972: **Trades Descriptions Act**. Imported goods must display on container the country of origin.

1973: **Supply of Goods Act**. The purchaser cannot be deprived of his right to be supplied with goods of merchantable quality and fit for their purpose. This law reduced the risk of consumers being 'conned' by misleading statements.

The growth of consumer organisation is also traced in Chapter 18; and in discussing **nationalised industries** (Chapter 40) we have seen how consumers' interests and viewpoints are studied by the consumer councils and advisory bodies appointed within each of these undertakings.

Consumer protection

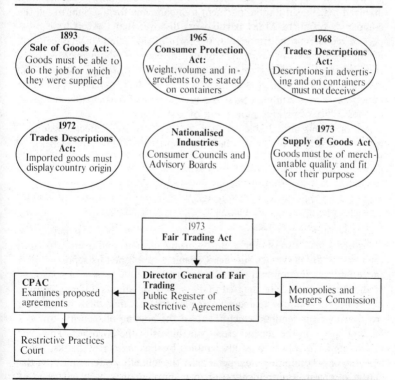

Under the **Fair Trading Act** of 1973 the **Director General of Fair Trading** may refer any unfair trading practice to the **Restrictive Practices Court**. Under this act, the **Consumer Protection Advisory Committee** (CPAC) was set up. The CPAC examines proposals that have come to the attention of the Director of Fair Trading. Full discussions between the members of the committee and all interested parties take place before a decision is reached on whether the matter should be referred to the Secretary of State. The first two practices examined by the Committee after it began its work in 1974 were:

1. The display of notices in shops worded in such a way as to imply that customers had no rights to the replacement of faulty goods; such notices were frequently worded: **No goods exchanged or money refunded**.
2. Manufacturers' guarantees and warranties, which frequently do not clearly state what the buyers' rights are.

Pricing. Legislation is currently planned to make pricing of goods in shops compulsory, and where applicable *unit pricing*, so that the prices of different sizes and brands may easily be compared.

Pyramid selling. The practice of pyramid selling is an abuse which has grown from the increase in recent years of direct selling. The salesmen involved make a substantial payment to a company for the right to sell the company's products. Many participants discover that there is little prospect of recovering their money in the form of sales, and they concentrate on the recruitment of new participants, for each of whom they receive a cash payment. These newcomers, in turn, put down a payment to the company for the right to sell their goods and they too try to get their money back by recruiting others. As the number of participants increases, the possibility of making money out of sales diminishes.

Although this undesirable practice does not adversely affect consumers, it is regarded as a matter for the intervention of the Director General of Fair Trading.

Consumer credit

The various types of credit offered to customers by the retail trade, and the laws governing hire-purchase transactions, are described in Chapter 16. Consumers may also obtain credit by means of loans and overdrafts from their banks. In 1971 the **Crowther Committee** published its report, after a thorough examination and much consideration of all aspects of consumer credit. The committee recognised that competition among different sources of credit will continue to increase; it also foresaw that there would be a trend away from lending which involved the holding of security, towards lending based on the general credit-worthiness of the borrower. This type of lending is already successfully handled by the commercial banks, which have the opportunity to assess personally the reliability of customers in the matter of credit. The tremendous growth in popularity in recent years of the **credit card** system testifies to the success of the system. These cards enable the users to have their signatures accepted on bills in shops, restaurants, hotels and other establishments participating in the scheme. The banks and other organisations that issue the cards meet the traders' bills promptly, and the card-holders settle their accounts at stipulated intervals.

The Crowther Committee recommended that this type of lending should be adopted for all credit transactions; that there should be a complete reform of existing consumer credit legislation; and that a uniform legal structure should be worked out to cover all types of consumer credit.

1974: **Consumer Credit Act.** Building on the foundations laid by existing legislation, the Act extends to a far wider range of transactions, covering hiring, rental and leasing agreements, the activities of credit brokers, debt adjusters, debt collectors and credit reference agencies. The Act aims to provide 'a complete framework within which consumers can take credit, and creditors can grant it, with confidence and ease'. Its recommendations and provisions will be introduced in easy stages over the next few years.

Questions

1. What protection is afforded to the consumer to help him obtain value for his money?

2. Indicate briefly the case for consumer protection, and as fully as possible the existing safeguards for consumers provided by the central and local Government and other bodies.

3. Outline the provisions of the Fair Trading Act of 1973 in relation to the responsibilities of the Director-General of Fair Trading and those of the CPAC.

4. Give some account of the laws that protect consumers from buying adulterated food and receiving short weight. How are the laws enforced?

5. Describe in general terms the recommendations of the **Crowther Committee** Report on Consumer Credit. How do existing laws protect the consumer in regard to hire purchase?

6. (*a*) Why do consumers require protection?
   (*b*) Indicate **three** ways in which the Government endeavours to protect them.
   (U.C.L.E.S.)

7. Mention some of the conditions covered by the Offices, Shops and Railway Premises Act of 1963.
   How does the Government ensure that the provisions of the Act are carried out: in the factories? In railway offices?

8. What may the food inspectors do, and what is the work of public analysts in respect of food?

Chapter 42

The workforce · Division of labour · Automation · Redundancy · Trade unions · Employers' Associations · Chambers of Commerce

The rapid development of factory production in the early part of the nineteenth century transformed the pattern of life of the working people in Britain and undermined the traditional relationships between employers and workers.

Before the Industrial Revolution, when many industries were home-based, a weaver or potter would produce as much cloth or pottery as he could, helped perhaps by members of his family or by some paid help from outside. The installation of large-scale machinery in workshops and factories enabled many more goods to be produced, since workers could be organised so that each could specialise in one part of the production process. A potter, therefore, would not produce a finished pot himself: he would be responsible for one operation – putting on the handles perhaps, or painting a coloured rim around the pots.

This **division of labour** made possible the **mass production** of goods. Modern industrial installations with highly developed machinery call for more and more specialisation, so that many workers spend their days performing a repetitive task that occupies only a few minutes, and to do this they may stand before a moving belt or a machine which regularly places before them the task they have to do. This breakdown of labour into small components reduces the difficulty of the work. The job is simple to do, it probably calls for little physical strength and little or no mental exertion. Because it is repetitive, the worker becomes swift and adept at it. Some large machines are able to manufacture an entire product without human intervention; one operator 'feeds' the machine with stacks of raw material, another 'minds' the machine during the manufacturing operation, pressing an emergency 'stop' switch if anything goes wrong with the normal process, and a third collects and stacks the finished products.

Machines speed up work and ensure that each product conforms to an expected standard. On the other hand, the interest and pride that the individual weaver and potter of the old days experienced in doing their work are lost: many factory workers find their jobs unspeakably boring. A worker who settles into this type of work for a period of years may find that he is unwilling, and perhaps even unable, to adapt to any change of job.

Automation

The introduction of machinery where work has previously been done by human labour has been the cause of much industrial unrest in the past. In recent years, **automation** has carried **mechanisation** a step farther. By means of electronic control, a sequence of processes can be integrated into one whole, which is virtually self-controlling. Automated systems do away with such deadening jobs as machine feeding and machine minding. In the sphere of communications, automation has brought about subscriber trunk dialling in the telephone system and electronic sorting of mail. In the office, electronic accounting systems using computers have introduced entirely new concepts into office organisation and procedures.

Redundancy

Large-scale mechanisation and the growth of automation have caused much redundancy among workers. New opportunities for employment have been created but in most cases these call for special training and considerable personal adjustment by the worker to the new conditions. In any case, the number of workers displaced by automation is usually greater than the number needed to staff the new systems. It has been predicted that the widespread application of automation that is bound to come to industry will eventually bring about a reduction in working hours and an increase in leisure time. Provided that an acceptable standard of living is assured, many people would regard such a prospect as welcome progress, but there is little doubt that such a change in working patterns will also bring some problems. In the meantime, workers whose jobs have disappeared because of automation are protected by the Redundancy Payments Acts of 1965 and 1969. These acts provide for the payment of lump sums to the workers if the employers are unable to offer them suitable alternative work, provided the employees have completed at least two years of service.

Growth of the trade unions

In the early nineteenth century the low rates of pay and long and arduous hours of work in the factories, mines and mills, as yet uncontrolled by any laws providing protection for the workers, brought about the growth of trade unions.

For many years the banding together of workers for the purpose of securing higher wages and better working conditions was outlawed as conspiracy, but gradually trade unions were permitted and many were formed among skilled and semi-skilled workers. In 1868, the first Trades Union Congress was held.

In 1875 legislation was passed recognising the legal status of trade unions and the right of workers to strike if they had a grievance against an employer. It also gave employers the right, if they were aggrieved, to lock workers out. During the next twenty-five years there were many great strikes – of colliers, cotton workers, iron workers, railway employees, shoemakers, dock labourers and others. The strike of dock labourers encouraged other groups of unskilled workers to support the growing trade union movement. Objectives sought by the workers were higher rates of pay, better working conditions and the establishment of an eight-hour working day.

Employers' associations

During this period employers also began to organise themselves, associations of employers being formed in several industries to represent the views of manufacturers and traders in a particular industry in their dealings with the trade unions and the Government.

Since those early days, the work of the associations has considerably widened. Regular journals and year books are published containing articles and comments contributed by members, reports of meetings and other news and information of interest to members. Statistics are compiled of trends and developments in the industry concerned and the prospects for overseas trade. Advisory services are available to members, and some associations organise courses in management training. Cooperative advertising is sometimes undertaken for a whole industry (see p. 77). On all issues that are important to member firms, particularly any Government measure which may affect members, a united front is presented to the Government, the trade unions and the public.

With the growth and development of industry during the twentieth century, the employers' associations have increased in size and number. Associations are generally organised according to industry, and where there are local or regional associations these are combined in a national federation. Similarly, in large industries involving a number of different products there may be local associations with national and regional federations for each of the different sections of the industry. There are about seventy national associations, to which these smaller organisations are federated, and almost all of them are members of the Confederation of British Industry.

The Confederation of British Industry (CBI)
The Confederation of British Industry was formed in 1965 and was the result of a merger between the three employers' bodies then existing. It deals with all matters affecting the interests of employers and represents its member organisations in negotiations with the Government at national level, and in discussions at the international level, for example, at the conventions of the International Labour Organisation (I.L.O.) (see ch. 55, p. 280. Members of the CBI include over 10 000 individual companies, over 200 employers' associations, and 16 nationalised industries.

The chambers of commerce
A chamber of commerce is to be found in every industrial and commercial

centre in Britain. Membership is open to all the producers and traders within the area, the chamber existing to promote the interests of *local* industry and commerce. In this, the chambers of commerce differ from the employers' associations, each of which watches over the interests of members in a certain industry or trade. In matters of common interest, there is frequently cooperation between the CBI and the chambers of commerce. The central organisation is the Association of British Chambers of Commerce, founded in 1860; ninety-two local chambers of commerce are affiliated to it. Chambers of commerce in Scotland and in Northern Ireland have their own central bodies.

The work of a chamber of commerce includes meetings of members at which local matters affecting business are discussed and speakers on a variety of topics are heard; the publication of papers, reports and journals; and the maintenance of an advisory service to give information to members on such matters as: laws and local regulations affecting industry and trade; exporting opportunities, including import duties and other regulations imposed by foreign governments; laws regarding trademarks and patents; company taxation; taxation on goods.

The International Chamber of Commerce was founded in 1919 and now has a membership drawn from over sixty countries. There are also nineteen British chambers of commerce operating abroad. This international network of people whose common interest is the promotion of peaceful trading conditions between nations is a potentially valuable factor in the maintenance of friendly international relations.

Questions

1. What is the meaning of the term 'division of labour'? Describe (*a*) its advantages, and (*b*) its disadvantages, in the organisation of production. (L.C.C. & I.)

2. Why do textbooks on economics and commerce put considerable stress on the 'division of labour'? (L.C.C. & I.)

3. Explain: (*a*) division of labour, (*b*) mass production, (*c*) mechanisation, (*d*) automation, (*e*) redundancy.

4. Write an account of the growth of trade unions. Why did workers seek to form unions in the first place? Have the unions now outgrown their usefulness and become too powerful, or are there still good reasons for their continuance?

5. What are chambers of commerce? How do they differ from employers' associations? In what ways are they useful to business people?

6. Describe the structure of the CBI and the help offered to members by the employers' associations.

Chapter 43

The workforce · Trade union organisation · The Donovan Commission report · The Social Contract

With a total membership of over eleven million, trade unions today represent a substantial body of working people. There are around 500 unions, some of them having only a few thousand members; the nine largest unions, however, each have a membership of over a quarter of a million, and more than 70 per cent of unionists are members of the twenty-four largest unions.

Union membership is sometimes on an occupational basis, such as fitters or electricians working in a variety of industries; sometimes members are workers from a particular industry such as railwaymen, mine workers or boilermakers; and the two large general unions, the Transport and General Workers' Union and the National Union of General and Municipal Workers, draw their members – who are semi-skilled or unskilled – from many different industries. Some unions of professional and clerical workers have also been formed, such as those in the teaching profession and among clerks in government and municipal offices. The National Union of Teachers, the Association of Teachers in Technical Institutes, the various Civil Service trade unions and the National Association of Local Government Officers (NALGO) are examples.

In the large unions, the centre of the organisation is the **National Executive Council** elected by annual conferences of delegates from the local branches, and responsible to them. Branch organisation is by region, district or area, and the individual unionist is a member of his local branch. He is entitled to attend its meetings, put forward his views and suggestions, take part in the election of branch officers and vote on motions put forward.

Shop stewards
These are accredited trade union representatives who look after the interests of union members in their places of work. In times of grievance or dispute, it is the union representatives who negotiate with the employer on behalf of the union members. Shop stewards also recruit new members for the unions and see that members are kept informed on union matters.

Some unions are affiliated to a confederation of unions representing all the unions in an industry; this arrangement strengthens their bargaining power in negotiating with employers.

Members' benefits

Besides seeking better working conditions and rates of pay for their members, trade unions have funds for the payment to members of sickness, accident and death benefits; there are superannuation schemes, strike pay in time of dispute, and unemployment benefits.

The Trades Union Congress (TUC)

The TUC is the national centre of trade unionism in Britain. Most unions are affiliated to it. It meets every year, those who attend being elected delegates of the member-unions, and each year it elects the General Council, which acts as its executive body throughout the ensuing year. Its activities include acting as mediator in the event of inter-union disagreement, and intervening in cases of unauthorised work stoppages if requested by a member-union.

The TUC and some of the larger unions provide educational services for trade unionists. These include general and vocational courses as well as courses on industry, trade unionism and industrial relations. Summer schools, weekend courses and correspondence courses are organised; and scholarships, for one year, are available at certain university colleges.

Affiliation to the TUC is open to trade unions throughout Britain, but Scottish trade unionists have set up their own national centre – the Scottish Trades Union Congress, which holds its own annual congress and conducts its own negotiations with the Government.

Traditionally, bargaining between employers and workers has taken place at national level, between the national associations of employers and the trade unions, and national collective agreements for an entire industry or type of worker have been carried out. This procedure may still apply, but in recent years there has been a growing tendency for negotiations to take place at 'shop floor' level, i.e. in the individual plant, factory or site, groups of workers being led and represented by the shop stewards. The ability of workers to organise and negotiate in this way at their place of work and frequently to bring about through their action the improvements they sought, led to growing tension between managements and workers and to many unofficial strikes.

The Donovan Commission Report

In 1965 a Royal Commission under the chairmanship of Lord Donovan was appointed:

> 'to consider relations between managements and employees and the role of trade unions and employers' associations in promoting the interests of their members and in accelerating the social and economic advance of the nation, with particular reference to the law affecting the activities of these bodies, and to report.'

In June 1968 the **Donovan Commission Report** was published.

The Commission drew attention to the two conflicting systems of industrial relations that existed in Britain – the formal system operated by the official institutions, and the informal system (the actual behaviour of the management, shop stewards and workers on the spot) that frequently overrode the collective agreements made under the formal system. Many of the informal agreements arrived at were the result of local 'custom and practice' and were unwritten understandings between shop stewards and managements. From this state of affairs, chaotic pay structures and frequent unofficial strikes had resulted. The Commission therefore recognised the need to accept that bargaining was frequently taking place between managements and unions in individual places of work, and to provide a framework within which such negotiations could be an official part of the collective bargaining structure.

Recommendations of the Donovan Commission
Collective bargaining machinery should be established at **company and factory level** and managements should work out with union representatives suitable procedures for the rapid settlement of grievances and disputes.

Industry-wide agreements should be confined to questions that can be appropriately settled at that level; such agreements should provide guidelines for company and factory agreements.

Managements and union representatives should work out agreements on the position of shop stewards and the treatment of redundancies, and should establish effective rules and procedures for industrial discipline.

There should be regular discussions between managements and workers' representatives on safety measures.

Management should work out constructive policies on recruitment, promotion, training and re-training, and keep workers' representatives fully informed.

Employers' associations should assist their members in the development of good industrial relations and join with the trade unions in working out industry-wide agreements designed to facilitate collective bargaining at company and factory level.

Trade unions should improve their organisation and procedures, and if necessary re-define the position and sphere of authority of shop stewards.

Trade unions should consider the possibility of further mergers between unions, and there should be closer union cooperation in such matters as disputed rights of representation (disputes of the 'who does what?' variety).

'In Place of Strife'

The Government White Paper '**In Place of Strife**' was published in January 1969. It endorsed the Donovan Commission's findings and agreed to its recommendation to set up a **Commission of Industrial Relations** (CIR). This was done in March 1969. The White Paper also published the Government's proposals for an **Industrial Relations Bill** based on the Donovan Commission's recommendations. The change of Government brought about by the British general election of June 1970 delayed the preparation of the bill, and the **Industrial Relations Act** was passed by the new Government in 1971.

This Act introduced voluntary unionism – the right of an employee to belong or not to belong to a trade union, set up a National Industrial Relations Court for the settlement of disputes, introduced registration of trade unions and employers' associations, and empowered the Secretary of State for Employment to order a sixty-day 'cooling-off' period if a dispute threatened to cause a serious national emergency. A Code of Industrial Relations set out guidelines for management, trade union officials, and workers on good industrial and human relations.

Many parts of the Act (especially the sixty-day cooling-off period and the question of voluntary unionism) were not acceptable to trade union leaders. With the change of Government in the spring of 1974, **the Act was repealed**, and the NIRC, together with the Code of Industrial Relations, was abolished.

Another general election in the autumn of the same year delayed the introduction of fresh legislation, but measures introduced during 1974–5 gave workers protection against unfair dismissal and required suitable payment to be made to employees when work was not available (except as a result of a strike).

Under the **Industry Act** 1975, trade unions were granted access to information concerning the future plans of any enterprise that played an important part in the national economy, unless this would not be in the public interest.

The most significant development at this time was the **Social Contract** – a voluntary agreement concerning wage restraint entered into by the government and the trade unions. This is dealt with in more detail in Chapter 53, The Government and the economy.

The public sector

Industrial employees in Government service and in the nationalised industries are encouraged to join the appropriate unions. Non-industrial employees, whose salaries and conditions of service are the responsibility of the Civil Service Department, belong to the various Civil Service trade unions.

In Local Government service there are separate national joint councils for the manual, clerical and technical grades of employees, which are responsible for negotiating wages and conditions of service with regional and district councils below the national level.

The Department of Employment

This Government department, headed by the Secretary of State for Employment, is responsible for employment, the maintenance of good industrial relations, the carrying out of pay policies, training and related activities.

Questions

1. Write an account of the work and importance of trade unions at either shop floor level or national level. (L.C.C. & I.)

2. Write briefly about: (*a*) the TUC, (*b*) Wages councils, (*c*) Shop stewards.

3. Write briefly about the Donovan Commission Report, mentioning at least six of the recommendations made by the Commission.

4. In relation to the settlement of industrial disputes, explain the terms: national (or industry) level; shop floor (or company/factory) level.

5. Describe some of the financial and other incentives that employers offer to their office staffs. Why do employers find it necessary to offer these benefits over and above good wages?

6. Outline the organisation and functions of the Department of Employment. (R.S.A.)

7. 'Trade Unions are not only concerned with increased wages but many other aspects of the economic and social well-being of their members.' Describe these wider functions and responsibilities of trade unions. (A.L.S.E.B.)

Chapter 44

Money

Goods are bought and sold for money. Without money trade would take place by **barter**, goods being exchanged for goods. Suppose that I want a pair of boots in return for a coat. I have to find someone who not only wishes to possess a coat like mine, but also has boots with which he is willing to part. I may discover that the boots and coat are too big or too small. To enable the exchange to take place there must be a double coincidence of wants. Even if the coat and boots are the right sizes, I may think that my coat is worth twice as much as the boots, but I cannot tear it into two in order to give one half of a coat for one pair of boots. Coats and boots are indivisible. They cannot be split up without losing their value. I must either make a bad bargain or begin another search for suitable boots and carry the coat from person to person.

The disadvantages of barter, the need for a double coincidence and the indivisibility of goods, are avoided by exchanging the goods for **something everyone is willing to take, i.e. for money**. I can sell my coat to anyone for money and be certain that someone who has boots to sell will take money in exchange for them. If the boots cost half as much as I obtained for the coat, the money can be divided without losing its value. £1 can be exchanged for 100p which, again, can be exchanged for £1, but if a coat were divided into 100 parts, the parts would be worth nothing.

In a barter transaction I deal with one person, giving goods to him at the same time as I receive goods from him. Money enables me to sell to any person at any time and to buy from a different person at a different time. By using money, selling can be quite separate from buying. Money is thus a **medium of exchange** or a means of payment and without it trade as we know it today would be impossible. How could we pay in goods and services for all the things we buy?

Instead of having to say that a coat is worth so many boots or chairs or anything else for which it might exchange, we can now give its value and the value of all goods in one thing, namely, money. We use money to **measure values**. The value expressed in money is the **price** and because we can give money prices to all things exchange is made much easier.

If we measured distance in paces, I would measure a cricket pitch as twenty-three paces long but you might make it twenty-one paces. We both use the pace as the unit of measurement, but my pace is not the same length as your pace. In the same way we might measure values in gold coins called pounds, but £1 made in some parts of the country might contain more gold than £1 made in other parts. When measurements varied like this, it was inconvenient and bad for trade and it became necessary to fix or to standardise the units so that they were the same all over the country. The gram was standardised by making it equal to the weight of a piece of metal kept in Paris and enacting that all gram weights should equal the weight of this standard gram. £1 was standardised in the form of a sovereign, a coin containing a fixed weight of gold, and by enacting that only the Government could mint coins. Money, as well as being a measure of value, is a **standard of value**. Not only are prices measured in money, but in money which has been given a standard unit which means the same to all, and this again makes trade easier.

In order to be a medium of exchange, money had to be originally some material that all people wanted. Many materials have been used as money, but the most important was **gold**. People all over the world will take gold in return for goods and services. Most countries have now learned how to use paper money instead of gold. England has its own system of paper money which enables trade to be carried on within the country just as easily as it was when gold coins were used. Foreigners, however, may not be prepared to accept our paper money, and for foreign trade gold is still important. It would be a great help to foreign trade if all countries adopted the same standard units of measurement. Many countries now use the metric system, but each country still has its own money system.

We measure coal by the kilogram and oil by the litre. We cannot add kilograms to litres to give a total that will mean anything, but we can add prices or money values when they are expressed in the same standard units of pounds or francs to tell us the total value of all kinds of things. Money serves as a **common denominator** for comparing, counting and adding together values of different things. When cash is not used, then money is merely a unit of account, something by means of which values can be recorded in books.

If, instead of buying a car worth £1000, I lend the money for one year, I expect that when it is repaid it will still buy a similar car and that I shall not need twice as much money for the purpose. Otherwise I would not lend the money, but use it to buy a car now. Neither would traders be willing to give credit if money were to lose its value quickly. Money, as well as being a standard of value, is a **standard for deferred payments**.

For the same reasons money is a **store of wealth**. A fruit-grower cannot keep the crop for long, but if he exchanges it for money he can store his wealth for as long as necessary. If he thought that in a year's time the money would become worthless, he would spend it now and save nothing.

Because money serves as a medium of exchange, a measure and a standard of value, a store of wealth and a standard for deferred payments, it makes **specialisation** possible. There is no need for a teacher to grow his own food. He can give all his time to teaching because he is paid in money which he knows people are willing to take for the goods and services that he requires and he can save some of it for future needs. By specialising and becoming experts at our jobs we can produce more and raise the standard of living.

Money **differs from other standards** of measurement in one important way. Imagine an island that has been carrying on trade by means of barter deciding to adopt a money system. Its government prints £1000 of money. This is the total supply of money in the island and nothing can be sold for more than £1000 in money. When 1000 articles are offered for sale at any one time, the sum obtained for them cannot be greater than £1000 and the average price per article no more than £1. If 500 articles are sold, the average price can be £2 and if 2000 articles are sold it can be £0.50. As the quantity of goods decreases or increases, prices rise or fall.

If the supply of money is increased to £2000, then 1000 articles could sell for an average price of £2 each and 500 articles for £4 each. An increase in the quantity of money leads to an increase in prices. In the same way a decrease in the quantity of money would cause prices to fall. Only by increasing or decreasing the quantity of goods and services sold and the quantity of money to the same extent would average prices remain the same.

This example shows that the **value of money alters**. The metre is not only the same length everywhere, but it is the same length at all times. If we buy a metre of ribbon today, we get exactly the same length as we did years ago and as we shall get years hence. £1, however, does not always buy the same length of ribbon. The value of the money unit alters from time to time, whereas the weight and length units do not alter. The length, width and weight measurements of this book do not alter but its value measurement or price does alter.

When prices rise the pound depreciates in value and will buy less. This process is inflation. In times of falling prices the pound appreciates and will buy more: then deflation is taking place. **Inflation and deflation** have important effects on business and employment, and governments must try to prevent these processes from taking place too rapidly, as we shall see from what happened in this and other countries.

Before the First World War this country used gold coins, sovereigns and half sovereigns. During the war it needed goods from abroad but could send very little in return. As foreigners were prepared to take gold in payment, the Government asked people to give up their gold coins so that they could be used for buying foreign goods. In return for the coins the Government gave notes promising to exchange the notes for gold coins whenever people wished to do so.

As long as the Government printed a note only when it received a gold coin, there would be no more money than previously. However, it is much easier and cheaper to get paper for printing notes than it is to get gold to be made into coins, and once a government starts printing notes there is a danger that it will print too many. A government has heavy bills to pay and normally it finds the money by taking it away from people in taxes. By printing notes a government could spend as much as it liked and settle its debts to its own people by using notes that it had printed at hardly any cost to itself.

When this happens **inflation** begins and prices rise higher and higher. After prices have risen workers demand more wages, but almost as soon as they have obtained them they ask for a further increase because higher wages cause prices to rise still more. Traders who are able to buy goods and labour at the lower prices and sell when prices have risen gain, but people who cannot get wages increased quickly and those who live on fixed pensions lose. Prices may rise so much in a short time that money becomes worthless.

In Germany in 1922–3 prices rose by more than 500 000 000 times. People spent their money as fast as they could. One day they could buy something with it, but the next day they would require many times as much money to buy the same thing. The faster they spent the faster prices went up. Finally, German money became worthless and had to be scrapped and another beginning made with new money. Wars are the most important causes of inflation because governments spend much more in times of war than in times of peace.

During inflation money loses its importance as a store of wealth and a standard of value and deferred payments. When prices rise very quickly, people will not save as much and are unwilling to lend and to give credit except at very high rates of interest. If prices in this country rise much more than prices in other countries, our goods become too dear for foreigners to buy and we ourselves buy more of the cheaper foreign goods causing unemployment here and difficulties in paying for imports.

Printing unlimited quantities of notes does not make a country richer. It is what money will buy that matters. As we learned in the chapter on capital, the only way in which all of us can become wealthier is by baking a bigger cake, i.e. by producing more goods and services to share among us. More money without more goods and services just leads to inflation.

After the war had ended in 1918 Britain decided to go back to the 1914 system and began preparing by cancelling some of the notes and building up a stock of gold. Reduction in the quantity of money meant deflation. Prices and profits now fell and employers wanted wages reduced but the workers refused and there were many long and serious strikes. In 1925 the old system was restored, but with one important difference. As people were now accustomed to paper money, gold coins were no longer to be minted. The gold was kept in the Bank of England and the coins that could have been made out of it were represented by pound and half pound notes which were much cheaper to make than gold coins. The notes were convertible, i.e. they could be exchanged for gold bars at the Bank of England.

In 1929 there was worldwide unemployment. Britain was not considered a safe place for money and so much gold was being taken out of the country that in 1931 the Government stopped further export of gold and the Bank of England was ordered to refuse to exchange notes for gold. The notes became inconvertible and have remained so ever since.

From what happened in the past we can learn that the quantity of money, although it is not the only cause of inflation and deflation, is very important and must be controlled. In this country prices have been rising at an average of 7 to 8 per cent per annum, but in some countries prices may rise by more than 100 per cent in one year. When the Government thinks that we are spending too much it may take some or all of the following measures. It may take more money away from us by increasing the taxes, or it may raise the rate of interest to make borrowing and hire purchase more expensive and to encourage people to save more, or it may force the banks to lend less.

In February 1971 the new **decimal money** became the official currency.

Money is, then, a means of exchange, a standard of value and of deferred payments, a store of wealth, a common denominator for comparing, counting and adding values, and a means whereby we can specialise. The quantity of money must be controlled to avoid the evils of inflation and deflation.

Questions

1. What is barter? What are the disadvantages of trading by barter?

2. Define money. Why is it much easier to trade with money than without it?

3. 'Money is a medium, a measure, a standard, a store'.
   (*a*) For what is money a medium?
   (*b*) What does it measure?
   (*c*) What is meant by a 'standard'?
   (*d*) For what is money a standard?
   (*e*) Why is it a store?
   (*f*) Has money any other functions?

4. How does £1 as a standard differ from 1 kilogram as a standard? Give reasons for your answer.

5. What is price? Why may the prices of houses rise or fall much more than other prices? Why may prices in general rise or fall?

6. What is inflation? What causes it? Why is it described as a 'vicious spiral' and as 'too much money chasing too few goods'?

7. What effects does deflation have on trade and employment? Who benefits by deflation?

8. Show, by means of an example, why the quantity of bank notes in circulation is important.

9. Give an account of the changes which have taken place in the British money system since 1914. (See also page 245.)

10. Which is best for trade (*a*) stable prices, (*b*) falling prices, (*c*) rising prices? Give reasons for your answer.

11. (*a*) Explain the functions of money in a modern society.
    (*b*) What constitutes the supply of money in the UK?
    (*c*) How does the Bank of England regulate the supply of money? (R.S.A.)

12. What is the meaning of the term 'money'? Explain whether or not 'money' is the same as 'legal tender'. (L.C.C. & I.)

Chapter 45

Bills of exchange and promissory notes

In Chapter 6 a cheque was described as a note to a banker ordering him to pay somebody a certain sum of money on demand. There are three parties to a cheque, the drawer, the drawee and the payee, the drawee always being a banker. Now other people besides bankers can be ordered to pay by means of written orders. When the drawee is not a banker the order is known as a bill of exchange. When, too, the order does not require payment on demand, but states a future time for payment, it is not a cheque, but a bill of exchange, even although the drawee is a banker.

The Bills of Exchange Act, 1882, **defines a bill of exchange** as an 'unconditional order in writing addressed by one person to another, signed by the person giving it, requiring the person to whom it is addressed to pay on demand or at a fixed or determinable future time a certain sum in money to or to the order of a specified person or to bearer'.

This definition includes everything we have said about cheques. In fact, a cheque is a special kind of bill of exchange, the Act defining it as 'A bill of exchange drawn on a banker, payable on demand'.

The order to pay must be unconditional. It must be 'pay' and not 'pay if' or 'pay but'. The sum to be paid must be 'certain', i.e. it must be definitely stated as £100 and not 'about £100'. The time of payment must be determinable. If payment is not to take place any time it is demanded, there must be some means of fixing the date, and either a definite time must be stated or it must depend on an event that is certain to happen, such as 'one month after the death of A'. 'One month after the marriage of A' is not enough because it is not certain that A will get married, but it is certain that he will die at some time.

In the bill given here A. Seller is the drawer and he had 'drawn' on

---

Bill of exchange

£50

53, Bridge Street,
Birmingham
1 September 19 . .

Three months after date pay to me or my order the sum of fifty pounds. Value received.

To B. Buyer,
28, Queen Street,
Stratford

A. Seller

B. Buyer, the drawee, who owes him money. In this case the money is to be paid to the drawer himself, and he is therefore the payee as well. He could, if he wished, order B. Buyer to pay the money to somebody else.

The draft, as the bill is now called, is given to the debtor to 'accept'. If the debtor or the drawee is willing to carry out the order he writes 'accepted' across the bill and signs it as shown below. The bill is now an 'acceptance' and is returned to the drawer.

Bills offer **advantages to debtors and creditors**. A bill provides a creditor with written **evidence** that the debtor has agreed to pay on a definite date and, if the debtor's reputation is good, people will be prepared to take the bill in return for money or goods knowing that they can obtain the money by presenting the bill to the drawee on the due date. Like cheques, bills can be endorsed and passed on, and are negotiable instruments, but the provisions for crossing cheques do not apply to bills.

Bill of exchange

£50

53, Bridge Street,
Birmingham
1 September 19 . .

Three months after date pay ~~Accepted B. Buyer~~ me or my order the sum of fifty pounds. Value received.

To B. Buyer,
28, Queen Street,
Stratford

A. Seller

Instead of passing on the bill the one who holds it **can discount it**. He takes it to a banker who will give him the sum named on it, less interest on that sum, for the number of days still to run before the due date. On the due date the bank will collect the full value of the bill from the drawee. In arriving at the due date months are always taken to be calendar months.

In the above example the bill is dated 1 September and the tenor is three months. The due date is therefore 1 September plus 3 months, i.e. 1 December. If on 19 September, 73 days before the due date, the bill is discounted at 5 per cent per annum the banker will give for it £50 less interest on £50 for 73 days.

$$£50 - \left(£50 \times \frac{73}{365} \times \frac{5}{100}\right) = £49.50$$

The discount taken by the banker is known as 'banker's discount' to distinguish it from true discount. The discount is calculated, not on the money paid by the banker, but on the sum named on the bill. The one who discounts the bill is therefore paying more than 5 per cent on the money he borrows from the banker on the security of the bill. He is paying £0.50 for the use of £49.50 for one-fifth of a year which is:

$$\frac{1}{2} \times \frac{2}{99} \times 5 \times 100 = 5.05 \text{ per cent per annum.}$$

If, when the bill is presented to the debtor on the due date, he does not pay, he is said to **dishonour** the bill. The holder of the bill must then act in accordance with the rules laid down by the Bills of Exchange Act. If he wants certain proof of the dishonour, he can note and protest the bill. To do this he asks a notary to present the bill again to the debtor and to 'note' on the bill when presentation took place and the answer given. The notary then prepares a document known as a 'protest', giving particulars of the bill and of the dishonour. A bill can be dishonoured by non-acceptance as well as by non-payment if the drawee had, on buying the goods, agreed to accept a bill.

When a bank has discounted a bill that is later dishonoured, it will demand payment from the person who brought it to the bank for discounting. The one who holds the bill when it is dishonoured will expect the person who passed it on to him to be responsible for seeing that he is paid.

In the event of the drawee wishing to pay the bill before it is due, he **can retire it**. If he pays before the due date, he will be losing interest on his money and therefore, when a bill is retired, interest on the sum mentioned on the bill is deducted for the time between the date of retiring and the due date. If B. Buyer retired his bill on 19 September, he would pay, taking interest at 5 per cent per annum, £49.50 instead of £50.

Besides discounting bills, banks will pay them on behalf of their customers. When accepting the bill, the debtor can write 'Accepted payable at Midland Bank, Stratford', and then instruct the bank to pay the bill out of his funds. Similarly, the holder of a bill can arrange for his banker to present it and collect the money which will be credited to his account. The drawee may bind himself to pay only a part of the sum stated on the bill by writing, for example, 'Accepted for £30 only'.

By the use of bills of exchange, the debtor can buy goods and sell them before he has to pay, while at the same time the seller of the goods can obtain cash by discounting the bill or he can pass it on in settlement of his own debts. This is why bills of exchange are so important in foreign trade where transactions take place between people living in different countries and who may know nothing about one another. The importer may be unwilling to pay before the arrival of the goods and the exporter may be unwilling to send them without being paid first. This difficulty can be overcome by the use of bills of exchange as will be explained later. In the home trade, bills are not so important as they used to be, having been replaced to a great extent by the use of cheques and banker's loans.

The Bills of Exchange Act makes a distinction between inland and foreign bills. An inland bill is one which is 'both drawn and payable within the British Islands or drawn within the British Islands upon some person resident therein. Any other bill is a foreign bill'. Most countries, other than the United Kingdom and Commonwealth countries, do not allow days of grace.

The Act also deals with **promissory notes**. It states that a promissory note is 'an unconditional promise in writing made by one person to another, signed by the maker, engaging to pay on demand or at a fixed or determinable future time, a sum certain in money to or to the order of a specified person or to bearer'.

There are only two parties to a promissory note, namely, the maker of the promise, and the one to whom the promise is made or the payee. There is no acceptance for promissory notes as is the case with bills. £1 notes, and all bank notes are promissory notes.

Cheques, bills of exchange and promissory notes form part of the country's currency. **Currency** includes anything that is generally accepted as a means of payment and of settling debts. Money orders and postal orders, and even stamps, are other instruments that do the work of money. But none of these, except bank notes, are legal tender. Coin and notes alone are legal tender.

Questions

1. What is the legal definition of a bill of exchange? How does a cheque differ from other bills of exchange?

2. On 1 January 19 . . H. Mills draws a bill at two months for £1000 on R. Stone. R. Stone accepts the draft, making it payable at Martins Bank.

    (*a*) Prepare the acceptance adding any necessary details.
    (*b*) Name the parties to the bill.
    (*c*) On what date must Stone pay the bill?

3. What are the advantages of a bill to (*a*) the buyer of goods, (*b*) the seller?

4. If H. Mills discounted the above bill on 26 January at 6 per cent per annum, how much would he receive for it?

5. A bill broker purchases a £1000 bill with 93 days to run, on the basis of a discount rate of $3\frac{1}{2}$ per cent per annum, and sells it to a bank on the same day at a discount of $3\frac{3}{8}$ per cent. What profit does he make?   (R.S.A.)

6. What must be done when a bill is dishonoured?

7. What is a promissory note? How does it differ from a bill of exchange?

8. Explain: tenor of a bill, retiring a bill, inland bill, negotiable instruments.

9. What makes up British currency? Which parts of it are legal tender currency?

10. Why are bills of exchange not so important in home trade as they used to be? Why are they still important in foreign trade?

Chapter 46

Bank loans · Money market · Base rate · Minimum lending rate

The legal tender currency of notes and coins equals about £70 per head of the population. The country needs several times this amount of money, and notes and coins must be supplemented by the other forms of money mentioned in the previous chapter and by 'bank money' (or loans). Bank money is by far the most important part of the money supply. **How banks 'create money'** by lending can be understood by making the bookkeeping entries for the following transactions.

1. I am prepared to let certain pupils in my school draw cheques on accounts opened with me. A. North, who wants to buy a cycle for £8 from B. South, asks for a loan. I do not give North any money, but credit his account and debit loans or advances to customers account with £8. I am now liable to give £8 according to North's instructions which he will give in the form of cheques.
2. A. North gives B. South a cheque for £8. South does not need the money at the moment and lets me keep it for him, paying the cheque into his account instead of cashing it, on the understanding that I am to pay the money out when he orders me to do so. Now I debit North and credit South with £8.
3. B. South buys a bat from D. East and gives him a cheque for £2. East pays the cheque into his account. Debit South and credit East with £2.
4. D. East buys £2 worth of books from A. North paying by means of a cheque which is paid into North's account. Debit East and credit North with £2.
5. B. South buys back the cycle from A. North for £6, North paying the cheque into his account. Debit South and credit North with £6.
6. A. North cancels the loan. Debit North and credit advances to customers account with £8.

Now there is no balance left on any of the accounts. I owe nothing to my customers and they owe nothing to me. The transactions have been carried through without the use of any cash. The loan and the cheques have done the work just as well as if I had lent eight £1 notes to A. North. This is why banks are said to create money when they grant credit or loans.

In the example we have just considered, no one asked for cash, but in practice some people will want to take cash out of the banks. Experience has shown that on an average only 8 per cent of what the banks owe to customers is asked for in cash. For every £100 cash paid into the banks, it

A. North

2.	B. South	£8	1.	Advance	£8
6.	Advances to customers	8	3.	D. East	2
			5.	B. South	6
		16			16

B. South

3.	D. East	£2	2.	A. North	£8
5.	A. North	6			
		8			8

D. East

4.	A. North	£2	3.	B. South	£2

Advances to customers

1.	A. North	£8	6.	A. North	£8

can be assumed that only £8 of it will be asked for in the form of cash. The other £92 will be allowed to remain in the bank being transferred from one account to another by means of cheques. The need to keep some cash places one limit on bank lending. Another limit is enforced by the Bank of England.

Suppose I start a bank and a depositor pays £100 into a savings account. The balance sheet is then

Balance sheet 1

Liabilities	£	Assets	£
Deposits	100	Cash in hand	100

The Bank of England requires a bank to open a current account at the Bank of England and pay into it an amount equal at least to $12\frac{1}{2}$ per cent of the bank's deposits. My bank decides to pay £75 into its current

Balance sheet 2

Liabilities	£	Assets	£
Deposits	100	Cash in hand	25
		Cash at the Bank of England	75
	100		100

account at the Bank of England and to keep £25 in the till. Cash at the Bank of England can be withdrawn on demand and is considered to be as good as cash in the till.

My bank must pay interest on the £100 savings deposited with it but cash in the till and money at the Bank of England earn nothing so my bank must find some way of making the deposit earn for it.

Cash at the Bank of England is one of the reserve assets that a bank must keep and the Bank of England is satisfied if the **reserve assets** are never less than $12\frac{1}{2}$ per cent of deposits. Thus my bank with reserve assets of £75 can owe £$\dfrac{75}{12\frac{1}{2}} \times 100 = £600$. It already owes £100 so it can owe another £500. It does so by lending, not by giving cash of which it has only £25, but by entering or depositing £500 on the credit side of borrowers' accounts and debiting loans or advances account with £500. These loans earn interest for the bank.

Balance sheet 3

Liabilities	£	Assets	£
Deposits (including advances)	600	Cash in hand	25
		Cash at the Bank of England	75
		Advances	500
	600		600

Suppose now that a customer takes £10 cash from my bank which replenishes its till by withdrawing £16 from its account at the Bank of England.

Balance sheet 4

Liabilities	£	Assets	£
Deposit	590	Cash in hand	31
		Cash at the Bank of England	59
		Advances	500
	590		590

The reserve assets are now $\frac{59}{590} \times 100 = 10$ per cent of deposits which is well below the minimum of $12\frac{1}{2}$ per cent demanded by the Bank of England.

Of course the bank will take steps to prevent the percentage falling below $12\frac{1}{2}$. It can

1. lend only to customers who can offer the best security and refuse others;
2. refuse to renew loans and press for repayment of loans outstanding;
3. raise the rate of interest so that
   (*a*) loans cost more and customers will borrow less and
   (*b*) savings earn more, which will encourage depositors to leave their money in the bank and may attract new savings.

The banks fix their own rates of interest. Each bank has a **base rate** which may be raised when money is scarce or lowered when it is plentiful. The rates charged for borrowing are determined by adding so much to base rate. A business offering the best security may be charged 1 per cent more than the base rate while someone with poor security may be charged 3 per cent more than base rate. Interest paid on savings also goes up or down with the base rate. Because the banks compete, the rate charged by one bank cannot differ much from the rates charged by other banks.

If the bank had adopted the above measures in time instead of having to pay out £10 cash it might have received £10 more which could have been paid into the Bank of England or used to acquire other assets. **Reserve assets** include, besides cash at the Bank of England, money at call and short notice, Treasury and other bills, and certain government and local authority securities. A bank may possess different kinds of government securities but on any date the only ones eligible to count as reserve assets are those which the Government must repay within one year of that date. The liabilities to be counted are mainly deposits.

It takes time for an alteration in the rate of interest to make itself felt. The extra money required by the banks cannot be saved and paid in immediately, nor can all loans be repaid at once. To meet this difficulty the banks make some of their **loans repayable at call or short notice**, lending for twenty-four hours only. Borrowers who receive a loan today, may be asked to repay it tomorrow morning. If the bank has no need of the money, the borrowers will be allowed to keep it for another day. Money at call is lent at low rates of interest. It does not earn much, but forms a first line of defence for a bank in need of more cash.

The borrowers are bill brokers and **discount houses** in London – about a dozen firms – who use the money to buy and sell bills of exchange and Treasury bills. They buy at one rate of discount and sell at a lower, thus making a profit after allowing for the interest on the borrowed money.

The **Treasury bill** is one of the means by which the Government borrows money. It is a promissory note promising to pay at the end of three months £5000 or £10 000. Buyers tender for the bills stating how much they are prepared to give for them. As there is no risk attached to the bills, the buyer being certain of receiving his money back on the due date, the Government may obtain the money at a very low rate of interest, sometimes at less than 1 per cent per annum. When, however, the Government takes steps to halt inflation, and forces up the rate of interest, less will be offered for bills. £98.50 given now for £100 to be received in three months gives a profit of £1.50, which is equivalent to a rate of over 6 per cent per annum before deducting expenses.

Many of the bills handled by the brokers and discount houses are sold to the banks after being selected and arranged in parcels containing bills that fall due on different dates so as to bring in a steady stream of cash. The bill dealers are expert middlemen, saving the banks the trouble of selecting and arranging bills into suitable lots for bringing in a regular supply of cash.

Each day bill brokers try to borrow as much as they have spent. When the banks do suddenly ask for the repayment of the loans and refuse further loans, the bill brokers must go elsewhere for the funds they need to carry on business. The only place they can go to is the Bank of England which is prepared to discount first-class bills at a rate fixed by itself, a rate which may be considerably more than that which was charged by the other banks.

The Bank of England's rate for discounting is known as the **minimum lending rate**. It is at least $\frac{1}{2}$ per cent higher than the average discount rate demanded by discount houses when they tender for Treasury Bills and is announced every Friday. The Bank is not bound to charge this rate but it will do so when it wants to restrict other banks. The Bank does not lend to anyone except the discount houses and they will borrow from it only when they must because of the high lending rate it charges. It is the **lender of last resort**.

The existence of the money and discount market, dealing in bills, enables the banks to reduce their lending and to increase their cash at very short notice. Without such a market they might have to borrow from the Bank of England, which could lay down its own terms and conditions for lending. The Bank of England, however, has other means of influencing the commercial banks as we shall see in the next chapter.

All reserve assets are liquid assets, i.e. they can be turned into cash quickly. If there is a big demand for cash the banks can find enough of it to pay at least $12\frac{1}{2}$ per cent of what they owe. Their **liquidity rate** is at least $12\frac{1}{2}$ per cent.

The ways in which a bank uses its money are shown in the balance sheet on page 239, the assets being arranged according to the ease with which they can be turned into money. Cash at the Bank of England, being obtainable on demand, earns nothing. The discounting of bills was dealt with in Chapter 45. As well as discounting bills, a bank is prepared to accept them on behalf of its customers. A creditor may not be prepared to trust his debtor's acceptance of a bill, but if a bank undertakes to pay it he can be certain of payment and will be able to discount the bill at a low rate. The acceptance of bills involves the bank in liabilities. As the debtor agrees to pay the amount of the bill to the bank before the due date, his undertaking is an asset. Thus, the same figure appears on both sides of the balance sheet. The banks earn a commission by lending their names in this way. They also use their financial standing by issuing bankers' drafts, in cases where a creditor will not accept a cheque. A banker's draft works in the same way as a money order. The debtor pays the money to the branch he uses and obtains a draft ordering another branch to pay an equivalent sum. He sends the draft to his creditor who is then certain of payment.

Questions

1. Why is the amount lent by the banks important to the country? Why may the Government want the banks to lend less?

2. When a bank lends £100:

   (a) Does it give the borrower notes?
   (b) If not, how does it give the loan?
   (c) How does the borrower spend the loan?
   (d) How much is he likely to ask for in cash?

3. What is the difference between 'bank money' and 'legal tender'? What is meant by the phrase the 'value of money'? Explain whether or not the value of money has changed in this country in recent years. (J.M.B.)

4. If a bank has £1 million in cash, how much could it lend? Explain how it could lend more than £1 million.

5. What is (a) money at call and short notice, (b) a Treasury bill?

6. Why does a bank prefer to lend for short periods? Why does it invest some of its funds instead of keeping them and lending more?

7. Describe the functions of the merchant banks and the discount houses in the London money market. What do you mean by the phrase the 'London money market'? (R.S.A.)

8. The balance sheet below shows a bank's assets as percentages of current and deposit accounts. (These percentages may change. Advances, for example, will be less than 50 per cent when there is a severe 'credit squeeze' and more than 50 per cent when there is no squeeze.) What would the proportion of cash to current and deposit accounts be if:

   (a) £1 million were taken out of the bank in cash?
   (b) £1 million in cash were paid into the bank?
   (c) What might be the result on the rate of interest in each case?

Balance sheet

Liabilities	£ million	Assets	£ million
Capital	3	Cash in hand and at the Bank of England	8
Reserve	1	Cheques in course of collection	6
Current, deposit, and other accounts	100	Money at call and short notice	13
Liabilities for engagements and acceptances on behalf of customers	6	Bills discounted (including Treasury Bills)	10
		Special Deposits	2
		Investments	13
		Advances to customers	50
		Liability of customers for acceptances	6
		Premises, etc.	2
	110		110

9. For what main purpose does a bank use its funds? What other uses does it make of them? Which use is (a) the most profitable, (b) the least profitable?

10. Banks maintain the total of reserve assets at not less than $12\frac{1}{2}$ per cent of deposits. Why is this 'liquidity ratio' important?

11. 'It is a sign of good trading conditions if many businessmen are overdrawing their current accounts.' State, with reasons, whether or not you agree.

    How do (*a*) the businessmen, (*b*) their customers and (*c*) the banks, benefit by the granting of loans and overdrafts by the commercial banks? (R.S.A.)

12. A small industrial firm has decided to buy an additional machine costing £700 for its factory. The balance at the bank is not sufficient to cover outright purchase. What advice would you offer?

(A.E.B.)

Chapter 47

The Bank of England

The Bank of England was set up in 1694 for the purpose of lending money to the British Government. Besides receiving interest on the loan the Bank was granted certain privileges, one of which was **the right to print bank notes** equal in value to the sum lent to the Government. These notes were for £5 and upwards, and like the present £1 notes were promises to pay on demand. Some other banks also printed notes and used them for making loans (the system of credits and cheques described in the previous chapter developed later).

Originally, bank notes had been receipts given by the banks for money deposited with them. When people began using the notes instead of the money which remained in the banks, the bankers found they could lend some of the money, or instead of lending the money, print more notes to give to borrowers. One who borrowed £100 from a bank would be given £100 in notes which the banks acquired merely for the cost of paper and printing. Interest was charged on the loan so that the more notes the bank printed and lent the more profit it made. There was, therefore, a strong temptation to print many more notes than represented the gold coins in the bank.

The notes were not legal tender but creditors would accept them and pass them on so long as they had confidence in the bank making the promise, just the same as they accept cheques today. As soon as anything happened to cause people to suspect that the bank was not as safe as they had supposed, they would refuse to accept its notes and all those who had notes in their possession would at once take them to the bank and demand gold coins instead. If the bank had printed too many notes, it would be unable to find enough gold coins to meet the demand, and its notes might then become worthless pieces of paper, causing loss to many who had trusted the banker's promise. So frequent did such bank failures become that in 1844 the Bank Charter Act was passed to deal with the matter of notes.

The **Bank Charter Act** provided that in future only the Bank of England should be allowed to print notes. Existing banks issuing notes were to be allowed to continue to do so, but when they gave up or lost the right the Bank of England could take over two-thirds of their note issue. It was not until 1921 that the Bank of England became the only note-issuing bank in England and Wales. It then had a **monopoly of note-issuing**, but the profit made by using the notes had to be paid to the Government.

The Bank was allowed to print notes to the value of £14 million, even if there was no gold in the Bank. But for every note above this figure there had to be an equivalent amount of gold in the Bank. If the Bank printed a total of £20 million in notes, it would have to keep £6 million in gold; if it printed £30 million, it would have to possess £16 million in gold, and so on. This meant that the Bank was at any time able to give gold for all the notes issued except for £14 million. This £14 million without gold backing was known as the **Fiduciary issue**. It had no gold behind it, but it was covered by securities which in case of need could be sold in order to pay cash for the notes.

As well as being obliged to give gold in return for notes, the Bank was also bound to buy at a fixed price all gold offered to it.

The fiduciary issue is now much greater than it was in 1844. It is 160 times as much as it was in 1914. Two world wars brought about such an increase in the notes required that they are now practically all fiduciary. During the wars most people were working and earning and so there was a demand for more money to pay wages. More notes were put into circulation while, at the same time, goods were becoming scarcer, and, as we should expect from what was said in the chapter on money, prices rose.

The granting of a monopoly in notes to the Bank of England in 1844 meant that the commercial banks had to find some other ways of earning. The result was the development of the system of credits and cheques described in the previous chapter. Instead of printing promises to pay and giving these to borrowers, the bankers allowed borrowers to make notes or

---

Bank of England return, ... 19 . .

Issue Department

Liabilities	£ *million*	Assets	£ *million*
Notes issued:		Government debt	11.0
In circulation	3157.4	Other Government securities	3188.0
In banking		Other securities	0.7
department	43.0	Coin other than gold bullion	0.3
		Fiduciary issue	3200.0
		Gold coin and bullion	0.4
	3200.4		3200.4

Banking Department

Capital	14.5	Government securities	537.5
Rest	3.8	Other securities:	
Public accounts	13.3	Discounts and advances	89.7
Special deposits	221.1	Securities	30.4
Other deposits:		Notes	43.0
Bankers	311.0	Coin	0.4
Other accounts	137.3		
	701.0		701.0

cheques ordering them to pay. In both cases the banks undertook to pay more cash than they possessed.

The Bank Charter Act also provided for the division of the Bank of England into two departments, **the issue and the banking departments**, which had to be kept entirely separate. Once a week the Bank has to publish a return or balance sheet showing the notes issued and the value of the gold held. The return is prepared every Thursday and appears in the newspapers on Friday.

A **bank return** is given on page 242. The capital and the rest (a reserve of profit) belong to the Bank, so that the amount due to customers is £682 million, while the Bank has only £43 million in notes, i.e. its reserve of notes equals 6 per cent of its debts. The Bank can never pay all its debts at once. Like the commercial banks, it trusts that all will not ask to be paid at the same time. If all the banks were to ask for the £311 million due to them, there would not be enough notes to pay them. When people are spending more, they take more notes out of their banks; the latter then obtain more by drawing on their current accounts at the Bank of England. The more the Bank pays out, the more its percentage or proportion of its notes to its debts falls. If the percentage continues to fall, the Bank will take steps to check the demand for notes.

One means of checking the demand is to raise the **Minimum Lending Rate** which is the rate at which the Bank of England will discount bills of exchange, i.e. the charge it makes for lending money on the security of bills of exchange. In recent years it has varied from 4 to 14 per cent. At present it has dropped to $6\frac{1}{2}$ per cent. When the rate is raised, other banks increase their rates of interest, so that people are more inclined to leave their money in the banks and are less inclined to borrow. In this way the Bank can protect its reserve of notes and influence the lending of the other banks.

Another method is that of **open market operations**. The Bank of England is the **bankers' bank.** In the return on page 242 the Bank of England owes £311 million to the other banks. This balance at the Bank of England is considered by the other banks to be as good as cash in hand, because they can obtain it whenever they like. If the Bank of England now sells £20 million worth of securities, they will be bought by the other banks and their customers, and be paid for by drawing cheques in favour of the Bank of England. The other banks now owe the Bank of England £20 million for the securities, and this sum is deducted from the £311 million that the Bank of England owes them, leaving a balance of £291 million. Thus, the reserve assets of the commercial banks have been reduced and may now be less than $12\frac{1}{2}$ per cent of what they owe to depositors and borrowers. As a result, they are not so ready to lend, and charge more for loans and give more interest for money left with them. When cash is plentiful and the Bank of England thinks more lending is necessary, it will increase the amount it owes to other banks and add to their reserve assets by buying securities.

Under the newer method of **special deposits**, the commercial banks are ordered to place a percentage of their deposits in the Bank of England.

These special deposits are kept quite separate from the balances which the banks regard as part of their cash in hand. They earn interest, but cannot be touched until the Bank of England thinks it safe to relax the credit squeeze. The advantage of special deposits is that they reduce the reserve assets and the lending power of the banks at once, whereas the older methods take some time to become effective. The amount of the special deposits, and the rate of interest paid on them, can be varied to suit the circumstances.

Notes taken out of the Bank of England are **in circulation**. They are withdrawn from the banks, and after passing from hand to hand find their way back to the banks. Every week, for example, employers cash cheques for wages which their employees spend on food and other requirements, the shopkeepers paying most of the notes they receive into the banks, to be withdrawn again in the following week. When more notes than usual are required, the banks draw cheques on their accounts at the Bank of England and take out notes. If the increased demand persists, it may be necessary for the Bank to obtain Treasury consent to increase the note issue. It can buy coins whenever it likes from the Mint, the Government's account being credited with the value of the coins received.

When the demand for notes decreases, they accumulate in the banks, which pay the surplus into their accounts at the Bank of England, which may then seek permission to reduce the note issue. The Government itself may bring about an alteration in the demand for notes. When, for instance, it thinks that there is too much money chasing too few goods, and that there are signs of inflation, it may take some of the money away from us by increasing the taxes, and by borrowing more from the banks and from the public, leaving us with less money to spend.

Besides looking after the note issue and being a bank for the bankers, the Bank of England is also the **bank for the Government**. It raises loans for the Government and pays the interest. It is an agent for the Mint, collecting up coins that are worn and sending them back to the Mint. It keeps the country's gold reserve (not shown in the return) which is important for foreign payments, and it controls the amount of British money exchanged for foreign money. Ordinary banking is still carried on, but is only a very small part of the Bank's work, and only a few customers selected by the Bank are now accepted.

The Bank of England is the **centre of the money market** for short-term borrowing and lending. The lenders are the banks, insurance and investment companies. The borrowers are the Government, discount and acceptance houses, bill brokers and stockbrokers.

In 1946 the Bank was nationalised and became the property of the Government. It was then given power to issue certain instructions to other banks. It can now tell these banks not to grant loans if it is intended to use them for certain purposes.

Here is a **summary** of the Bank's work.

It acts as banker for the Government.

It looks after the country's supply of notes and coin.

It is the bankers' bank.

It is the centre of the money market and controls the lending of the commercial banks by altering its minimum lending rate and by other means.

It keeps the country's reserve of gold and foreign money.

It exercises foreign exchange controls.

It does a little ordinary banking.

It is the lender of last resort.

Historical Survey

1694	Bank of England founded to lend to the Government. Allowed to print notes.
1816	Gold standard adopted.
1833	Bank of England notes made legal tender.
1844	Bank Charter Act. Note issues to be controlled. All notes except fiduciary issue to be backed by gold.
1914–	First World War. Gold coins called in and replaced by Government notes.
1918	Increasing fiduciary issue. Rising prices.
1918	Further amalgamation of banks, without Government consent, forbidden to prevent a banking monopoly.
1920	Silver in coins reduced from 92.5 per cent to 50 per cent.
1921	Bank of England gained complete monopoly of bank note issue in England and Wales, but Government notes issued during the war still in existence.
1925	Return to the gold standard, but gold coins not to be minted. Coins that could have been made from the gold kept at the Bank to be represented by notes. Falling prices. Strikes.
1928	Currency and Bank Notes Act. Government notes amalgamated with Bank of England notes. Bank of England now responsible for all notes in England and Wales.
1929–	Worldwide depression. Unemployment on a large scale.
1931	Gold being taken from the Bank of England in large quantities.
1931	Britain abandoned the gold standard and notes could no longer be exchanged for gold.
1932	Exchange Equalisation Account set up to steady the value of the pound in foreign monies. Foreign traders then knew what they would receive for exports and pay for imports. Encouraged foreign trade.
1939–1945	Second World War. Quantity of notes increased. Rising prices and wages.
1946	Bank of England nationalised. Silver coins replaced by cupro-nickel coins.
1949 1967	The pound devalued. A dollar now bought more pounds and so more British exports. Imports discouraged.
1971	Decimal currency adopted.
1971	Rising unemployment – Government eased credit restrictions; more money available to consumers. Prices rose sharply.
1972	£ became a 'floating' currency; undue fluctuations prevented by activities of Exchange Equalisation Account.
1972–1973	Special deposits increased on three occasions to discourage lending by commercial banks; high level of inflation.
1974	World oil prices quadrupled.
1975–1976	Minimum Lending Rate rose to unprecedented high levels; credit hard to obtain; rise in unemployment.
1976–1978	Minimum Lending Rate reduced by steady steps to $6\frac{1}{2}$ per cent at the time of writing.

Questions

1. Why and when was the Bank of England founded? What special right was granted to it? Did other banks have the same right?

2. In what ways does the Bank of England differ from a commercial bank?

3. Give the main provisions of the Bank Charter Act of 1844. Why was the Act necessary? Do all its provisions apply today?

4. What is the fiduciary issue? How does the fiduciary issue today differ from that of 1844? What were the main causes of the changes? Is there any connection between changes in the fiduciary issue and prices?

5. What are the functions of the Bank of England? Which do you consider the most important?

6. The Bank of England is the bankers' bank. Why do commercial banks have current accounts at the Bank of England? Of what importance is this to the Bank of England?

7. 'If the Bank of England wishes the economy of the country to contract it will make borrowing dearer by increasing the Minimum Lending Rate.' Explain this quotation and describe the effects of an increase in the Minimum Lending Rate. (R.S.A.)

8. In what ways can the Bank of England control the lending of the other banks?

9. The following items appear on the liabilities side of the banking department account:
   rest, public deposits, special deposits, other deposits. What do you understand by each of these items? (R.S.A.)

10. The Bank of England controls the monetary policy of the country by making changes in the *Minimum Lending Rate*, by *open market operations*, and by means of *special deposits*. Write brief explanatory notes on the three phrases in italics. (R.S.A.)

11. In what ways does a central bank differ from a commercial bank?
    (L.C.C. & I.)

Chapter 48

The Clearing House

The joint-stock banks settle any claims they have on one another through the Bank of England and the Clearing House. The receiver of a cheque usually pays it into his account. If he happens to use the same bank as the drawer of the cheque, all the bank has to do is to debit the drawer and credit the one who paid in the cheque. When different branches of the same bank are involved, the branch receiving the cheque credits its customer and then sends it to the drawer's branch where the debit is made in the drawer's account. Where different banks are concerned the matter is not so simple, but can be dealt with by means of the **Clearing House** as explained below.

1. A of Plymouth gives B of Derby a cheque for £100. B pays it into Lloyds Bank, Derby, to be added to his balance there. But A has his money in the Midland Bank, Plymouth. The Derby bank sends the cheque to its Head Office in London from where it goes to the Clearing House.
2. C of Derby gives D of Plymouth a cheque for £120. This also finds its way through the Midland Head Office to the Clearing House.

At the Clearing House a representative of Lloyds Bank will hand over the cheque drawn by A of Plymouth to a representative of the Midland Bank and claim the £100 due to their customer B. Similarly, the Midland representative will hand over the cheque drawn by C, a customer of Lloyds Bank and claim the £120 for their customer D. On balance Lloyds Bank owes the Midland Bank £20. When the representatives have agreed the figures, particulars are sent to the Bank of England which transfers the amount by way of the Clearing House account from Lloyds account to the Midland account without using any cash.

After being passed through the clearing, the cheque drawn by A is sent back to Plymouth where it is debited to his account and the balance in his account reduced by £100. The other cheque is sent to Derby where C's account is debited with £120. If, when the cheque reaches the drawer's bank, it is found that the drawer has no money in his account, notice must be given to the other bank in accordance with rules drawn up by the Clearing House. Unless this notice is received within a certain time, the cheque is assumed to be good for payment.

When the amounts due to or from each bank have been determined, they are listed as shown below. Figures are in millions of pounds. The second column tells us that Bank A is to collect £5 million from Bank B, £2 million from

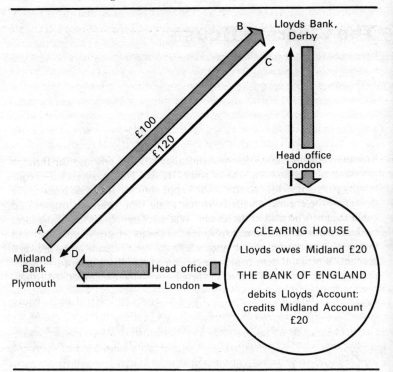

Bank D, but owes £1 million to Bank C. On the whole it is to receive a net sum of £6 million. The other banks must therefore owe it £6 million which is shown by the −6 in the right-hand column.

	Due from (+) or to (−) banks in first column				Net sum due from (−)
Bank	A	B	C	D	or to (+) all banks
A	—	−5	+1	−2	−6
B	+5	—	−4	−1	0
C	−1	+4	—	−2	+1
D	+2	+1	+2	—	+5
	+6	0	−1	−5	0

The third column shows that Bank B is neither a debtor nor a creditor, what it owes being equal to what is due to it. On balance Bank C owes £1 million and Bank D £5 million.

The total due to all banks must be equal to the total due from all banks. If the figures are correct the horizontal and vertical totals should equal 0.

In adjusting the accounts there is no need to make separate entries for each figure in the table. The Bank of England makes one entry in A's account, a credit of £6 million, and one debit of £1 million in C's account, and one debit of £5 million in D's account. No cash need pass because tomorrow Bank A might owe £6 million and the position will be restored by reversing the entries.

The clearing is, of course, much more complicated than appears from the above example. All banks and their branches are involved, and cheques totalling millions of pounds are dealt with, and have to be sorted, bundled and checked by representatives before the sums due to or from each bank can be agreed. Some cheques are exchanged directly between Head Offices instead of being sent forward through the Clearing House. Banks which are not members of the Clearing House employ one of the big banks as their agent. In one year more than 700 million cheques worth over £700 000 million pass through the London Clearing House.

There are two clearings each day. The *town clearing* deals with cheques paid into and drawn on banks quite near the Bank of England. If these are for £500 or more they are cleared in one day, i.e. it is possible to cash the cheque the same day as it is paid into the bank. Other cheques pass through the **general clearing**; it takes normally three days to clear these.

The cheque clearing is known as the debit clearing. **Giro credits** go through the credit clearing which deals with about 200 million credits worth more than £13 000 million in one year.

The **Clearing House returns** show the state of trade. When the figures are increasing, they indicate that trade is improving, and vice versa. In studying the figures it must be remembered that all cheques do not go through the London Clearing House. Allowances must also be made for Stock Exchange transactions which, at times, may cause a big increase in the figures without there being any improvement in trade. Rising or falling prices will also cause the Clearing House returns to increase or decrease while the volume of trade remains constant.

Clearing Houses for setting off debts and settling the differences only are used by other businesses as well as by banks. The Stock Exchange and air line companies, for instance, have Clearing Houses for settlement of the sums due between members.

Questions

1. With the help of a diagram show how the Clearing House works.

2. Why is it necessary to clear cheques? What difference would it make if there were no Clearing House?

3. How does the Clearing House save time and work? How do smaller banks, which are not members of the Clearing House, have their cheques cleared? Which other businesses make use of 'clearing'?

4. What are the (*a*) general clearing, (*b*) town clearing, (*c*) debit clearing, (*d*) credit clearing?

5. What can be learned from the monthly totals of cheques cleared? What allowances must be made when studying the figures?

6. Black, who banks with the Westminster Bank, Penzance, sends a crossed cheque, marked 'account payee only' and bearing the letter 'R', to White who banks with Barclays Bank, Carlisle. Describe what happens to the cheque after it has been received by White.

Chapter 49

Foreign trade · Free trade · Protection · Visible and invisible exports · Balance of trade and payments

For Britain, foreign trade is very important. A small island **cannot produce all it needs**. Cotton, coffee, rice, etc., cannot be grown here, and we have no gold, no copper, nor many other important products. If we are to obtain these things we must buy them from other countries and sell abroad the goods we can produce here.

Foreign trade is carried on, not only in those goods we cannot produce ourselves, but also in some goods we could make quite well. It pays us to concentrate on those things we can do best, in the same way as it pays Lancashire to concentrate on cotton and Yorkshire on wool.

If England can make article A for £1 and article B for £2 and if France can make article A for £2 and article B for £1 the total cost of making one of A and one of B in both countries would be £6. But if England makes two of A and France makes two of B the total cost is only £4 plus the expenses of exchanging one of A for one of B. As the cost of transport is small, and cheaper mass production may be possible, both countries gain by **specialisation** and exchange, instead of making everything themselves.

Free traders believe that this principle should be applied as far as possible, and that we should not make anything ourselves if we can obtain it cheaper from abroad. **Protectionists** believe the opposite, and want us to make all we can in this country. They point out that what happens in foreign countries is beyond our control, and changes there may cause serious unemployment in this country when foreigners no longer want to buy or cannot buy our goods. In time of war we may be unable to import goods which are essential if we rely on other countries to produce them for us. Some things could be made here just as cheaply as they are made abroad, if foreign competition did not kill the industry before it had a chance to establish itself. 'Infant industries' should be protected until they have grown up, according to the protectionists.

Before the First World War Britain was a free trade country, but during that war it began to protect its industries and within a few years it became, like most other countries, a protectionist country, restricting the imports of certain foreign goods in order to encourage their manufacture at home.

The chief way of **restricting imports** of foreign goods is to impose **customs duties** on them. Their cost is then increased by the amount of the duty, and, if the homemade goods can be sold for less, no one will buy the foreign goods. The duty may be levied on the value of goods, as, for example, 22 per cent on motor-cars, when it is said to be an *ad valorem* duty, or it may be charged on the quantity or weight of the goods, as 4p per litre on petrol, when it is termed a specific duty. When a duty is levied for the purpose of raising money for the Government and not for keeping out foreign goods, it is a revenue duty. The more revenue a duty brings, the less effective it is from the point of view of the protectionists.

Goods made in this country may also be taxed, for example, spirits. Such duties are **excise duties**. When an excise duty on any article equals the customs duty, it is a countervailing duty, neither the homemade nor the foreign product being given an advantage.

Britain and its partners in the Common Market admit some goods from certain undeveloped countries free or at a lower duty than is charged on similar goods from other countries. Such duties are called preferential duties.

There are other ways in which the Government can protect home industries besides by taxing imports. A limit or **quota** is sometimes placed on the quantity to be imported in any year. Those who use foreign goods can be compelled to use a certain percentage of British goods. Cinemas, for instance, must show a certain proportion of British films, and millers have agreed to use a certain quantity of British wheat. Instead of putting up the price of the imported goods by the imposition of a customs duty, the Government can allow them to be sold cheaply and if home producers cannot then make a profit, **subsidies** can be paid to them, as is the case with beetsugar which has to compete with sugar made from cane. Some countries stipulate that some of the money they pay for imports must be used to buy goods for export.

Details of the goods imported and exported must be given to the Customs Offices on forms known as 'entries', so that the goods can be checked and the amount of the duty calculated. No goods can be taken away from the docks without the permission of the customs officers. If the importer is not ready to pay the duty, he must store the goods in a bonded warehouse.

A **bonded warehouse** is one whose owner has signed a bond with the Government to the effect that he will not part with the goods until he has been informed that the duty has been paid. While lying at the bonded warehouse, the goods can be weighed, sorted, graded and packed just as at any other warehouse, the owner of the warehouse charging for storage and for any work done in connection with the goods. The goods can be sold while still in bond, the seller stipulating that the buyer must pay the duty. In this way an importer can avoid having to keep capital idle as he need not pay the duty until he is ready to use the goods. Excise duties paid on goods that are later exported and customs duties paid on goods that are re-exported, can be recovered. The shipper makes a declaration that the goods have been sent out of the country on a document known as a 'debenture' which, after being certified by the customs, entitles him to the refund or 'drawback'. If such goods are stored in a bonded warehouse to await shipment, no duty need be paid at any time. This is a great help to merchants carrying on a large entrepôt trade.

Entrepôt trade is the name given to the re-export trade that is done in commercial centres throughout the world, where foreign goods arrive for trans-shipment to other destinations. London, Liverpool and Hull are three of the British ports where entrepôt trade is carried on. It may be defined as the export trade done by a country in another country's products.

Free ports, like Copenhagen and Hong Kong, allow imports to be landed without paying any duties. Within the free area, materials can be stored, repacked and manufactured, and then re-exported, without having had to pay and reclaim customs duties.

Since the Second World War there has been a movement towards freer trade. In 1947 a number of countries, including the most important trading countries, signed the **General Agreement on Tariffs and Trade** for the purpose of reducing customs duties and promoting world trade. Headquarters were set up in Geneva where representatives of various countries meet to discuss alterations in duties.

In 1957 Belgium, Holland, Luxembourg, France, West Germany and Italy agreed by the Treaty of Rome to form the European Economic Community. Duties between the 'Six' were gradually reduced and finally abolished in 1970. The 'Six' formed the **Common Market** in which goods from any of these countries could be sold without having to pay import duties. As a result of the greater freedom and competition, industry and commerce in the Common Market were expected to increase considerably.

The 'Six' also agreed to form a **Customs Union**, i.e. they have a common tariff of duties on goods imported from non-members, but with free trade within the Union.

In 1959 Austria, Denmark, Norway, Portugal, Sweden, Switzerland and the United Kingdom signed the Stockholm Convention and set up the **European Free Trade Association** for manufactured goods only. Duties on such goods between member countries were reduced and finally abolished in 1966. Each of the 'Seven' (which were later joined by Iceland) reserved the right to please itself as to what duties it levied on goods from other countries, i.e. they did not propose to form a Customs Union, with a common tariff on goods from countries which are not members of the Association. In 1973 Britain and Denmark left the Association and, together with Eire, joined the Common Market.

An outline of the organisation of the EEC is set out in Chapter 54.

From the customs entries supplied by individual traders, the total figures for the whole country are compiled. When the results, such as those given in the table on page 254, show that the country is buying more foreign goods and services than it can afford, the Government may take steps to remedy matters.

The difference between the two totals is known as the **visible balance**. In this case it is an adverse or unfavourable balance because the imports are greater than the exports. When the exports are greater than the imports, the balance is favourable.

The visible balance is the difference between the imports and exports of **goods only**.

Goods	Imports £ million c.i.f.	Exports £ million f.o.b.
Food, beverages and tobacco	1904	398
Basic materials	1142	172
Minerals, fuels, lubricants	973	174
Manufactured goods	3773	5278
Others	107	153
Total	7899	6175

Services too are imported and exported, and this kind of trade is called **invisible** trade. Services imported by Britain include money spent abroad by holidaymakers, the cost of maintaining units of the armed forces abroad and money sent out of the country by immigrants and others. British services exported include shipping, banking and insurance, dividends on foreign investments and interest on foreign loans, and the considerable earnings from the expanding tourist industry. Britain's invisible exports are usually much higher than her invisible imports, and this favourable balance usually makes a significant difference to her balance of payments, as there is almost always an adverse balance of visible imports over visible exports.

Here are some of the terms used to describe a country's final balances at the end of the fiscal year:

Balance of trade: The difference between the total value of *goods* exported and *goods* imported.

Balance of payments, Current account: The difference between the total value of exports and imports of *goods and services* added together; in other words, the difference between the total value of all export and import *trade*.

Balance of payments, Capital account: The difference between the total value of *capital* moving into and moving out of the country.

Over-all balance of payments: This figure takes into account all movements of money into and out of the country, and is an indication of the country's economic soundness. If the over-all balance of payments shows a credit balance, the country is said to have a *favourable* balance, but if it shows a deficit the country has an *unfavourable* balance.

Countries, like individuals, must pay their way, and if there is an unfavourable balance the government takes steps to correct it. It may:

Limit the number of import licences issued;
Place limits on credit to reduce consumer spending (see pp. 70, 243);
Limit wage increases to keep costs and prices down so that people will buy home-produced goods in preference to imports;
Devalue the currency. When the £ is devalued in terms of the American

dollar, for example, British goods in America cost less in dollars and American goods in Britain cost more in sterling; therefore, exports to America tend to rise and American imports into Britain to decrease.

But the most positive step a Government can take is to increase the value of its exports by giving as much help and encouragement as possible to firms to expand into overseas markets.

Balance of trade and payment

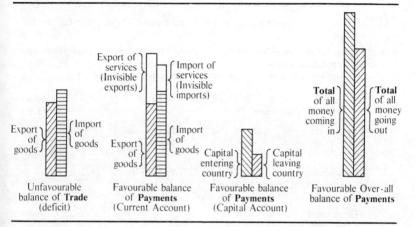

Questions

1. Why is foreign trade so important to Britain?

2. Argue in favour of (*a*) free trade, (*b*) protection.

3. Describe two similarities and four differences between home and foreign trade.   (W.J.E.C.)

4. Distinguish between the following duties and state why they are levied: (*a*) customs, (*b*) excise, (*c*) *ad valorem*, (*d*) specific, (*e*) revenue, (*f*) countervailing.

5. In what ways can British industry be protected?

6. What are bonded warehouses? Why are they advantageous to (*a*) exporters, (*b*) importers?   (W.J.E.C.)

7. What do you know about GATT, EFTA, EEC?

8. Home trade has been defined as trade within the same customs area.
   (*a*) How then in similar terms would you define foreign trade?
   (*b*) What is a customs area?
   (*c*) Why are the activities of HM Customs important in connection with foreign trade?   (W.J.E.C.)

9. What are invisible exports? Why are they important to Britain?

10. Explain visible balance of trade, balance of current account and balance of payments.

11. Why did Britain want to join the Common Market?

12. (*a*) Explain clearly the difference between visible and invisible items in foreign trade. (*b*) Briefly describe the main groups of items which comprise Britain's visible trade. (*c*) Comment upon the importance of invisible trade to Britain. (A.E.B.)

13. Explain: (i) Entrepôt trade, (ii) free ports, (iii) Customs drawback.

14. (*a*) In what ways does trade between countries differ from trade within a country?
    (*b*) What are the main benefits derived from trade between countries? (R.S.A.)

15. Explain, giving examples, the term 'invisible exports'; can there be invisible imports? (L.C.C. & I.)

16. Foreign trade has been defined as trade between the inhabitants of two Customs areas.
    (*a*) How then, in similar terms, would you define home trade?
    (*b*) What is a Customs area?
    (*c*) Why are the activities of HM Customs & Excise of importance in connection with home trade? (W.J.E.C.)

17. You are employed by a firm which manufactures and exports clothing. The pound is devalued. Briefly, what are the possible effects on your firm's sales abroad? (R.S.A.)

18. The following figures are available for UTOPIA for the year 1975–6, relating to its trade with the rest of the world:

	£M
Money spent on goods imported	4480
Money spent on goods exported	4000
Money spent by Utopia on use of foreign transport	239
Money spent by foreigners using Utopian transport	275
Money spent by Utopia on use of foreign insurance and financial services	300
Money spent by foreigners on use of Utopian insurance and financial services	375
Money spent by Utopians on foreign travel	250
Money spent by foreigners visiting Utopia	400
Money spent by Utopians on private transfers to foreigners	150
Money spent by foreigners on private transfers to Utopians	75
Money spent by Utopian Government overseas	200
Money spent by foreign Governments in Utopia	300
Money paid out by Utopian firms to foreigners in interest, profit and dividends	200
Money received by Utopians as interest, profit and dividends on investments in other countries	600

Draw up a statement in tabular form to show:

(*a*) the balance of visible trade
(*b*) the balance of invisibles
(*c*) the overall balance of payments

of Utopia, stating in each case whether the balance is favourable or unfavourable.

(Marks will be awarded for presentation.) (R.S.A.)

Chapter 50

Exporting and importing · Market research · Government aid

A maker whose goods can be sold abroad may, as in the home trade, employ several channels of distribution. He can make use of middlemen or he can adopt more direct methods of trading. We shall first discuss a manufacturer who has decided to make goods for export and to do his own marketing by setting up an export and foreign sales department.

Before making goods for a new market it is necessary to discover first of all if the goods can be sold profitably in that market. To answer that question is one of the objects of **market research**. We have already discussed the importance of market research in selling on the home market, and it is vital to success in overseas markets. The exporter must consider, for example:

Physical and climatic conditions: The suitability of his products: heavy clothing is not worn in hot climates; mountaineering equipment would not be in demand in a flat country.

Social conditions: If there is a low standard of living with poor wage levels, there may be no market for television sets or cars or luxury products. It may be desirable, even necessary, for pricelists and sales promotion literature to be translated into a local language, with local units of measurement and currency. If there is a high level of illiteracy, advertising matter may need to be in pictures and symbols rather than in words.

Traditions and customs: Habits of work and play and dress may affect the goods bought. Imported cricket, baseball or tennis gear would not sell in a country where these games are not played. Religion may also affect the situation – certain foods may not be eaten on religious grounds.

Existing products and structure of trade: If there is a satisfactory locally-made product at an acceptable price, there will be no sale for an imported one. Attention must be given to sizes of products and to the suitability of packaging. If machinery is to be sent to a certain area, it will be necessary to ensure after-sales service. Some estimate of the efficiency of local agents should be obtained beforehand.

The legal aspect: Such matters as safety regulations for vehicles and machinery; left- or right-hand drive for cars; restrictions on the sale of drugs; and any import quotas that exist.

It is possible to learn from income tax statistics how many people earn £5 a week, £6, and so on. From such figures the maker can obtain an estimate of the number who can afford to buy his goods and are possible customers. Census returns, showing the number of men and women in various age groups, are further guides. Questionnaires can be sent to a few selected people and their answers considered as samples to show what can be expected in the country as a whole.

Attention must be given to the methods of trading adopted in the foreign markets. Wholesalers and other traders may be more or less important than they are at home and more credit may be demanded. At home the maker may leave the provision of spare parts and an after-sales service to others, but if no such facilities are available abroad he must be prepared to organise them or to open a branch abroad. Certain goods may be subject to heavy duties, making it almost impossible for the exporter to compete with foreign producers. Imports may be limited by quotas and other restrictions.

The Central Office of Information in London publishes booklets and reports on the industrial development and social conditions in many foreign countries; and the **Export Intelligence Department** of the Department of Trade has branches in all the main cities of Britain to supply information to firms interested in exporting.

The British Overseas Trade Board (*BOTB*)

The Board is made up of people especially experienced in export activities, including representatives of commerce and industry together with representatives of the Department of Trade and the Commonwealth Office. Its main task is to direct export intelligence work, to work on the promotion of British goods overseas through trade fairs and other similar activities (British 'weeks', for example), to give financial support to encourage overseas firms to visit Britain, and to help British firms to participate in trade missions overseas.

Intending exporters may also obtain information from:

The Banks, which nowadays form part of a world-wide network of banking and are in a position to obtain information about markets and the financial standing of foreign companies and agents through their own branches and agents in many parts of the world;

The Confederation of British Industry, the Chambers of Commerce, and the various Trade Associations, all of which have information available to their members on export markets, problems of distribution, foreign agents, tariffs and other restrictions, and so on. The work of these associations is discussed in detail in Chapter 42.

After deciding that there are good prospects for his goods abroad the maker may advertise. The kind of advertising that has proved successful at home may not be suitable elsewhere. The native language must be used and prices and measurements must be given in the foreign units which may not be pounds and metres. Where the population is mainly illiterate, pictures and symbols must be used.

The **Government aids** exporters in many ways. It has set up Export Boards to study various regions and to give information and advice to firms which could sell their goods in those areas. It helps to arrange exhibitions and fairs advertising British goods and pays some of the cost. The **Department of Trade** has formed an Export Intelligence Department with branches in the main cities to answer queries from firms who wish to export.

Insurance companies insure the risk that debts will not be paid, but they do not cover non-payment resulting from wars, or from political changes, such as new laws making it impossible for the importer to pay. The **Exports Credit Guarantee Department** of the Department of Trade insures these risks so that banks are readier to lend to exporters who offer policies covering such risks as security. The department guarantees bank loans made to exporters to enable them to give credit and when banks reduce their lending they must give preference to exporters.

The Department of Trade collects information of value to exporters from its representatives in all parts of the world. It publishes books and journals like the weekly *Trade and Industry* which gives news of opportunities abroad and draws attention to changes in tariffs, customs regulations and documents required.

Over 80 per cent of our exports are provided by less than 30 per cent of the firms. To help small firms sell abroad, big firms with experience in exporting and owning special export departments are being encouraged to help them to market their goods abroad. Ten firms have joined with the Government to form an **Export Corporation** to act as an export merchant for small firms. The corporation buys suitable goods and exports them on its own account.

Foreigners will not buy British goods if they can buy cheaper elsewhere. To prevent prices rising faster than foreign prices the Government tries to limit increases in wages, costs and prices. To keep down imports the production of more food and goods at home is being encouraged.

Questions

1. Discuss the part played by market research and advertising in the marketing of goods.   (R.S.A.)

2. Suppose you are a small manufacturer of engineering products. What would you have to do if you wished to enter the export market?   (W.J.E.C.)

3. Chambers of commerce, trade associations and the Confederation of British Industry, are all concerned with the promotion of trade. Discuss the work of any two of them.   (R.S.A.)

4. What factors tend to discourage a British manufacturer from exporting? How does the Government help to overcome these difficulties?   (A.E.B.)

5. In what ways does the Government at present assist exporters? Suggest other ways in which the Government could encourage exports. (W.J.E.C.)

6. What is devaluation? What difference does it make to (*a*) prices of exports, (*b*) prices of imports, (*c*) prices we pay in the shops?

7. 'To sell abroad successfully, we must remain competitive.' Competitive in what ways? (L.C.C. & I.)

8. The directors of a small manufacturing company have decided to explore the possibilities of selling their product abroad. The directors wish to seek your advice on help available to exporters from (*a*) the company's bank, (*b*) the chamber of commerce, (*c*) the Department of Trade and (*d*) any other useful sources. Prepare a report to the directors. (R.S.A.)

9. The Department of Trade is charged with the promotion of the country's overseas trade. What services does it offer to the exporter and how is it organised to provide them?

10. Give three reasons to explain why international trade is so important to Britain. What steps can be taken to increase exports? (A.L.S.E.B.)

11. An exporter faces marketing problems which are not found in home trade. Describe the nature of these problems. (L.C.C. & I.)

12. (*a*) Indicate how the consumer is affected by foreign trade.
    (*b*) Comment on the statement: 'Home and foreign trade differ in details but fundamentally they are similar.' (W.J.E.C.)

13. Discuss the importance of market research to a medium-sized manufacturer of office furniture, (*a*) in the home trade, and (*b*) in the export trade. Mention the various data which are required. (L.C.C. & I.)

Chapter 51

Exporting and importing · Bills of lading · Export merchants · Customs procedure

When an order, or **indent** as it is known, is received from abroad the exporter gets the goods ready for the journey. It is most important to see that they are suitably packed. The indent may give instructions as to the type of packing to be used. Goods that must be stowed in a ship, travel through different climatic zones, and then, perhaps, be taken long distances overland, must have packing that will stand up to all risks of rough handling and weather. To save space it may be better to send certain goods, such as cycles, in parts and assemble them after arrival. The packing must be marked clearly in accordance with the instructions on the indent, the marking being durable and able to stand up to the journey. Some countries demand that cases should bear marks required by their customs regulations as well as the usual markings for delivery.

The goods having been packed, arrangements for **transport** must be made. Shipping companies issue lists giving the sailing dates, ports of departure and destination, etc., of their vessels. The exporter selects a suitable ship and obtains a shipping note from the owners and returns it to them with particulars of the goods to be shipped. Later, he receives a calling forward notice telling him when the goods should be at the docks ready for loading. Unless the goods arrive by that date, the ship may sail without them, involving the exporter in storage expenses and delays. The carrier who delivers the goods at the docks obtains a weight note stating the weights and measurements of the goods delivered, or, if the goods are delivered to a warehouse to await loading, he obtains a wharfinger's receipt. Goods arriving by canal or river are transferred directly from the barge to the ship, a mate's receipt being given for them. These documents are receipts for the goods, the details of weights and measurements they contain being required for calculating the cost of carriage by sea.

Meanwhile the exporter has obtained from the shipowners or their agents, **bills of lading** setting forth the terms of carriage and leaving blank spaces for inserting the name of the ship, ports of departure and destination, name and address of the consignee, description of the goods, weights and measurements, number of cases, their markings, etc. These are filled in and returned to the shipowners. As the goods are taken on board, they are checked by tally clerks and any defects recorded. The bill is signed by the shipowners and returned to the exporter in exchange for the weight note obtained when the goods were delivered at the docks.

Had any faults been found in the packing or in the goods, these would be noted on the bill in order to safeguard the ship-owner against claims for damage. A bill bearing such notes is known as a 'dirty' bill as opposed to a 'clean' bill. Unless the goods have been actually taken on board when the bill is issued, it will be a 'received for shipment bill' instead of an 'on board bill'. Clean and on board bills are obtained if possible.

'Through' bills of lading make the shipping company responsible for arranging any further transport that may be required after the goods have been unloaded at the destination port in order to send them to the consignee. A 'grouped' bill of lading is one used when several lots of goods are sent together, but are destined for different consignees.

The bill of lading is the document of title to the goods, which cannot be claimed without it. When the goods arrive at the foreign port, the bill must be produced before they can be claimed. The bill can be made out to a certain person only, or to order, when it can be endorsed and passed on like a cheque, ownership of the goods being transferred from one person to another. Unlike a cheque, however, it is not fully negotiable, because the bearer's claim to the goods can never be better than the claim of the person who passed on the bill to him. Had a bill been stolen before being passed on, it would not confer a legal right to the goods.

An exporter who has quoted c.i.f. terms has to insure the goods for the sea journey and obtain a policy of marine **insurance** as explained in Chapter 39. The indent may contain instructions as to the insurance of the goods.

Details of the goods exported must be sent to the **customs** authorites on forms known as shipping bills (for dutiable goods requiring an export licence) and specifications (for other goods). The goods must be described in accordance with the Import and Export Lists issued by the customs. Values must be f.o.b. values and weights must be net. Duty paid on the goods or on the materials from which they are made may be refunded when they are exported, the exporter being responsible for claiming the drawback before the goods are shipped and for obtaining the debenture entitling him to repayment.

The exporter must send to the importer at least three documents – the invoice, the bill of lading and the insurance policy. The **invoice** is the bill stating what goods have been sent, their weights, markings, prices and values, together with any other charge that may be due to the exporter, such as freight and insurance premiums paid by him. The importer requires the invoice to see for what he owes and how much he owes and for checking with his copy of the indent. He may ask for several copies to be sent to him. He must have the bill of lading to claim the goods, and the insurance policy enables him to claim from the insurance company the value of the damage, if any, suffered by the goods during the voyage.

At least three copies of the invoice, bill of lading and insurance policy are required. One set is sent to the importer by ship or airmail, and, in case these go astray, another set is forwarded by a different ship, the exporter keeping one set for himself.

Some countries demand **special invoices** and certificates of value and of origin. These can usually be obtained from consuls representing these countries. They are required for customs purposes. When a duty is *ad valorem* the customs authorities want to be satisfied that the values stated are the true values in case the exporter is trying to avoid paying the full amount of the duty. The purpose of the consular invoice is to certify that the values given are the true values and the values charged to the buyer on the commercial invoice sent to him. In cases where some countries are given preferential duties it is necessary to make certain that the goods were actually made in those countries and are entitled to the lower duty by demanding a certificate of origin signed by a consul or other responsible person.

Enough has now been said about exporting and importing, without mentioning the problems connected with payment to be discussed in the next chapter, to show that it is a difficult business involving a great deal of work and detailed knowledge about goods, markets, packing, transport, currencies, and laws and regulations enforced by various countries. Many manufacturers, especially the smaller ones, have no wish to undertake the work if they can avoid it. They would rather give all their time and energies to manufacturing and rely on others to send and sell their goods abroad.

Instead of trying to obtain foreign orders himself the maker can place the work in the hands of foreign **agents** who will collect the orders and transmit them to him. The agent, too, will send any information that may be useful to the exporter, and may receive goods to keep in stock and for distribution to customers. Goods can be consigned to agents for sale at a commission as explained on page 172. Occasionally, foreign makers of similar goods will undertake the marketing.

The exporter may also receive orders from buying agents in this country employed by foreigners to obtain goods for them. These agents receive indents from abroad stating what is required. If the indent leaves it to the agent to choose the maker, it is an 'open' indent. A 'closed' indent names the makers to whom the agent must forward the indent. These agents keep their principals informed of the prices and market conditions here and work on a commission basis.

The work of packing can be delegated to a firm of experts who may also be prepared to arrange for transporting the goods abroad. They are known as 'packing and forwarding agents'.

Shipping brokers can be employed to find space in a ship or plane that will take the goods at the right time to the right place. The great market for shipping is the Baltic Exchange, London.

The manufacturer can rid himself of all export troubles by dealing with the **export merchants**. The merchants are in business on their own account, though they also act as agents for foreign buyers. The manufacturer sells his goods to them and is paid promptly in the same way as when he sells to the wholesaler in the home trade.

The export merchants claim that they serve the maker in three important ways:
1. They are market experts who know what the foreign buyers need and they can advise the maker as to what kind of goods will sell best.

2. They know all there is to know about the procedure of exporting goods, what forms to fill in, what the customs regulations are, how to insure the goods, etc.

3. They pay the manufacturer at once in British money, while giving credit to the overseas buyers.

As they deal in goods supplied by many makers, they can spread the expenses over a large turnover. They can also send several makers' goods in one shipment on one bill of lading, thus saving in shipping, banking and insurance costs. It may be cheaper for the manufacturers, particularly the smaller ones, to use them instead of setting up their own exporting departments. The part played in foreign trade by the import and export merchants can be compared with that of the wholesalers in the home trade.

The **British importer** can obtain his goods through the same channels and he can pay for them in the same way. When the foreign goods arrive at the docks, he claims them by producing the bill of lading. Before he can take them away, he must give details to the customs authorities who check them with the ship's report of the cargoes carried. For goods not liable to duty, he fills in three copies of an entry for free goods. One copy is retained by the customs and one is required to present to the customs officer who examines the goods when they are unloaded and who then signs an out of charge note enabling the goods to be taken away from the docks.

For dutiable goods an entry for warehousing must be completed, naming the warehouse where the goods are to be stored. Storage for such goods must be in a bonded warehouse so that they cannot be removed until the duty has been paid. The warehouse acknowledges that it holds the goods by issuing a dock or warehouse warrant to the importer. The dock warrant can be endorsed and passed on. It is a document of title and the person who produces it claims the goods, but he has no better right to them than the person from whom he took the warrant.

To take away dutiable goods as soon as they are landed from the ship, an entry for home use ex ship is made out. After checking and payment of the duty the goods can be removed from the docks.

Although imports of manufactured goods are increasing, the bulk of **British imports** still consists of foods and raw materials, many of which are sold through brokers and Exchanges as described in Chapter 36.

Questions

1. What middlemen may be connected with the export of goods?

2. What arrangements must be made for shipping exports?

3. What is a bill of lading? Why is it important in foreign trade?

4. Describe the nature and uses of the (*a*) commercial invoice, (*b*) consular invoice, (*c*) certificate of origin.

5. Which documents must be sent to a foreign importer? Explain why these documents are required.

6. Describe the various ways in which exporters obtain orders. Give three reasons why trading abroad is more difficult than trading at home. (J.M.B.)

7. What are the advantages and disadvantages to a maker of selling to export merchants instead of setting up his own export department?

8. Describe what happens when goods liable to customs duties arrive at a British port.

9. Write notes on (a) open indent, (b) entry for home use, (c) weight note, (d) dock or warehouse warrant, (e) dirty bill of lading, (f) mate's receipt.

10. How does the export trade of Britain benefit from the services of (i) export merchants, (ii) the Exports Credit Guarantee Department? (L.C.C. & I.)

11. Explain briefly four of the following and illustrate their importance in foreign trade: (a) the Exports Credit Guarantee Department, (b) a bill of lading, (c) the procedure for release of 'free-entry goods', (d) Customs and Excise drawback, (e) discounting bills of exchange. (L.C.C. & I.)

12. A manufacturer who is considering entering the export trade must decide whether he should use direct or indirect export. What are the main considerations to be borne in mind by the manufacturer in deciding which method to use? Give reasons for your answers. (A.E.B.)

13. Explain the meaning and importance of direct and indirect export, stating the chief considerations which a motor car manufacturer should take into account when deciding which method to employ. (L.C.C. & I.)

14. A business is operating successfully in the home market. The Government is urging businessmen to export. Discuss the extra problems which may face a businessman when deciding whether to try to enter the export market for the first time. (R.S.A.)

Chapter 52

Payment in foreign trade · Bills of exchange · Documentary credits · Insurance

An exporter has to secure payment from a debtor who may live on the other side of the globe and about whom he may know nothing. He is loath to ship the goods without being reasonably certain of payment, while the importer does not wish to pay without some guarantee that he will receive the goods. To add to the **difficulties**, various countries use different kinds of money, such as dollars and francs, while disturbed political and economic conditions, strikes and wars may make foreign trade with some countries a very risky business.

The exporter can learn something about the financial position of his debtor through the banks and the Exports Department of the Board of Trade, which can make inquiries through their agents abroad. If the replies are satisfactory he can ship the goods and mail the documents direct to the importer in the hope that he will pay upon receipt of the goods. This process takes time, possibly months, during which the exporter has to find more capital to finance further transactions and is losing interest on the money outstanding. If the debtor does not pay, recovery of the debt through the courts of a distant country whose laws differ from ours may prove to be a difficult and costly matter.

By drawing a **bill of exchange** on the importer, the exporter may obtain a promise of payment on a certain date and a means of raising funds in the meantime. Three copies of the bill are made, two being sent with the documents by different mails, in case one is lost or delayed. When one has been paid, the other two are void. This method again takes time, and there is no guarantee that having accepted and returned the bill the debtor will honour it on the due date. If the debtor's reputation is good, the exporter can obtain funds at once by discounting the bill or by using it as security for an overdraft or a loan.

£1000

10, Station Street,
Birmingham
1 April 19 . .

Sixty days after sight of this First of Exchange (Second and Third of the same date and tenor unpaid) pay to Lloyds Bank, Birmingham, the sum of One thousand pounds. Value received.

To John Ashton,
42 High Street,
Cape Town

Robert Bell.

By availing himself of the **services offered by the banks** the exporter can make certain that his customer either accepts or pays the bill before obtaining possession of the goods. In this case he lodges the documents at the bank together with written instructions as to what he wishes the bank to do. The bank sends the bill of exchange with documents attached to a suitable bank in the importer's country. On receipt of the documents the foreign bank notifies the importer who must accept or pay the bill before the bank hands over the bill of lading and the other documents which he must have to get possession of the goods when they arrive. If acceptance only is required, the bill is known as a **D/A** (documents against acceptance) bill, if payment is demanded first it is a **D/P** (documents against payment) bill.

There is no certainty that a D/A bill will be paid on the due date merely because a trader has accepted it. The exporter may therefore require the importer to obtain someone of a greater financial standing to undertake payment of the bill. The importer then asks his bank to accept the bill on his behalf. Before agreeing to do so, the bank will expect the importer to pay to it the amount of the bill at once or it will satisfy itself that he will be in a position to pay by the due date. The bank binds itself to pay the exporter and the importer binds himself to pay the bank. The foreign bank is in a much better position than the exporter to judge the debtor's ability to pay.

It is not always necessary to send the bill abroad for acceptance because a foreign importer can arrange for a bank in Britain to accept bills on his behalf. Certain businesses in London have specialised in this kind of work, lending their names to traders in return for a commission. The names and reputation of these **acceptance houses** or **merchant banks** are well known throughout the world, and creditors are satisfied that bills accepted by them will be paid. Originally, they were traders who were asked by smaller and less well-known traders to accept bills on their behalf. As their acceptance work was profitable and increased, they gradually gave up trading and developed into bankers. Bank bills, or bills accepted by banks, are much safer than trade bills, or bills accepted by individual traders, and can be discounted at lower rates of discount.

When the exporter has drawn a D/P bill, the bank is responsible for seeing that payment is received before it releases the documents. It sometimes happens that the importer is not in a position to pay at the time the goods arrive. In such a case the bank, if it is satisfied that he can sell the goods and will pay, forwards the amount due to the exporter and obtains a **trust receipt** from the importer guaranteeing that he will make good the amount as soon as the goods have been sold. Otherwise the bank would have to store the goods until it had notified the exporter and received his instructions as to what to do with them.

To prevent such delays and expense the exporter, when he lodges the documents at his bank, can include a **letter of hypothecation** authorising it, in the event of failure to accept or pay the bill, to sell the goods and remit the proceeds less expenses. The letter of hypothecation is also used when an exporter discounts a bill with his bank or obtains an overdraft or a loan on the security of the bill, and when he has an acceptance credit from a merchant bank. When granted an **acceptance credit**, the exporter hands the documents, including the bill drawn on the importer, to the bank and draws another bill on the bank. He then obtains funds by discounting this bank bill at a low rate. The bank will have to pay anyone who brings this bill to it on the due date and it expects to collect the money for doing so from the importer when he is presented with the bill drawn on him by the exporter. If the importer fails to pay the bank can, under the letter of hypothecation, sell the goods to recover its money.

A safer and quicker method of obtaining payment, but one that is more expensive to the importer, is that of **documentary credits**, whereby the importer arranges for a bank in Britain to open a credit in favour of the exporter. If the credit can be altered or cancelled at any time, it is said to be a revocable credit, whereas a credit that cannot be altered or withdrawn during a certain period, usually six months, is an irrevocable credit and is, of course, much safer. To make an irrevocable credit safer still, it may be confirmed or guaranteed by a British bank. This added precaution is necessary because in some countries banking is not well developed, the banks being smaller and much less secure than they are here. With a confirmed irrevocable credit, the British bank must pay the exporter, whatever happens to the importer and the foreign bank.

Before opening a credit, the importer's bank will inquire into his financial position and make certain that he will be able to pay; there is no need for the exporter to make any such inquiries. It will insist that the exporter is to be told to make out the bill of lading either in the bank's name or that it be endorsed to the bank, while the importer must sign a letter of hypothecation. By these means, the bank retains control of the goods which, in the event of the importer failing to pay as agreed, it can sell to recover the amount it paid to the exporter.

When the credit has been arranged, the London bank notifies the exporter by sending him a **letter of credit** telling him what he must do to use it, such as making out the bills of lading to the bank. The exporter must comply strictly with these instructions. He then draws a bill of exchange and presents it, together with the invoice, bill of lading, insurance policy and any other documents required, at the bank. If the bill is payable at sight, the exporter receives his money immediately. If it is payable so many days after sight or date, the bank accepts it and he can discount it at low rates because it is a bank bill and a **clean bill**, i.e. a bill without any documents attached to it, as opposed to a documentary bill. The bill of lading and other documents are sent to the importer's bank abroad.

In trade with the East, importers, instead of opening credits, often arrange for a London bank to **negotiate the bill**, i.e. to buy or to discount it. The exporter takes all the documents to the bank which discounts the bill at once before sending it to the foreign bank. Before he can obtain the documents, the importer must pay the bill. The exporter obtains immediate cash, but as he is discounting a trade bill, accepted by an importer and not by a bank, he will not receive as much for it as for a bank bill and if the importer fails to pay the bank may claim the full value of the bill from the exporter.

To **summarise** we can say that the four chief methods by which an exporter secures payment are:

1. Sending the bill of exchange and documents direct to the importer and running the risk that he is to be trusted, as well as waiting for his money. Sending the documents to a bank first to make sure that the debtor accepts or pays the bill and to obtain funds more quickly.
3. Requesting the opening of documentary credits which may be:
   (*a*) revocable:
   (*b*) unconfirmed irrevocable;
   (*c*) confirmed irrevocable.
   This gives immediate payment, (*c*) being the safest method of all.
4. Authority to negotiate gives immediate payment, but the bank may recover this if the debtor fails to pay. Discount rates are higher than in 3.

An exporter who has to give about two years' credit can secure immediate payment by selling the debt to **factors** or finance companies who then collect instalments from the foreigner. Sometimes the exports are first sold to the factors who then appoint the manufacturer as their agent to send the goods abroad and to collect the money. This method enables the manufacturer to keep in touch with his customers who do not know that the real creditor is the factor. This system is known as 'undisclosed factoring'.

As stated on page 259 the exporter can insure foreign debts with insurance companies or with the Exports Credit Guarantee Department of the Ministry of Trade and Industry. The **ECGD also guarantees bank loans** made to exporters who give up to five years' credit. When an export is very costly, such as a steelworks worth many millions of pounds, the importers may want to spread payment over more than five years, possibly over ten to fifteen years. In such cases the department may guarantee loans made *to the foreign importers* to enable them to pay the instalments to the exporters. The rate of interest on loans made under these guarantees to help exporters is less than the rate on loans for other purposes and is fixed for the whole period so that exporters and importers know from the outset what the transaction will cost. In certain cases the department itself may make loans to exporters.

Payment between persons in different countries need not involve the passing of any actual cash. A bank asked to collect £1000 from an importer may at the same time be asked to pay out £1000 to an exporter. What the banks receive from importers, they pay out again to exporters, the transactions balancing one another to a great extent, much as the amounts due between British banks cancel out at the clearing. The British exporters are paid through the banks by the British importers and the foreign creditor is paid by the foreign debtor.

Funds are transferred from one country to another by crediting and debiting accounts in the banks' books. They can be transmitted by telegraphing in code (telegraphic transfer or T/T), or, if there is no hurry, notice can be sent by airmail or by ship (mail transfer or M/T). The cheapest is mail transfer, but it is also the slowest.

Methods of payment in foreign trade

Method	Procedure
Bill of Exchange	Exporter sends Bill of Exchange to importer; Importer accepts and signs Bill and returns it to exporter; Exporter discounts Acceptance with Merchant Bank (Discount House) (Trade bill)
Bill of Exchange through banks	Exporter lodges Shipping Documents with his bank; Bank's branch or agent in importer's country releases documents against payment or acceptance of the bill by importer (D/A or D/P) (Trade bill) Payment simplified if importer's bank holds documents and guarantees payment (Bank bill)
Bill of Exchange through British banks	Bill of exchange passes from exporter's bank to British bank acting for foreign importer – bill need not leave country (Bank bill)
Documentary credit	Foreign importer opens credit with a bank in Britain so that payments may be transferred to exporter's bank
By instalments	For large installations (power stations, roads, bridges, dams) exporter usually protected by insurance through underwriters or the ECGD; or debt may be taken over by finance or foreign Government

Note: When banks are involved in guaranteeing payment, they usually require a letter of hypothecation, empowering them to sell the goods to recover the money due.

Questions

1. What difficulties are connected with payment in foreign trade as contrasted with home trade?

2. What is a foreign bill of exchange? What purpose does the bill of exchange serve in foreign trade?

3. How can the exporter make certain that the importer accepts or pays the bill before he gains possession of the goods?

4. Explain (*a*) documentary bill, (*b*) clean bill, (*c*) D/A bill, (*d*) D/P bill, (*e*) bank bill, (*f*) trade bill. Say, with reasons, which can be discounted for the lowest rates.

5. In what ways can an exporter protect himself against loss through non-payment for goods sold abroad?

6. What are (*a*) letters of hypothecation, (*b*) trust receipts? Of what use are they to (*c*) exporters, (*d*) banks?

7. Describe how the banks finance exports. What other services do they give to foreign traders?

8. Give a definition of a documentary credit and describe its general nature. Explain, in outline, the role of the banks when this method of payment is used.
(A.E.B.)

9. A *bill of lading is a document of title*; it is an essential document in connection with a *documentary credit* be that credit *revocable, irrevocable* or *confirmed*.
(*a*) Briefly explain the meaning of the phrases and words in italics.
(*b*) Why is a documentary credit of great importance to exporters and importers?
(W.J.E.C.)

10. In what ways are exporters helped to grant long periods of credit to their foreign customers?

11. Of what use are factors and finance companies to exporters?

12. 'In exporting there are three major disadvantages: competition from local production, delay in payment, and selling at a distance.' In what ways are these disadvantages overcome?

13. Mention *three* kinds of credits which may be opened in foreign trade, and explain one of these in more detail.
(L.C.C. & I.)

14. Name the chief documents which are usually required when a documentary credit is opened in foreign trade.

15. Select any **one** of these documents, and explain its use and purpose as fully as possible.
(L.C.C. & I.)

16. (*a*) Name **four** problems met with in foreign trade which are not met with in home trade.
(*b*) Describe briefly how **each** of these problems is overcome.
(M.R.E.B.)

Chapter 53

The Government and the economy · Gross National Product · Taxation · Inflation · Government policies

In Chapter 29, pp. 136–7, we examined the system of budgetary control by which large businesses plan and control their production and related activities. The Government, too, plans the economic life of the country by means of budgets. The **annual budget**, normally presented in March or April, is a set of proposals for financing Government expenditure in the ensuing year. The proposals are described in the Budget Speech, delivered to the House of Commons by the Chancellor of the Exchequer. Sometimes emergency or 'mini' budgets are put forward by the Government at other times of the year, when circumstances necessitate such action.

The total value of a country's products, including both goods and services, reckoned over a period of time, usually one year, is known as the country's **Gross National Product** (G.N.P.), and in preparing the Budget the Government seeks to provide for a satisfactory balance between this figure and the total of the claims likely to be made on it. The Budget deals, therefore, with the *financing of necessary expenditure*, and usually includes some changes in taxes.

Taxes that are paid by the consumer through the prices charged by suppliers of goods and services are known as **indirect taxation** (for example, Customs and Excise duties and V.A.T.); taxes that are levied on specific items and paid directly by the taxpayer are described as **direct taxation** (income tax, estate duty, car licences, dog licences, local rates and so on).

In 1973, far reaching changes in the structure of income tax, company taxation and purchase taxes were introduced, as follows:

A single graduated personal tax replaced the former system of income tax and surtax.
Corporation tax was levied at a single rate on all company profits, including both undistributed profits and those distributed as dividends.
An 8 per cent Value Added Tax (V.A.T.) replaced the former Selective Employment Tax and Purchase Tax.

Income tax: From April 1975, a basic rate of 35 per cent was levied on the first £4500 of taxable income (i.e. total net income after deduction of allowances). From £4500 to £5000 the rate became 40 per cent, and thereafter it increased by 5 per cent for successive 'bands' of income up to a maximum of 83 per cent reached at a level of £20 000. Special allowances for married people and in respect of children still apply.

Company taxation: The new single rate of corporation tax was fixed for 1974–5 at 52 per cent, with a reduced rate for small companies (defined in the Finance Acts). Capital gains made in any year are also taxable, but only a proportion of capital gains is included in the profit figure for tax purposes. The levels and basic procedures for the computation of these taxes are those laid down by the Board of Inland Revenue in accordance with Government policy.

Value Added Tax (*V.A.T.*): A detailed explanation of V.A.T. has been included in Chapter 3, pp. 11–12. V.A.T. is collected at each stage in the production and distribution process, and the final tax is borne by the consumer.

In addition to these taxes, there are direct taxes on specific goods such as petrol and oil, cars, alcoholic drink, tobacco and on betting. Capital Gains tax on the profits of sale of assets is also payable, subject to certain exemptions, which in the case of private individuals include the principal private residence, and private possessions worth less than £1000.

When the Chancellor of the Exchequer introduces the Budget to the House of Commons, he reviews the economic considerations which have led him to make his proposals, and he places before the House the accounts of the central Government for the year and the estimates for the year ahead. The accounts of the Public Sector are also put before the House; these include local authorities, the nationalised industries and other public corporations. A consolidated account for the entire public sector is also shown, so that the House may see, on balance, the financial requirements of the public sector as a whole.

The economy: We know that during the nineteenth century Britain emerged as a leading manufacturing country, and that because of her lack of natural resources she is compelled to import raw materials for her industries and basic foods. This large import bill is paid for by exports, not only of goods but also of services ('invisible' exports).

The years of war from 1939 to 1945 cost Britain about £3000 million in lost shipping, bomb damage and replacement of run-down industrial installations. In addition, new external debts amounted to another £3000 million, and the export trade was barely one quarter of what it had been in 1938. After 1945, production gradually returned to a peace-time basis, but the rate of Britain's economic growth compared unfavourably with that of some other countries in Western Europe. During the 1960s there was much industrial unrest. Many unofficial strikes took place, largely because of the confused situation then existing in industrial relations. Recent Government policies, as we have seen, have been aimed at providing a more realistic framework for cooperation between employers and workers. (See Chapter 43, p. 222.)

In order for the country to survive and progress, there must be an annual margin of growth reflected in the G.N.P. During the ten years from 1962 to 1972 Britain's G.N.P. rose by 30 per cent, but this annual growth rate of 2 to 3 per cent was not sufficient to correct recurring balance of payments deficits and to sustain full employment. The Government aimed to increase the growth rate to 5 per cent.

Inflation: **Inflation** and its opposite **deflation** are situations which basically arise from the operation of the **law of supply and demand**. Briefly, this law states that the price of a commodity is determined by the supply of it and the demand for it: if it is in short supply and many people wish to buy it, the price tends to rise; conversely, if the supply is plentiful and the demand small, the price tends to fall. When personal incomes rise and credit is easily and cheaply available, the demand for goods is high; unless the rate of production shows a similar increase, demand outstrips supply and this tends to inflate prices. In a country like Britain which has a large volume of imports, any increase in production to meet increased demand at home causes imports to rise, and unless this is accompanied by an expansion of exports, it has an adverse effect on the country's balance of payments. There are also psychological factors. When there is inflation, people fear for the value of their money; there is a tendency to withdraw savings in the form of investments in shares and interest-bearing bonds, and instead to buy houses, land, pictures, antique silver and furniture, and so on, which the buyers hope will at least retain their value and may even appreciate.

Deflating the economy also brings problems. If productivity increases without a comparable rise in demand because incomes have not been allowed to rise in the same proportion (possibly through wage restraints, increased taxes and credit restrictions), supply then exceeds demand and prices tend to fall. Unless the situation is remedied by a rise in exports or an increase in spending power at home, unwanted stocks of goods accumulate, output has to be reduced and unemployment results. In such a case, deflation of the economy leads to a trade depression.

From these brief explanations, it can be seen that in a highly developed economy many factors come into play, and a careful balance must be maintained if a country is to pay its way, maintain a good standard of living for its citizens and retain their confidence. During the 1960s, successive Governments in Britain attempted to achieve these aims by what came to be known as a 'stop-go' policy, placing restrictions on buying at home by curtailing credit and increasing purchase taxes, whenever an adverse balance of payments appeared to warrant such action, and lifting the restrictions when deflation threatened to be approaching depression, in order to avoid unemployment.

By the middle of 1971, unemployment in Britain had risen sharply, and the Government embarked on a number of policies to increase the rate of economic growth. Restrictions on credit were eased, tax reductions introduced, financial incentives were offered to industry to encourage capital investment, and a comprehensive programme of regional industrial development was planned.

Regional development: Generous grants were offered by the Government on new plant and machinery and towards new industrial building, these grants to be in addition to tax concessions on profits. Factories built by the Department of Industry may be leased, or bought on deferred terms. Grants to cover removal expenses to the scheduled areas were also offered.

Close cooperation between the Department of Industry, the Department of the Environment and the Department of Employment in the problems of economic development of the depressed regions testifies to the priority being given by the Government to this question.

Economic growth and counter-inflation measures: Rapid growth of the economy resulted from these Government measures, and by 1973 the growth rate had reached 5 per cent. Living standards rose and unemployment began to fall. Problems then arose in connection with the supply of money, which had been increased to meet the expected rise in output and consumer demand. Price levels, which had been steadily increasing since the end of the war, began to rise sharply with the increase in consumer spending. It became necessary to reduce the lending power of the banks. Special deposits were called for by the Bank of England on two occasions towards the end of 1972 and once in 1973.

Counter-inflation measures taken by the Government included setting up a Pay Board and a Price Commission to control prices and wages, but these provisions were unpopular and a change of Government took place.

In 1974, the new Government abolished the Pay Board and entered into a voluntary agreement with the TUC whereby the unions would refrain from asking for wage increases beyond the limits set by the Government. In return, the Government promised to work towards a more equitable society with increased opportunities and better standards of living, especially for the lower paid. This voluntary agreement became known as the **social contract**.

Under the Industry Act 1975, a **National Enterprise Board** was set up, under which agreements may be made between managements and the Board for long-term investment projects. Companies entering into such agreements will receive government finance to carry out agreed plans, in return for a corresponding share of the equity capital. The Board's plans are drawn up in consultation with managements and trade union representatives, followed by consultation with Government experts, and cover such important issues as investment, productivity, employment (especially in the development regions), exports, the saving of imports, prices and the interests of consumers.

The Board also encourages the reorganisation or expansion of an industry, where industrial efficiency and profitability would thereby be promoted.

It is clear that where public money is used in these ways an increase in public ownership in industry will be the outcome.

Advisory bodies: In formulating its economic policies the Government looks for advice to various sources outside the government. One important advisory body set up in 1962 is the **National Economic Development Council** ('Neddy'). Its members include representatives of the government, of management and of the trade unions, and they meet under the chairmanship of the Prime Minister. A number of Economic Development Committees ('little Neddies') dealing with specific industries and specific aspects of industry have also been established.

Questions

1. Explain briefly: (i) G.N.P., (ii) V.A.T., (iii) corporation tax, (iv) capital gains tax.

2. What is meant by (*a*) a hard currency, (*b*) a soft currency? What effects may a persistently hard currency have on the exports of that country?

3. Briefly, what do you understand by inflation?
   How may deflation be brought about?
   What might persistent deflation lead to?

4. What are 'Neddy' and the 'Little Neddies'?

5. What was the Social Contract?

6. The government receives and spends large sums of money. How is the private sector of business affected by the way it
   (*a*) raises the money and
   (*b*) spends it?

7. In Britain, the main types of tax are on income, on capital and on expenditure. Give examples of these taxes and indicate the difference between direct and indirect taxes. (R.S.A.)

8. Taxation may be classified as either 'direct' or 'indirect'. Giving examples, distinguish between the two forms.
   You are employed by a firm which assembles vehicles from imported parts at a time when corporation tax is increased and customs duty is reduced. Outline the possible effects on your firm. (R.S.A.)

9. Examine the ways in which the operation of a business concern can be influenced or directed as a result of the decisions of central Government.
   (L.C.C. & I.)

10. Explain clearly how a Government may use its budget as an important weapon to foster business activity. (A.E.B.)

11. Select a government department and describe how its work assists commerce. (L.C.C. & I.)

12. In 1972 a decision to 'float' the pound was taken. How does 'floating' differ from devaluation? What are the disadvantages of floating currencies? (R.S.A.)

13. Inflation has been described as 'the single biggest threat to our prosperity' and 'socially unjust'. How would you support these statements? (L.C.C. & I.)

Chapter 54

The European Economic Community

Public opinion in Britain concerning membership in the European Economic Community remained divided even after Britain was accepted as a member, and the Government that came to power in March 1974 pledged itself to re-negotiate the terms of Britain's entry and subsequently hold a national referendum. Negotiations were concluded in March 1975 and in June a national referendum voted to remain in the EEC.

A free trade association within Europe obviously creates a very large market for the kinds of manufactured goods that Britain can supply, but in return for such advantages Britain must turn to Europe for supplies of farm products such as butter, cheese and meat which have for many years been supplied to her by New Zealand and Australia. Sugar too presents problems, since cane sugar from the West Indies has always found a ready market in Britain, whereas beet sugar from Europe is now expected to become a serious competitor.

As a member of the EEC, Britain has also become a member of the European Atomic Energy Community (EURATOM) set up in 1957. This organisation coordinates members' atomic energy industries, aims to develop a coordinated research programme for peaceful nuclear activities, and to ensure the pooling of technical information among members.

A meeting of the heads of the nine member countries was held in Paris in 1972, at which the following aims were agreed:

Steady progress towards economic and monetary union;
Parallel progress in social and industrial policies;
Progress in regional and environmental policies;
Scientific and technological advancement;
Development of energy policies;
Joint action in external relations especially in the field of trade.

Organisation of the EEC

The Council of Ministers is the decision-making body, the ministers being appointed by member countries to represent their governments. Decisions (which should be unanimous on questions of major importance) are made on proposals submitted to the Council by the Commission. The Commission is composed of thirteen Commissioners nominated by member governments; it formulates policy proposals for submission to the

Council of Ministers. In doing its work, the Commission consults with officials of member governments, with representatives of producers, trade unions, employers' associations and others: it is pledged to act in the interests of the Community as a whole and in complete independence of national interests. The Assembly, or European Parliament, debates the major policy issues; the members are members of the parliaments of member countries (Britain nominates 36 out of the total of 198). The Assembly may question both the Council of Ministers and the Commission. The Court of Justice interprets and rules on the meaning of the treaties and of any measures enacted under them by the Council and Commission, and hears complaints and appeals brought by member states or individuals against the institutions of the Community. Its findings are binding on all members. It consists of nine judges and four advocates-general.

Some idea of the framework provided by the EEC organisation is given in the figure below.

The Assembly, or European Parliament, examines and approves the budgets for the various activities of the Community. It has powers of dismissal over the Commission.

Organisation of the EEC

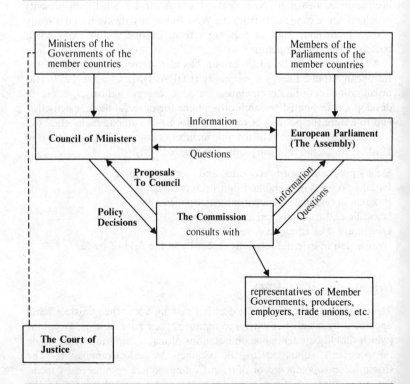

There are other Community institutions fulfilling a variety of functions. These include:

The Committee of Permanent Representatives, made up of representatives of member states of ambassadorial rank, whose duties include the preparation work in connection with meetings of the Council of Ministers.

The Economic and Social Committee, whose members represent employers' associations, trade unions and other interested groups. This committee advises the Council of Ministers and the Commission on matters arising in the making of policy.

The European Investment Bank;

The European Agricultural Guidance and Guarantee Fund;

The European Social Fund (occupational re-training programmes).

EEC finance

All members contribute to a common budget to cover administrative costs and the cost of certain specific services such as those provided under the European Social Fund. In the case of Britain and other new members, the contribution is graduated in steps increasing annually to reach a full contribution in 1980.

Questions

1. What do the initials EEC stand for? What was the Treaty of Rome?

2. Outline the principal aims of the EEC, and some of the obligations that member countries must discharge.

3. Give your assessment of the importance to the United Kingdom of entry into the EEC.   (L.C.C. & I.)

4. Describe some of the special trading problems that Britain has to solve in the light of her membership of the EEC.

5. How are the activities of the EEC financed?

6. Do you think customs unions are a stimulus or a stumbling block to world trade? Support your views with reasons, examples, etc.

Chapter 55

The work of the United Nations

The development of commerce throughout the world has brought together the peoples of many nations and raised the standard of living in many countries. Natural resources are being developed and harnessed, transport improved and expert knowledge and techniques shared. Money is made available on a world-wide basis to countries needing to extend their industries and modernise their facilities.

Behind these developments lies the work of the United Nations, of which a brief outline is given in this chapter.

Towards the end of the Second World War the United Nations came into being, having taken over the assets and interests of the former League of Nations that had been based in Geneva. UN headquarters are in New York. Its charter was signed by fifty-one nations, but today the number of member nations is more than twice that figure. In pursuing its aims of maintaining international peace and security and encouraging improved economic and social conditions throughout the world, the United Nations works through a number of subsidiary organisations and specialist agencies set up to meet certain needs.

International Monetary Fund (IMF)

This was set up as a result of the conference held at Bretton Woods in 1944. The Fund has its headquarters in Washington. Member countries make subscriptions to the Fund in their own currencies and have drawing and borrowing rights in the currencies they need. The aims of the Fund are to maintain orderly exchange arrangements among members by creating a multi-lateral clearing system of payments between members, which it is hoped will contribute to the stability of exchange rates, and to help to eliminate unnecessary exchange restrictions which might hamper trade development between the nations.

Recently, because of the large increase in oil prices in 1974, the IMF set up an arrangement called the 'oil facility' through which countries may borrow money lent to the fund by the oil exporting countries. This was followed in 1975 by a Finance Support Fund, set up by a group of twenty-four developed countries as a kind of 'safety net' for members whose financial problems are not adequately met by existing provisions.

International Bank for Reconstruction and Development (IBRD) – the 'World Bank'

This was set up at the same time, with the object of helping the economic development of member countries. Loans to members are of a long-term nature (whereas borrowings from the IMF are to meet the short-term needs of trading). Loans may be made to governments or to private enterprises – these usually being guaranteed by the Government of the borrowing member. The Bank may also guarantee loans made by private lenders. Loans have been made to member countries for the development of electricity supply, modernisation of ports, agricultural projects of various kinds, and other important improvements and developments, a great deal of this assistance going in recent years to the developing nations of Asia, Africa and South America.

Funds for lending are derived from the capital subscribed by members (about one-third of the total capital), from the sales of the Bank's own bonds, and from borrowings made in the capital markets. In the first twenty years of its existence the Bank made over 600 loans, totalling some $10 000 million, for capital projects in more than 80 countries.

Three other organisations supplement the work of the IBRD. They are:

International Finance Corporation (IFC): This was established in 1956, and is more elastic in its lending powers than the Bank itself. It encourages private investors, particularly the large institutional investors, to invest in private enterprises in the less developed countries. Certain safeguards apply, in that the money invested in an enterprise should not be more than half of the total cost of the enterprise, and the Fund must be satisfied that the enterprise is in the hands of competent management.

International Development Association (IDA): This was established in 1960. This organisation provides long-term loans (up to fifty-years) for large-scale developments in less developed countries. The loans frequently carry no interest, being subject only to a nominal administrative charge. Capital repayments usually do not start until after the first ten years.

Development Advisory Service (DAS): This was set up in 1961. This organisation provides resident experts to advise and assist the developing countries with their development projects and problems.

Other UN organisations include:

International Labour Organisation

The ILO was originally set up in 1919 under the League of Nations, to bring together representatives of governments, employers and trade unions to work out plans of action to meet the problems arising from industrialisation. In 1946 it was affiliated to the United Nations. Delegates and advisers meet at the annual conference. There is also a Governing Body, which does the work of an executive council.

ILO recommendations are guides to governments on desirable labour standards and conditions; **ILO conventions** are international treaties which member governments are asked to ratify and put into practice in their countries. They concern such things as the right of workers to organise, the abolition of forced labour, hours of work, protection against accidents, discrimination in employment and so on. Taken together, the Conventions and Recommendations are known as the **International Labour Code**.

The United Nations Conference on Trade and Development (UNCTAD)

First held in 1964, UNCTAD aimed at exploring new policies for enlarging the export trade of the developing countries, especially in connection with the protection of infant industries in those countries and the development of agricultural trade. Further conferences were held in 1965 and 1968 and will continue to be held from time to time.

World Health Organisation (WHO)

The Organisation aims to achieve the highest possible level of health throughout the world – headquarters in Geneva.

Universal Postal Union

This Union aims to perfect postal services by promoting international collaboration in postal matters – headquarters in Berne.

International Telecommunications Union

The ITU establishes international regulations for radio, telegraph and telephone services; aims to reduce costs of international services – headquarters in Geneva.

World Meteorological Organisation

WMO aims to standardise and improve world meteorological work – headquarters in Geneva.

International Civil Aviation Organisation (ICAO)

The ICAO promotes international standards and regulations to control civil flying – headquarters in Montreal.

Intergovernmental Maritime Consultative Organisation

IMCO promotes cooperation in technical problems of international shipping and in the removal of restrictive and other undesirable practices by shippers – headquarters in London.

International Atomic Energy Agency

The Agency is intended to develop peaceful uses of atomic energy.

United Nations Children's Fund

UNICEF helps countries in need to provide for their children, especially in times of disaster – headquarters in New York.

United Nations Educational, Scientific and Cultural Organisation

UNESCO aims to promote collaboration among nations through education, science and culture. Awards are made for study or training in Britain and other countries, and scientific cooperation between governments is encouraged.

Agencies of United Nations

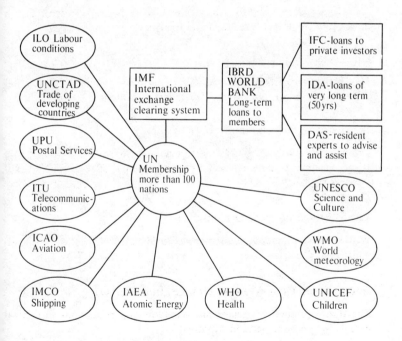

Questions

1. Write an essay on the establishment and work of the United Nations.

2. What is the IBRD? What other name does it have? Briefly explain its work.

3. What do the initials UNCTAD stand for? What are the aims of this particular organisation?

4. Explain the work and aims of the International Labour Organisation, and what is understood by the International Labour Code.

5. Describe any particular commercial or economic problems to which you think the United Nations should give priority.

285

Some additional examination questions

1. Commercial banks provide many services for both private individuals and business firms. Select five such services which would be of particular benefit to a large retailer whose customers buy largely for cash/cheque and on credit, and whose buyers travel regularly abroad in search of new lines. Give reasons for your choice. (R.S.A.)

2. Farmer Giles says: 'I am not engaged in Commerce. True, I have to buy seeds and young animals, fertilisers and feeding stuffs, and I have to store and sell my produce as well as arranging to transport it to market. But I have nothing to do with advertising or foreign trade. My job is food production.'
Comment on Farmer Giles's statement. (W.J.E.C.)

3. Briefly describe the functions and operations of **two** of the following: (a) Lloyd's Underwriters, (b) Members of the Baltic Exchange, (c) Export Credits Guarantee Department, (d) Finance houses concerned with hire purchase, (e) Stock Brokers. (U.C.L.E.S.)

4. State what you know of **three** of the following: (i) the Consumers Association, (ii) the Export Credits Guarantee Department, (iii) limited partnerships, (iv) mail order, (v) cable transfers. (W.J.E.C.)

5. Read the following passage and then answer the questions set on it. London is the centre of international insurance. There are several hundred British and overseas insurance companies located there together with Lloyd's underwriters. Britain ranks as the leading exporter of insurance services and the premium income received from abroad represents an important invisible export.
   (a) Who are Lloyd's underwriters and how are risks placed with them?
   (b) How are insurance services exported?
   (c) Explain the relationship between the premiums charged by an insurance company and the profit made by the company.
   (d) Explain the importance of invisible exports to the British economy. (R.S.A.)

6. **Briefly** indicate what you consider to be the purpose and dangers of advertising.
   Give **two** examples of named products or services which use the following in preference to other possible media. **Briefly** justify your choice where you think this necessary:
   (a) monthly women's magazines,
   (b) Sunday supplements,
   (c) posters in public transport,
   (d) sporting sponsorships,
   (e) house-to-house leaflets. (W.J.E.C.)

7. Give brief answers to the following, using examples where appropriate. Distinguish between: (a) Trade and barter, (b) a bill of lading and a charter party, (c) a standing order and a credit transfer, in banking practice, (d) a preference share and a debenture, (e) a country (or state) and a customs area. (W.J.E.C.)

8. In the course of their work traders are faced with problems relating to (a) finance, (b) distance, (c) risk, (d) time. What is the nature of each of these problems and what commercial activities help to overcome them? (A.E.B.)

9. Giving appropriate examples where applicable, distinguish between: (a) an invoice and a statement of account, (b) a postal order and a money order, (c) Customs duties and Excise duties, (d) insurance brokers and underwriters, (e) fixed assets and current assets. (W.J.E.C.)

10. James Thompson is a sole trader dealing in men's clothing. He has two retail shops in two medium-size towns (populations around 50 000–70 000), one run by himself and the other by a paid manager. His trade has been showing signs of steady expansion during the past five years, and his most recent results show the following figures:

	Last year £000	Previous year £000
Annual turnover	60	50
Cost of goods sold	48	40
Total administration expenses	9	8
Stock at beginning of year (cost)	5	3
Stock at end of year (cost)	3	5

Write a short report on these results, telling James Thompson as much as you can about what his business has recently been doing. He is considering the possibility of opening a third shop in another town, 45 km distant (population 80 000), and also the possibility of becoming a private limited liability company, and would particularly welcome your advice on these two points. He also wonders if he is holding enough stock, and whether he might improve his trade by changing his policy of selling all kinds of lines – made-to-measure suits, ready-made suits, casual clothing, etc. (R.S.A. – modified)

11. Distinguish between:

    (a) a jobber and a broker on the London Stock Exchange.
    (b) an insurance proposal and an insurance policy.
    (c) capital and working capital.
    (d) a broker and a factor, both dealing in commodities.
    (e) the effects of a general crossing and a special crossing on a cheque.

    (W.J.E.C.)

12. 'The *Customs Authority* does not *levy* duties on imports although it is concerned with the collection of duties. It is not, however, concerned with the collection of port, harbour or dock dues to *maintain the efficiency* of the port; that is the business of the *Port Authority*.'

    Explain this statement; pay particular attention to the terms in italics.

    (U.C.L.E.S.)

13. Indicate, and account for, **four** modern trends in retailing. (W.J.E.C.)

14. (a) Outline the ways in which public limited liability companies and publicly owned corporations obtain their capital.

    (b) Mention the main differences between public limited liability companies and public corporations with regard to: (i) control, (ii) use of profits.

    (M.R.E.B.)

15. Using appropriate examples, show how individuals and communities are interdependent. (W.J.E.C.)

16. Write an essay about **five** different methods of investing money which are available to the general public, stating their advantages and disadvantages. (W.M.E.B.)

17. Explain the difference between:

    (a) commerce and trade
    (b) a cash transaction and a credit transaction
    (c) commercial banks and building societies
    (d) cash discount and trade discount. (L.C.C. & I.)

18. State what you know of **three** of the following: (i) mobile shops, (ii) price maintenance, (iii) finance of hire-purchase, (iv) a Lloyd's broker, (v) retail trade associations. (W.J.E.C.)

19. Explain *the difference* between:

    (*a*) fixed capital and circulating capital
    (*b*) turnover and rate of turnover
    (*c*) gross profit and net profit
    (*d*) loan capital and share capital.

                                   (A.E.B.)

Answers

Ch. 3, no. 3. £386.66; £38.66.

Ch. 4, no. 3. 5%.

Ch. 8, no. 8. £7.39.

Ch. 12, no. 6. £600; £576.
7. 25%.
8. 21%; 18.5%, 12.1%.
9. 5% COD.

Ch. 14, no. 3. $16\frac{2}{3}$%; 20%; 23%; 25%; 28.5%; $33\frac{1}{3}$%.
4. 14.2%; 31.5%; 53.8%; 81.8%; 200%; 300%.
6. $33\frac{1}{3}$%; 50%.
9. (i) £8200; (ii) 2050, £1025; (iii) G.P. 25%. 20%, N.P. 12.5%. 10%.
10. (a) £70; (b) £30, £10; (c) £20.
14. 33%; 3%; 38%; 2% loss, 17%; 12%; 15%.

Ch. 15, no. 1. G.P. £25, £27, £32, £35, £45, £75.
N.P. £5, £7, £12, £13, £20, £45.
2. £5; 29p.
3. 80p; 79p.
5. 14%.

Ch. 27, no. 2. 4; 3 months; no.
3. (a) 4; (b) $33\frac{1}{3}$%; (c) £3000, $4\frac{1}{2}$.
4. £3000; £4000.
6. G.P. £10 400, 23.6%; N.P. £4800, 10.9%.
G.P. £12 600, 25%; N.P. £6200, 12.3%.
8.4; 9.
8. (a) £365.62$\frac{1}{2}$; (b) £375.
9. £4923.

Ch. 28, no. 7. (a) £2700, £3000; (b) £500, £2500; (c) £2700, £300;
(d) £2200.
8. (a) (i) £16 100; (ii) £10 000; (iii) £10 700; (iv) £5000;
(v) £5700; (vi) £5000.
(b) (i) £3000; (ii) 8.
11. (a) £120 000; (b) £20 000.
15. (a) £2714.285; (b) £3571.43.

Ch. 32, no. 11. 20%; low.

Ch. 33, no. 3. 4.16%.

Ch. 39, no. 3. £2000.
8. £3.50: £13.

Ch. 45, no. 2. 1 March.
4. £994.41.
5. 32p.

Ch. 46, no. 8. (a) 7%; (b) 8.9%.

Index